BLACK MONDAY

The Stock Market Catastrophe of October 19, 1987

By

Tim Metz

BeardBooks

WASHINGTON, D.C.

The original title of the work was:

Black Monday: the Catastrophe of October 19, 1987...and Beyond.

The title has been changed to facilitate electronic retrieval and/or to reflect current conditions in the subject area.

LIBRARY OF CONGRESS CATALOGING-IN-PUBLICATION DATA

Metz, tim
    Black Monday: the stock market catastrophe of October 19, 1987 / Tim Metz.
    p. cm.
Originally published: Black Monday: the catastrophe of October 19, 1987, and beyond. New York: W. Morrow, c1988.
    Includes bibliographical references and index.
ISBN 1-58798-214-5
1. Phelan, John J., 1931-2. New York Stock Exchange. 3. Wall Street. 4. Speculation. 5. Business cycles—United States. 6. United States—Economic conditions—1981–2001. I. Title: Stock market catastrophe of October 19, 1987. II. Title.

HG4572.M58 2003
332.64′273′09048—dc22

                                          2003062872

TO MARY VIRGINIA

ACKNOWLEDGMENTS

The author is grateful to the following people for assistance and encouragement that made this book possible: Cathy Fiducia, Edward Foldessy, Norman Pearlstine, John Prestbo, Richard Schuster, all at *The Wall Street Journal;* Pamela Altschul, Sonia Greenbaum, and Adrian Zackheim at William Morrow; Jane Dystel at Edward J. Acton Agency; Peter Bakstansky at the Federal Reserve Bank of New York; Catherine Maroney at the New York Stock Exchange; Jay Poole at Serfling & Associates; Joseph and Antoinette Burke. Most of all I am grateful to my wife, Mary Virginia, who saw and counseled from the beginning that my main task here was to tell the story of five very different men coping with cataclysmic fear.

INTRODUCTION

OCTOBER 19, 1987. ■ New York Stock Exchange, chairman's office, 10:45 A.M.: John Phelan searches the faces of the dozen men who are perched on the sofa and on the Chippendale chairs strewn haphazardly around his desk.

These are powerful men huddling with the Big Board chairman this morning, Wall Street's elite, commanding some of the richest and most influential securities houses on the planet. There is John Gutfreund of Salomon Brothers, Inc.; Bill Schreyer of Merrill Lynch & Company, also a NYSE vice-chairman, is here. So are Peter Buchanan of First Boston Corporation, Bob Linton of Drexel Burnham Lambert, Inc., George Ball of Prudential-Bache Securities, Inc., and Phil Purcell of Dean Witter Reynolds, Inc. All are chairmen of their firms. Top trading or operating officials from Goldman Sachs & Company, Shearson Lehman Brothers, Inc., and Bear Stearns & Company have also responded to a round of urgent phone calls placed a couple of hours ago by Robert Birnbaum, the stock exchange's quietly professional president.

Phelan is just over six feet tall and weighs 180 pounds. But his erect bearing and somber gray suit make him look taller. The fifty-six-year-old chairman's hair remains mostly dark, but it is thinning now, and salt-and-pepper sideburns frame his high, broad forehead. His eyebrows, though, are full and dark, arching above intense brown eyes. Phelan's hands are soft and white, his features refined.

Indeed, everything about his appearance insists that here is an Irish aristocrat. No one in the room knows yet how vital appearances will be in the days ahead. But today, as on all days, before this group, as before all groups, John J. Phelan, Jr., appears cool, maybe even a bit arrogant, but commanding and in control.

Ostensibly this morning's business is straightforward, simple.

Following last week's 235-point collapse in the Dow and the horrendous start of trading this morning, there is nowhere to run and so the exchange must turn and make a stand, Phelan knows. But he also knows you don't simply tell the industry's most powerful chief executives that you've decided the exchange will have to trade its way through this mess. There are too many billions of dollars of these firms' and their clients' investments hanging in the balance for that. No, Phelan knows he must seek a consensus.

"If I were the chief executive of an organization like the New York Stock Exchange, I'd want the intangible benefits of being sensitive to the times by meeting with the key people around the industry," says a top trading official who attended the meeting. "Here Phelan had a group that was responsible for a whole lot of the [securities] business."

Is it agreed, Phelan wants to know, that closing the exchange today probably will both broaden and intensify any panic among investors and produce even more selling pressure upon reopening?

It is.

One of the conferees floats a novel idea for trying to cope with today's selling pressure: a $1 billion superfund, created with capital advanced by the big member firms to help those traders designated by the exchange to maintain fair and orderly markets in their assigned stocks in the face of today's selling blitz.

However the idea dies a swift death. The moguls of Wall Street have better things to do with a billion dollars than turn it over to Phelan's market makers. And who can be sure anything close to that amount will be needed, anyway?

Well then, Phelan wants to know, is there a consensus that the exchange should continue operating today no matter how much blood flows?

There is.

CHAPTER 1

EARLY IN THE 1980s. ■ Harry's of Hanover Square, evening: But for the clink of glasses and the hearty laughter, you could mistake the roar for that on the NYSE floor. Animated revelers flood the room, pressed four deep around Harry's big mahogany bar.

All the rage at Harry's these days is risk arbitrage—the takeover stock trading strategy that is sweeping Wall Street, spread far and wide by Ivan Boesky and a growing band of imitators, large and small. They call themselves simply "arbs," and they think of themselves as the Green Berets, or maybe the Oakland Raiders of Wall Street. They figure there's not much they can't get away with.

Grizzled middle-aged brokers and traders anchor the crowd, using just enough muscle and savvy to take over the best bar space without triggering a fight. They come for little else but scotch or vodka on the rocks, and the chance to unwind and banter with the bartenders and pals, who include both Wall Street colleagues and a few rich syco-phants who circle the bar, angling for stock tips.

"Hey, Phillie! Here! Over here!" shouts a big, jovial man in his mid-thirties. Harry's isn't a celebrity bar and anyone but a superstar could probably drink here unrecognized. But to the crowd at Harry's in the late 1970s, Ivan Boesky's chief trader, Phil DiLeo, is Sly Stallone. Like the parting of the Red Sea, a path opens to the bar space beside Fran Bodkin, an independent arb who once worked at Edwards & Hanley, now defunct, when Ivan did.

A waiter eases by through the crowd holding a tray full of six-inch plates loaded with two-by two-inch squares of just-baked pizza. The six-foot five-inch, 250-pound Bodkin reaches down and grabs a couple of plates, then stuffs a bill into the waiter's shirt pocket. "Here, Phil,"

Bodkin says, offering DiLeo some pizza. "No thanks, Fran. I'll just have a little white wine," he tells the bartender, who produces a glass in a flash. Bodkin slurps the hot cheese toppings off a few pieces of pizza and puts the naked crust back on the plate. He's on a diet, he tells DiLeo, who is most of a foot shorter and not much over half Bodkin's weight.

The two men talk clothes, cars, restaurants, shows, anything, really, except business. Ivan doesn't allow his employees to talk about the business to outsiders. Also, after a day in the pressure cooker that is Boesky's trading room, business is the last thing DiLeo wants to discuss at Harry's.

DiLeo isn't a big drinker and rarely stays more than a half hour or so before heading uptown to dinner or home to Long Island. Other revelers swing by, not entirely by accident, to offer Phil a drink, share a joke, or just say hello. He nods, smiles, shakes hands with those dropping by like a don being paid homage. If strangers have the poor taste to ask him what's happening at the office, they are ignored as if they had not even spoken.

But the real don of Wall Street during these heady days in the early 1980s is DiLeo's boss. It is Ivan Boesky and risk arbitrage that make the sun shine on Wall Street and about $1 billion of investment capital is chasing the takeover target's stocks alongside Boesky's $100 million. By November 1986, when he agrees to pay the government $100 million to settle insider trading charges against him, Boesky will be managing a $2.3 billion pool of his own and others' money, or more than 15% of the estimated total of $15 billion that will then be committed to risk arbitrage in the U.S.

No one plays the game of risk arbitrage harder than Ivan. While others buy thousands or tens of thousands of shares of a takeover target's stock, Ivan buys hundreds of thousands or even millions of shares. The influence those shares give Boesky is enormous.

"Do you know what owning 500,000 shares of somebody's stock means?" an admiring competitor of Boesky's asks a companion at the bar. "It means Ivan can get any chief executive officer in America off the toilet to talk to him at seven o'clock in the morning."

Ivan's seven A.M. calls are already legendary, raising suspicions that he is cheating; wielding his huge stockholdings like truncheons to beat valuable information out of the corporate executives. Exactly when will the directors meet to consider the offer? Will you recommend that they approve it? What views have directors expressed so far? What do your lawyers say about possible antitrust obstacles or other defenses? Are you considering an economic defense such as inviting a competing offer from a company of your choice?

Boesky's private intelligence network is legendary, too. According to bar lore, one of his fifty employees does nothing but call airports around the country all day long, asking for the FAA registration numbers of arriving and departing private jets—numbers he has already arranged in order for a directory of U.S. corporate aircraft. So the sleuth supposedly justifies his existence by trying to confirm rumors of takeover talks by tracking the movements of rumored merger partners' corporate jets.

The crowd at Harry's never gets the details, but even Ivan's staunchest admirers at the start of the decade suspect he must be cheating big. Other risk arbitrageurs—even some cheaters—earned around 50% a year on their capital between 1975 and 1980, or less than two thirds of what Boesky's is making in the same market environment. And the other arbs realize that's just too big a discrepancy to be explained, year after year, by luck or brains.

Major arbs who compete with him head on are both envious and furious at Boesky's gall, and they fear he will one day bring down the wrath of Washington and Main Street. But many smaller arbs and other traders love it. To them, Ivan is a latter-day Robin Hood, spitting in the faces of the slow-witted tsars of business, even as he picks their pockets. So Washington and Main Street can go suck eggs.

Boesky often owns more shares of a target company's stock than all its whining managers combined. And in the black-or-white, binary logic of traders, that means Ivan should call the tune. As the many young arbs who admire Boesky see it, target company managers fighting takeovers are frustrating the legitimate interests of shareholders and plundering the assets of their companies in order to hold on to their jobs.

And indeed, the plunder will seem to increase right in step with the takeovers boom. Sibson & Company, the Princeton, N.J., compensation consultant that has surveyed U.S. chief executives' pay annually since 1964, would find that it accelerated sharply at a sample of 300 medium and large general industrial concerns, mostly manufacturers, in the decade ending in 1987. During that span, chief executives' salary and bonuses alone would rise an average 12.2%, compared with an average 6.5% increase in inflation, a 6.1% average gain in wages for the firms' hourly workers, and a mere 0.75% annual rise in the firms' earnings.

They do not suffer fools or opposition gladly, some of these swaggering Boeskyphiles. Besides the recalcitrant target company managers, their enemies include: the SEC for wasting their time with inside-information witchhunts that the arbs are sure aren't going to catch anybody; the IRS for auditing them even though every trader in the securities business knows how to defer income taxes indefinitely*; and just about anyone else who gets in their way, even by mistake.

Boesky himself almost never appears at Harry's. If he did, he would often get an eyeful. Take that middle-aged rogue standing at the bar near the front door, beside the wide-eyed young woman in the Lady Brooks charcoal pinstriped suit. She's an uptown girl in her early thirties, normally cool and assured, but now her face is flushed with excitement.

Her consort is a well-connected member of Wall Street's WASP elite. His age shows in the tiny wrinkles at the corners of his eyes and his stomach sags a bit, but he still cuts an elegant figure in his navy blue blazer and club tie. He's one of perhaps a dozen traders aping Ivan Boesky these days by managing their own risk arbitrage businesses.

It has been a good year. He made three quarters of a million dollars in the market in June, signed up a limo service, and played the weeknights away until just before Labor Day, when his wife and kids got home from the Hamptons. Their affair is going nowhere, the young woman knows. But he'll do until a real prospect materializes; he's pleasant company, a free spender, and he knows how to make the demons come and go. He will point to this spot at the bar in years to come and boast that he actually brought the young woman to orgasm here in the midst of a crush of revelers who never suspected what was happening. But who knows . . . ?

Viewed entirely from a traders' perspective, the way so many on Wall Street are beginning to view the world, there is a perverse logic

---

*Through year-end stock-options trading maneuvers called "tax straddles," which let them recognize any stock losses in the current year while pushing any gain into the following year. The loophole allowing the practice was closed in 1982.

to their behavior, even in matters of the heart. Casual sex is "the perfect trade": Both sides get back more than they invest, all in a matter of minutes and with no entanglements, no liabilities.

At the far corner of the bar a tousle-haired young arb, squat and as powerfully built as a badger, brags to fellow tipplers about the swift justice he has dealt to a woman who interrupted his trading with an errant phone call. "She thought she'd reached Beekman Downtown Hospital . . . gave her husband's name and asked about his condition," the arb says. "I waited a little while and told her I was sorry, he'd just died."

His companions roar with glee. To be an arb in this era is to be outrageous. The more outrageous the better.

The badger is introduced to a sinuous blonde from Salomon Brothers. He greets her as he does all the girls he meets:—with grunts of pleasure and a string of noisy half-bites, half-kisses up her arm, over her shoulder and, oops, that's enough for now. She laughs nervously and spends a few minutes trying to figure him out.

As Ivan's legend spreads, commercial liaisons push their way up the list of priorities around Harry's bar, and occasionally there are cryptic conversations to overhear. The form seldom varies much:

"What do you hear about Company X?"

"I hear fifty from Company Y." (Translation: He hears a $50-a-share takeover offer has been proposed to Company X by Company Y in language just vague enough to avoid a public announcement under SEC disclosure rules.)

"How well do you hear it?"

"Market rumor," or "not that well" sometimes is the reply.

Or the answer may be "I hear it pretty well," which means either he got it from a person who probably would know or he has access to someone who should know. Rarely, among close associates, the answer is: "I hear it perfectly." That means the informant is an official at one of the companies, or an investment banker, lawyer, or other adviser actually working on the deal.

Some even follow up on promising leads, pausing between drinks to call investment bankers, other arbs, or lawyer pals from the bank of phones along the front wall near the bar. Indeed, the reckless young arbs here seem more like Runyonesque caricatures than real people. Most other traders on Wall Street, even the house arbs at the large firms, are regimented Milquetoasts by comparison. They do their work, carry their briefcases home to the suburbs by 6:30, and come back on the seven A.M. train the next day.

The prosaic majority of traders includes Wall Street's army of "sales" or "position" traders whose role is executing brokers' orders from individual clients, soliciting and carrying out institutional block trades, trading for the firm's own investment portfolio, or helping distribute new stock offerings the firm underwrites. Traders on the stock exchange floor are part of that army, carrying out the trades transmitted to them from their counterparts. To be sure, there is horseplay aplenty on the trading desks and exchange floors, but sex or sensitive business in public? Never.

The arbs are descendants of the classic traders who have taken advantage of price discrepancies in different markets as long as there have been markets. If apples sold for 15 cents apiece in New York and 12 cents in Connecticut, why not go into the apple business, buy in Connecticut, sell in New York, and pocket the 3-cent difference? If you did, you were an arbitrageur, an arb.

The game sweeping Wall Street now, "risk arbitrage," involves the stocks of companies targeted for acquisition. The stock market is one of the two markets for these stocks, and the takeover offer price is the other. Buy on the stock market now, sell to the acquirer at a higher price under his offer, which expires a month or so hence, and pocket the difference.

The "risk" in risk arbitrage is that the acquirer might decide (or be compelled legally) not to consummate the deal. That risk is why the market price of a takeover target's stock is lower than the acquirer's offer price. Once the news of the impending takeover has been reflected on the stock market, the difference usually is only 5% or so. However, nowadays, would-be acquirers are commonly setting their prices as much as 50% or more above the target's preannouncement price in the market. So, risk arbitrageurs getting wind of an impending deal ahead of the announcement can make a killing.

Some do. Especially Ivan Boesky, whose name is on the lips of nearly everyone around Harry's big mahogany bar.

Ivan started Ivan F. Boesky & Company in early 1975 with $500,000. Five years later he had turned it into $100 million. Investors who wanted to ride Ivan's coattails had to put $500,000 into the limited partnership he managed and leave it there for the full five years. But what a ride they got: an average return on their investment of 80% per year.

And Boesky's success represents much more than just money. It will be one of the most important forces driving traders and trading into the spotlight in the Wall Street environment of the 1980s. Arguably, without Ivan Boesky—and Wall Street's adjustment to him—there would be no five-year runaway bull market and no Black Monday to end it.

Until Boesky, traders were regarded as an underclass on much of Wall Street. Few Wall Street houses, except those firms founded or dominated by traders, showed much respect for the trader's art.* Meanwhile, such firms as Morgan Stanley, First Boston, Kidder Peabody & Company, and Dillon Read & Company relied on fees collected for performing other services for their revenues. They operated trading desks primarily to attract and serve clients for these other services, principally capital raising and financial advice.†

Investment bankers typically were tweedy, wellborn, or well-connected Ivy Leaguers living on Park Avenue or in Manhasset, L.I., Short Hills, N.J., or Scarsdale, N.Y. Meanwhile, the stereotypical trader went to CCNY or NYU (if he went to college at all), lived in Brooklyn, Queens, or Garden City, wore polyester slacks, gold chains, and short-sleeved shirts open to the navel, and drank his soup out of the bowl.

But fundamental changes under way on Wall Street since the mid-1970s would give traders the last laugh. Fixed stock brokerage commissions, which had precluded price competition among the securities houses, would be eliminated by May 1975, under order of the Securities and Exchange Commission. For a variety of reasons, even as the brokerage business grew less lucrative, Wall Street's biggest and richest bank,

---

*Including Goldman Sachs & Company, Salomon Brothers, Inc., Oppenheimer & Company, and Bear Stearns & Company. Merrill Lynch also became a major trading firm by dint of the extensive buying and selling required to service the accounts of its huge brokerage client base.
†Among the most important fees were those earned in underwriting: providing financing for clients by helping them design and sell new securities. Trading was seen as mainly a service offered to attract and accommodate clients, and some felt that a firm that traded for its own account would inevitably come into conflict with its clients' interests. Trading took capital, too, and since these firms didn't have trading traditions, they hadn't amassed enough capital to be significant forces in trading. Besides the underwriting, their advisory and brokerage fees were good and they had the lion's share of them.

insurance company, mutual fund and pension fund clients would seek to trade their securities far more aggressively.

To service that demand and provide another profit base to help offset shrinking commission rates, Wall Street firms determined to expand their trading activities sharply. It would take big money to finance the stock and bond inventories needed for substantial trading operations, the firms realized. So, as exchange figures show, they embarked on a capital-building spree that lifted the total capital of all New York Stock Exchange member firms from $3.67 billion at the end of 1975 to $6.84 billion at the end of 1980.

One source of that additional capital was the soaring fees their investment bankers were earning by advising takeover participants. Another was risk arbitrage. By the late 1970s, Morgan Stanley, Kidder Peabody, and First Boston were all operating risk arbitrage departments, falling in step with Ivan Boesky's parade.

In the early 1980s, merger and acquisition advisory fees and risk arbitrage profits would be literally carrying the securities industry, accounting for more than one half of the earnings at some big firms.* Beginning in mid-1982, however, huge stock and bond market rallies will be fueled by aggressive Wall Street firms trading for their own accounts. Indeed, U.S. Senate Banking Committee investigators sorting through the market wreckage after Black Monday will find that in 1982 and every year thereafter, through 1987, Wall Street securities firms as a group made more money from trading than brokerage.

By the mid-1980s, nearly every larger-than-life figure on Wall Street will be a trader, and their exploits will speak volumes about the tenor of the times.

Take Salomon Brothers, Inc.'s John H. Gutfreund, a former Solly bond trader. Gutfreund was hand-picked by managing partner William R. "Billy" Salomon, who handed him the reins in 1978. In 1981, Gutfreund sold the firm for $554 million to Phibro, the big commodities concern, without even informing his old boss, let alone seeking his counsel. So Billy, who virtually created the modern Salomon Brothers

---

*Risk arbitrage and mergers and acquistions advisory services might fairly be viewed as part of the same profit base. Some investment bankers at firms that added risk arbitrage departments in the late 1970s explained that one motive was to make these departments more effective in the merger advisory business, as if this were some support service. But from a profits standpoint, risk arbitrage was the dog and M&A advice the tail in most firms. Ivan Boesky bought investment bankers, not vice-versa.

during a forty-year career, retained only a limited partnership interest and got $10 million in the sale, while Gutfreund was getting $32 million for his shares, according to John Taylor writing in *New York* magazine early in 1988.

As the mid-1980s approach, Gutfreund will be riding the crest of surging trading profits at Salomon and will be named co-chief executive of the merged firm, Phibro-Salomon, Inc. Soon after, he'll force out his only competitor, co-chief executive David Tendler of Phibro, and sell off several Phibro operations, reducing its employment by two thirds. In 1985, Phibro's name will disappear from the corporate title. Thus, in less than four years, a company that paid $554 million to take over Salomon will itself be taken over from within and all but liquidated.

In December of 1985, Salomon will be hailed on the cover of *Business Week* as the "King of Wall Street." Its huge stock and bond trading operations will account for the vast bulk of its 1985 earnings of more than a half billion dollars. And Salomon will have a staggering $38 billion securities portfolio, four times the size of any other Wall Street firm's.

In July 1983, Lewis Glucksman, Lehman Brothers Kuhn Loeb, Inc.'s top trader and co-chief executive, will demand sole control of the firm from Peter G. Peterson, who had elevated him to equal status barely two months earlier. And he'll get it. To save the firm from an irreparable rift, Peterson will do as he is told and resign. But by May 1984, some of Lehman's investment banker partners, angry over Glucksman's purported bias toward the firm's traders, will sell the firm from under him, to the American Express Company's Shearson/American Express, Inc. subsidiary.

Former Treasury Secretary William E. Simon, who once was a Salomon Brothers bond trading boss, will set the acquisitive standard of the decade. He'll turn a $330,000 stock investment in the mostly debt-financed purchase of RCA's Gibson Greeting Card division in 1981 into a profit of more than $70 million when Gibson is resold in 1984. Simon's Gibson deal would be among the most powerful influences spurring the 1980s explosion in such debt-heavy, so-called leveraged buyout transactions.

There were others, too, rising everywhere to the top of their firms. Morgan Stanley's Richard B. Fisher and Kidder's Max C. Chapman, Jr., will already have reached the presidency of their companies by the mid-eighties. And at Goldman Sachs & Company, former risk arbitrage head Robert E. Rubin and investment banker Stephen Friedman will be widely expected to reestablish the firm's tradition of co-chief executives when senior partner John L. Weinberg steps down.

The ascendancy of trading will help shape Wall Street and the investment world in the 1980s. So will an imminent worldwide explosion in available investment capital and the concurrent emergence of powerful new computer-driven trading strategies that will tie the stock market and a Chicago futures market together. The three forces and the men behind them will interact to create and sustain a historic five-year stock market rally and will then suddenly spin out of alignment to produce the catastrophe of Black Monday.

Catastrophe awaits Ivan Boesky and some of his friends, too.

One is young John A. Mulheren, Jr., who'd sold Merrill Lynch & Company on giving him a lucrative contract to establish its risk arbitrage business in the mid-seventies. Mulheren was only in his middle twenties then, and it wasn't yet clear how big the game would get. But by his late twenties, Mulheren was making $2 million a year, friends say, or four times the pay of Donald Regan, then Merrill Lynch's chairman.

It was the kind of performance Boesky respected, and he and Mulheren have had cordial dealings over the years. But the cordiality will end in 1987 after Boesky and Michael Davidoff, then Boesky's head trader, implicate Mulheren as an accomplice in allegedly illegal stock maneuvers. Early in February 1988, his lawyers will say, Mulheren will stop taking the lithium that has helped him avoid bouts of chronic depression over the years. On February 18, when police, tipped off by Mulheren's worried wife, stop his car near their Rumson, N.J., mansion, they will find weapons that include a loaded semiautomatic rifle. Mulheren reportedly will tell them he is on his way to kill Boesky and Davidoff.

Still, Boesky's purported testimony against Mulheren will be tame stuff compared with some of his other admissions. These will include six- and seven-figure payoffs to investment bankers Marty Siegel at Kidder and Dennis Levine at Drexel Burnham Lambert, Inc., in exchange for advance information on deals.

However, these days, early in the 1980s, no one yet dreams that the government's insider trading dragnet will reach someone with the power and resources of Boesky. There are just too many ways to hide illicit trading and illicit gains that even small-time cheaters know about. One arb's recipe:

"Take a few hundred dollars cash to Panama and hire a lawyer to set up a Panamanian bearer corporation [one that's registered to any bearer of the certificate of incorporation]. Use the Panamanian corporation to establish a Liechtenstein Anstalt [corporation] and the Liechtenstein Anstalt to open a brokerage account at a Swiss bank. Have the Swiss open trading accounts for you at banks in the Bahamas. If the Feds crack the Liechtensteiners, Swiss, and Bahamians, they may get the money. But they won't get you, because the Panamanian lawyer doesn't even know who you are."

Yet, through a freak set of circumstances, Boesky will be caught.

A pair of Merrill Lynch brokers in South America will be trading on inside information. An anonymous letter of accusation will arrive at Merrill's New York headquarters in May 1985. Merrill investigators in New York will examine the accounts of the two South American brokers and find small-scale trading in four stocks in advance of offer announcements. They'll also find that one of the brokers has sent a check to another Merrill broker in New York.

A review of Campbell's account will show he, too, traded in small amounts of the four stocks ahead of offer announcements, as well as in several others. Checking Campbell's customer accounts to see where he might be getting information, the Merrill investigators will see that one account, Switzerland's Bank Leu, has heavy preannouncement dealings in a dozen or more takeover stocks.

So, in June 1985, Merrill will take its findings to the SEC. Early in 1986, following negotiations with the SEC the substance of which hasn't been disclosed, Bank Leu will cough up certain accounts, including one, containing $12 million, that belongs to Dennis Levine of Drexel Burnham.

The SEC will drop the net on Levine in the spring of 1986 and he'll agree to disgorge the $12 million. Still, Levine* seemingly has an ace in the hole. Ivan still owes him $3 million for inside information previously furnished on a number of deals. But Ivan has better sources than Levine and he won't pay him the $3 million.

*In mid-1988 Levine was serving time at the Lewisburg, Pa., federal prison.

So, in retaliation, some on Wall Street would whisper, Levine will implicate Ivan. On November 14, 1986, Boesky and the SEC will announce a settlement, and Boesky will pledge to continue cooperating fully with federal investigators. On a February morning in 1987, Richard Wigton, the head of Kidder's arbitrage unit, who had worked with a Boesky accomplice, Marty Siegel, will be arrested in his office. Federal marshals will handcuff him and lead him out, in tears, under the gaze of shocked fellow workers.* In mid-1987, Kidder will settle the SEC insider trading charges by agreeing to disgorge $13.7 million of illicit profits and pay a $11.6 million penalty.

But traders and trading will only tighten their grip on Wall Street. Although Kidder will quit the risk arbitrage business in mid-1987, the pool of risk arbitrage money on Wall Street will return to nearly the pre-Boesky level by then.

Yet risk arbitrage will already have been displaced, even upstaged, by a whole generation of computer-driven trading strategies—strategies Boesky's young friend John Mulheren had helped to pioneer in the late 1970s and early 1980s. Reflecting the ascendancy of the trader, ambitious young MBAs will flock to Salomon Brothers and other trading-oriented firms in the mid-1980s, drooling at the prospect of landing jobs that their forerunners had so long scorned.

Former Treasury Secretary William E. Simon will be puzzled by the trend. In the early 1950s, when he entered investment banking, "trading was not a respectable profession. Now kids out of B-school are dying to get on the trading desk, but I never hired a B-school guy on my desk in my life," he will tell an interviewer late in 1987. "I used to tell my traders, 'If you guys weren't trading bonds you'd be driving a truck. Don't try to get intellectual when you're in the marketplace. Just trade.'"

Oh, they would.

---

*In May 1987 the U.S. attorney in New York would drop the indictments against Siegel, his former Kidder colleague Timothy Tabor, and Goldman Sachs & Company arbitrage department head Robert Freeman, indicating plans to refile more specific charges later. By mid-1988, that still hadn't happened.

CHAPTER 2

FRIDAY, OCTOBER 16, 1987. ■ Islamorada, the Florida Keys, 3:30 P.M.: Now in their early sixties, Donny Stone and his wife, Jean, view the freedom to be together again—away from the pressures of the city in their unpretentious cottage with the unremarkable fifteen-foot boat moored outside—as the most profound source of contentment and joy.

Often when they are here, the Stones put their fishing rods in the boat, and Donny, cigar in mouth and wearing cutoff jeans, poles out over the Florida Bay sandbars near the cottage. There they expertly snap the rods like whips, whizzing artificial flies a few inches above the placid surface of the water, teasing the bonefish that swim just below.

They are an unlikely pair in some ways. She is a gray-eyed blonde with a wide mouth and a southerner's full lips, the strong-willed Scotch-Irish daughter of a Texas state politician. Stone's face is rounder now and his torso thicker than when he courted her thirty-eight years ago. He parts his hair low on the left and pulls the strands straight across the balding crown of his head.

The eyes, those dark, steady eyes, are everything. To strangers, they are a one-way mirror, showing them nothing but their own reflections. But to his confidants, the mirror is reversed. Knowing him, they see in his eyes a man who is refined but not prissy; proud and prosperous but not pretentious; patient and loving, but nobody's pushover; deeply principled and loyal, but nobody's fool. They see the son every Jewish mother dreams of having, a mensch become a grandfather now.

The setting may be tranquil, but bonefishing is tremendously exciting because success is always a surprise. The surface explodes for an instant and there is the silvery flash of the bonefish's side as he strikes. Then comes the scream of the reel, the arching rod, and the helter-skelter duel like no other in sport fishing. In these waters, a big bonefish weighing up to fourteen pounds can feel like a marlin on such light tackle, and his odds of defeating the angler are higher. Strong and slippery as stainless steel, he can reach between thirty and forty miles per hour in mad runs for freedom, breaking lines and spitting out hooks or even snapping them.

Against the Stones, the bonefish always wins in the end. Even if he is caught, they will set him free, wiser and stronger for the next encounter. They do not come to Islamorada for trophies, but for the joy of the struggle, the sun, and to push the vexations of New York life out of their consciousness for a while. Like his father before him, Donny Stone makes his living as a specialist trader amid the tumult of the New York Stock Exchange floor. And Jean is run ragged by a community service schedule that befits a former mayor of Scarsdale, the first woman ever elected to the post.

There's been no bonefishing and precious little sun on this visit, which they'd begun in high spirits just before the Columbus Day weekend.

How different the prospects had seemed last Friday. He and Jean had flown from New York, motored south down Route 1 onto Upper Matecumbe Key and off again a mile across the causeway to this tiny two-square-mile speck of land on the imaginary line where Florida Bay meets the Atlantic Ocean.

The air was sticky and the skies leaden, but surely that would soon pass. For, almost always it seemed, Islamorada shimmered under the brilliant Florida sunshine. At least that was the way the Stones always thought about it when they daydreamed of their hideaway here.

There would be two glorious weeks of freedom for Jean from the constant round of meetings back in Scarsdale, from the bottomless list of people to call or see and things to check, things to do. For Donny it would mean two weeks of freedom, too: freedom from standing six and a half hours a day on the hard oak boards of the New York Stock Exchange trading floor; freedom from the thunderous roar of the crowd that itself was enough to exhaust a man. And freedom, too, from the tension of watching, always watching the screen of the electronic monitor hanging above Post 8 for signs of a sudden tidal wave of buy or sell orders that may deal him punishing losses.

Two days after they arrived, the Sunday *New York Times* weather forecast noted: "Tropical storm Floyd will slowly strengthen as it moves toward the southern Gulf of Mexico just east of the Yucatan Peninsula. Moisture from the storm will be funneled into southern Florida."

Thunderstorms did strike on Sunday as Floyd picked up speed and headed toward Florida's west coast. By Monday, Columbus Day, the *Times* was warning that "gale-force winds and heavy rain will threaten the Keys and spread north along the western coast. Rising tides and heavy surf will erode beaches as increasing winds from the south force Gulf water into bays and inlets." Indeed, the storm struck the southwestern coast near Fort Myers by mid to late morning. Since neither Donny nor Jean had ever been through a hurricane, they discussed whether to leave Islamorada for the mainland. "But the forecast was for the storm to miss us by a bit and we were sort of curious," Donny recalls.

About ten A.M. on Monday, Floyd, now a hurricane packing eighty-mile-per-hour winds, suddenly veered away from its course to Fort Myers and headed directly along the northern edge of the Keys— directly over Islamorada, "right up Route One," Donny recalls. Howling winds and sheets of stinging rain buffeted the cottage and ripped away at the palms and shrubs through the morning; then suddenly the Stones' power and telephone lines went dead.

The weather had begun to break on Tuesday. (Power was restored by midweek, but the telephone at the cottage would stay out of commission into the weekend. So, twice a day from Tuesday on, Donny walked the four hundred yards across the sand to call his office from the pay telephone outside Tiny's one-pump gas station.)

In fact, the dramatic weather was upstaged by another drama to the north. Donny could not put New York and the stock exchange out of his mind. On Wednesday the Dow Jones Industrial Average had fallen 95 points, more than on any other day in its ninety-one-year history. At this point, according to later gossip among Wall Street's elite, a concerned Donny Stone quickly moved to offset his firm's losses by investing in a type of stock index options whose value rises as the stock market falls. He will not discuss this purchase, how it was effected, or how he knew to place it.

On Thursday buyers had moved into the market following an early 20-point drop in the Dow, and by late afternoon the average was only down 4 points. But then came a sickening slide in the final half hour that widened the day's loss to 57 points.

Indeed, if Donny and Jean had ever spent a more miserable vacation in their seventeen years of owning the little white cottage on the water, he could not recall it.

On Friday, Stone stares aghast at the stock market statistics streaming in a white line along the blue band at the bottom of his television screen. There had been Floyd, the power and phone outages. Now this. Having already fallen 152 points on Wednesday and Thursday, the Dow is down another 130 points today. A buying flurry in the final half hour will narrow the loss to 108 points at the close, but the die is cast.

Today's market mayhem has been triggered partly by an eight A.M. report on the Dow Jones News Service that a U.S.-flagged tanker in the Persian Gulf has been hit by an Iranian missile attack. Periodically during the morning there had been "rumors of a war between the U.S. and Iran," as a presidential task force under investment banker Nicholas Brady will report three months hence.

Donny will get up now and trudge over to Tiny's to let the office know he's ending his vacation a week early and will be back at Post 8 on the floor come Monday morning. By Sunday afternoon, he and Jean will be back in Scarsdale, preparing for the toughest week of his life.

On the newsstands at the airport in New York, a color picture of Alan Greenspan, the newly appointed replacement for Paul Volcker as chairman of the Federal Reserve Board, graces the cover of the latest issue of *Fortune* magazine. The headline reads: Why Greenspan is Bullish.

FRIDAY, OCTOBER 16, 1987. ■ Chicago Mercantile Exchange trading floor, 3:45 P.M., EDT: Scott Serfling, boyish-looking, with a compact, athletic frame and a shock of blond hair, peers down from a bank of traders' desks raised a few feet above floor level.

He is looking into the seething mass of 550 traders, mostly scrubbed midwestern lads in their twenties, who are shouting and jostling one another in the carpeted, three-tiered trading pit whose northern rim lies just a few yards away.

Serfling is trying to catch the eye of a friend who trades near the west rim of this pit each day, mostly in behalf of Kidder Peabody & Company, one of the big Wall Street securities firms. Scott wants the young pit trader to help him make a $287,000 gamble. A bet, yes, but something more, too.

The traders below, and 2,000 other Chicago Mercantile Exchange (CME) members elsewhere in this huge room, actually are dealing in promises. Not idle promises but contracts. If you give me X dollars on the third Friday of December, I'll give you 30,000 pounds of live hogs that day. For Y dollars on the third Friday of next June, you can have the hogs then. You don't actually have to pay me all the money until the expiration day, and I don't have to give you the hogs until then, either. Meanwhile, we'll both deposit a little earnest money, say 5% or 10% of the price we're agreeing on, with a third party as an added incentive to keep our promises to each other.

These are futures contracts, literally, contracts to deliver something at a specified time in the future. In addition to hogs, pork bellies, and live cattle, the futures contracts traded here are based on half a dozen foreign currencies, on such other financial instruments as Eurodollars, Treasury bills, bank CDs. And some futures contracts here are based on the stock market.

Well, sort of. The "stock market" futures here are actually contracts on an amount of money that is related to the level of Standard & Poor's 500 stock index. For decades, the S&P 500, developed by the New York-based credit-rating and financial-information concern of the same name, has been the most widely followed measure of stock market performance among professional investors.

Assuming the same $287 price that Scott Serfling sees in the pit now, this is how this market works:

For openers, while $287, may be the quoted "price" on the December S&P 500 contract, the cost of each contract will be 500 times that, or $143,500. Why? Because the CME says so in its specifications for the contract, which were designed to attract institutional investors and high-rolling individuals.

When you agree to purchase a December S&P 500 contract from me, you are promising to pay me the $143,500 on the third Friday of December, the expiration date the CME has specified. (The other three S&P 500 contracts traded here expire on the third Fridays of next March, June, and September, respectively.)

As the seller, I promise to pay you, at expiration, an amount of money neither of us can be sure about at present. For I'll have to pay you 500 times the value of the S&P 500 index at that time. In the meantime, the price of your contract will fluctuate as the S&P index changes, on a minute-to-minute basis, right up to expiration. In the simplest of the many games that can be played in this pit, you, the buyer, are betting that the stock market will go up. The seller is betting it'll go down.

It's like off-track betting except the payoff can be a lot bigger. To be sure, the S&P 500 future is only one of a number of ways to bet on the stock market without actually trading there.* But it was the S&P 500 futures contract, first traded on the CME in early 1982, that triggered the bonanza. It's the S&P 500 that has drawn the biggest, richest players, and it's the action that has made this the hottest game with the highest stakes in any town.

When visitors come to see him on the floor, Scott Serfling shows them the pit from his trading desk perch and regales them on its majesty. The S&P 500 market "is the king," he says. "It's the most aggressive, volatile market in the entire world. There is nowhere you can make or lose as much money as quickly."

The trading badge Serfling wears on his red jacket is one of the first issued for the S&P futures market back in April 1982. That first month

---

*In addition to another futures contract based on an S&P index of 250 smaller stocks traded on the Chicago Mercantile Exchange, traders at the nearby Chicago Board of Trade deal in a futures contract based on the American Stock Exchange's Major Market Index of twenty big blue-chip stocks, which acts very much like the Dow. There's also a futures contract on the Value Line Index of some 1,700 stocks traded at the Kansas City Board of Trade; and on the New York Stock Exchange Composite Index as well as on three other very broad stock market indexes traded at the New York Futures Exchange.

Similar but more limited contracts called "options" are traded in Chicago, New York, and Philadelphia. These are based on the S&P 500, another S&P index of 100 industrial stocks, the Major Market Index, the NYSE Composite, the Value Line, and five other narrow indexes. Stock index options involve the *right* to amounts of money at expiration, depending on the level of the index involved.

Buyers of "call" options on a stock index will profit based on any amount that the index itself may exceed the option's specified so-called strike price at expiration. Conversely, owners of index "put" options profit based on any discount of the index level to the "strike" price at expiration. Sellers, or "writers," of puts are betting on a rising market and sellers of calls bet on a falling market. Like index futures prices, index options prices fluctuate during their term based on movements in the underlying index.

At expiration, if the index is below the strike price, a call option is worthless. If it's above the strike price, a put option is worthless; and if the index is the same as the strike price, both puts and calls are worthless. In contrast, futures contracts always have some value at expiration.

of trading, about 27,500 of the contracts, worth about $2.9 billion, changed hands here. In September 1987, the total had exploded above 1.9 million contracts, worth more than $315 billion.*

The S&P 500 trading dominates the southeastern quadrant of this gleaming, space-age trading facility whose fourth birthday is now just a month off. It is a carpeted acre of column-free space, four stories high, the largest such trading facility on earth and half again as large as the New York Stock Exchange's cavernous trading floor. There are half a million electrical outlets in this room, more than 6,300 phone lines, 11,000 miles of communications wire. As many as 4,300 people can work in this room, backed up by a room full of computers that is nearly the size of a basketball court.

This afternoon, as always, the place is a color-coded beehive. The members, consisting of speculative traders, or "locals," and brokers called "futures commission merchants" wearing bright red blazers issued to them by the exchange. Traders operate only in their own behalf, but FCMs, who must be licensed by the federal government's Commodity Futures Trading Commission, can trade for others, too. Exchange employees in powder-blue smocks oversee the trading, keeping detailed records of the proceedings.

The largest group is the members' clerks, clad mostly in yellow smocks. They answer phones and run messages and orders between the traders at the banks of desks crammed nearly everywhere in the room and those in the four big trading pits.

A smaller group in green smocks with black patches on the backs are the "out-trade" clerks. They represent members in resolving disagreements over the terms of trades. In a system where business is conducted by jostling crowds of shouting, gesticulating traders, there is no shortage of out-trades to be reconciled.

No one here during these past five years has watched the twists and turns of the trading below more closely, or thought about them more carefully, than Scott Serfling.

After trading most days, he repairs, monklike, to his small bachelor's apartment on the city's near North Side to pore over computer charts

---

*Chicago Mercantile Exchange figures. April 1982: volume, 27,544 contracts; average settlement price, 213.05. September 1987: volume 1,937,420; settlement price, 325.85.

for up to three hours. His tools are two personal computers and the telephone, and he taps into the CME's central data bank to produce the charts from that day's complete trading data.

Many of the less-experienced young traders know this and so, even at the tender age of thirty-five, Serfling has already achieved guru status.

But this guru is about to break one of the cardinal rules among the locals trading here: "Always go home flat." If you want to be among the 15% of traders who can last three years in the pit without losing all their money, you must always close out any S&P 500 position within the same trading day you take it.

But Scott catches the Kidder Peabody trader's eye in the pit and signals him to buy two December contracts that he will not sell back in the remaining fifteen minutes of trading. They are bought at 287—a cool $287,000 gamble that Serfling can secure with an initial margin deposit barely above $20,000.

It is a calculated risk. Today the S&P contract price has already cascaded down more than 11 points, or $5,500 per contract. Minutes ago, Scott had crossed over to the east edge of the pit to check the bank of CME computers drawing real-time charts with live trading data. "At around 287, the December contract was so cheap, and the computers showed it so oversold, I couldn't believe it," he recalls. "I'd never seen a bargain like that in five years here." The price just had to snap back like a rubber band, he'd reasoned, and decided to buy.

Yet, far from snapping back, the price will plunge a further 4.75 points after Serfling's purchase and will settle at 282.25, down 16 points for the day. Across the 146,563 contracts still open at the end of Friday, today's paper losses total almost $1.2 billion.

Serfling will not sleep well this weekend, but surely the rebound will come on Monday.

FRIDAY, OCTOBER 16, 1987. ■ American Express Tower, World Financial Center, 4:15 P.M.: Cat-quick, graceful, and still hard-bodied at forty-six years old, Peter DaPuzzo, Shearson Lehman's charismatic head of retail stock trading, has used up one of his nine lives here in the trading room at Shearson Lehman Brothers, Inc. today.

His is the typical Wall Street trader's success story. Unlike the snooty young investment bankers upstairs with their Harvard and Stanford MBAs and their Harvard law degrees, DaPuzzo earned just a good, serviceable BS—cum laude, mind you—from Rutgers back in 1965. Seven years earlier, fresh out of high school, he'd begun on Wall Street as a clerk at Carl M. Loeb Rhoades & Company. Within three months he was a trainee in the over-the-counter stock department, buying and selling the shares of mostly emerging young companies whose managements didn't yet have the time or money to apply for New York or American Stock Exchange listings. At twenty he was a full-fledged trader in the OTC department, and eleven years later, he became the youngest man yet to be made a partner of the venerable, old-line securities house.

Years later, when Loeb Rhoades was acquired and its name was changed to Shearson Loeb Rhoades, DaPuzzo stayed and rose higher. Then, following the firm's 1979 merger into American Express Company, he rose to be executive vice-president, and developed Shearson's OTC department into the largest and most powerful on the Street, bigger even than arch-rival Merrill Lynch's. His rewards as the bull market began in 1982 had been promotion to senior executive vice-president, responsibility for all stock trading in behalf of individual investor customers, and command over an army of 350 traders and support personnel.

But DaPuzzo always has been closest to his sixty-five OTC traders, and this afternoon is no exception. Wednesday was brutal for them, Thursday almost as bad, and now today's 108-point bloodbath was the coup de grâce. Most of the traders are still kids, as he was many years ago, but without his early experience in trading down markets. And he can see in their eyes that they are shaken.

Now DaPuzzo finally smells the bottom. He is sure this nasty market break climaxed today. So he moves among his exhausted young traders, smiling encouragement, toasting the end of the market break with the champagne he has ordered in.

FRIDAY OCTOBER 16, 1987. ■ Paris, Left Bank, bedtime: Norman Pearlstine, the managing editor of *The Wall Street Journal,* closes his eyes and drifts off to sleep in a charming little hotel whose name he will soon forget.

It has been an exhausting week. First it was Frankfurt and a speech to a group targeted by the *Journal*'s international advertising sales people. Then London and consultations with the *Journal*'s bureau chief, Kathy Christensen, and her staff as well as another speech for international ad people.

Monday there will be negotiations on news-sharing arrangements with *La Tribune de la Économie*. This newspaper is published by the L'Expansion Group, Jean-Louis Servan-Schreiber's go-go empire in which the *Journal*'s publisher, Dow Jones & Company, has just bought a 14% interest. Tuesday he'll lunch with Paris Bureau Chief Phil Revzin and then move on to Brussels to visit the staff of the European edition, which he was said to have agreed to launch for Dow Jones in 1982 in return for the *Journal*'s top news job.

But in the meantime, there'll be a weekend in Paris in the fall. A weekend to stroll and to shop. And rest. Especially, to rest.

CHAPTER

3

OCTOBER 19, 1987. ■ FDR Drive, lower Manhattan, 7:00 A.M.: The traffic is a lot lighter than it will be an hour from now, the time when Donny Stone is normally delivered to his Broad Street office next door to the stock exchange.

It is a spectacularly beautiful early autumn morning with a cloudless sky; a high of 70 degrees is predicted in this morning's *Times*. Donny is at least grateful for that, as the Stones' young driver wheels off the South Street Seaport exit ramp from the FDR Drive and rolls onto Water Street toward Battery Park and the Staten Island ferry landing.

No one recognizes the arriving Donny Stone as the wealthy man he is. His chauffeur isn't uniformed and the car is no limousine. It's not that Donny and Jean Stone try to hide their wealth, but they have always gone out of their way to avoid flaunting it.

Donny doesn't tell people how much money he makes. However, industry sources say that even if his firm's profitability is only average among specialist firms, it earns about 20% on its capital, or close to $5 million a year. Donny's share, as senior partner, is obviously enough to make him a rich man by any standard.

What Donny Stone has always treasured far more than money is respect. And the respect of his New York Stock Exchange colleagues has made him one of the exchange's most powerful officials. Beginning in 1978, the exchange's members elected him to three straight two-year terms as one of two vice-chairmen and as one of four "floor directors." He'd served on all of the board's most important committees throughout that period. And while exchange by-laws required him to step down after three terms, he was back again as vice-chairman, and again a member of the top board committees in June 1986, as soon as it was legal.

Long a close friend of exchange Chairman John Phelan, Donny is in some ways his alter ego. Phelan is tall and slim, sometimes sarcastic and petulant, and so frequently serious-faced that exchange wags call him "the undertaker." Donny is 5 feet 8½ inches tall, a stocky, almost jolly 180 pounds. Ever courteous, self-deprecating, and quick to smile, he is eminently approachable. No one calls Phelan Johnny, but nearly everyone calls Stone Donny.

Yet there is steel in Stone, too, and he is not to be trifled with, floor officials say. "When Donny starts calling you sir, or mister, watch out," says Arthur Cashin, a trader for PaineWebber, Inc., and a "floor governor" assigned by the exchange to enforce its rules and settle trading disputes. Cashin and fifteen other floor governors report to Stone and three other floor directors, who are the highest-ranking exchange officials consistently present on the trading floor. "On matters of honesty or fairness, he's tough as nails," Cashin says.

Lasker Stone & Stern, the partnership Donny and Bernard Lasker formed in 1968 to continue the business of E. H. Stern & Company after its founder's death, is far from the largest securities firm on Wall Street. Indeed, its $23.9 million of capital at the beginning of 1987 ranked only 107th in the industry, according to Securities Industry Association figures.

Lasker Stone is an NYSE "specialist" firm. It, and fifty-four other specialist firms or their subunits do business at seventeen posts on the trading floor. As provided by NYSE rules, they are responsible to the exchange for conducting "fair and orderly markets" in the more than 2,200 stocks traded there. Besides Donny, Lasker Stone has seven other full-time registered specialist traders on the floor. Together they handle a total of twenty-five stocks, including those of Coca-Cola Company and Johnson & Johnson.

The specialist's hoary craft originated with the explosion of stock trading in the speculative surge during and after the Civil War. Prior to 1869, the vice-president of the exchange would read the entire list of NYSE stocks to the crowd of brokers on the exchange floor three times a day. Brokers wishing to trade in a stock would have to wait for its name to be read to call out their bid and be offered prices. A merger in 1869 with two other exchanges doubled the NYSE's membership to more than 1,000, far too large a crowd to continue central trading. Instead, as noted in a history of the exchange, "Brokers dealing in particular stock or kind of stock remained at one location on the trading floor. This spot was indicated by a sign on a pole. Thus emerged the role of the 'specialist' at a 'trading post,' to whom other brokers came with their orders to buy and sell."

A specialist wears four hats at various times to accomplish his market-making function: broker, dealer, auctioneer, and catalyst.

His most obvious function is as a broker. When another broker on the floor has an order that can't be executed at the moment at the price stipulated by the customer, he can ask a specialist to hold the order and execute it for him when and if possible, instead of waiting around the specialist's post himself for the trading opportunity to materialize.

The rules also require specialists to act as dealers in their assigned stocks, risking their own firms' capital by buying and selling for their own accounts whenever there is a temporary imbalance between buy and sell orders. To narrow the spread between the bids and offers of the buyers and sellers in such cases, the rules require him to offer to sell at a lower price than anyone else is offering, or buy at a higher price than anyone else is accepting. He plays this dealer role at the margin of the market. The SEC will report that, for example, in the first nine months of 1987, the sum of all shares bought and all shares sold by specialists equaled just 12.63% of all shares bought and sold on the exchange for the period.

Specialists act as auctioneers when they establish an opening price for the stocks at the start of each trading session, or a reopening price following exchange-ordered trading halts for the dissemination of important corporate news or order imbalances too large for the specialist to correct. And the specialists serve a traffic-cop function, too, managing order flows, sometime smoothing them by seeking and sharing information about the price and size of orders.

Once specialists, wearing one or another of their hats, were personally involved in the trading of every share on the floor. But these days, so-called upstairs traders at big securities firms arrange "block" trades of tens or hundreds of thousands, or even millions of shares that account for the major portion of daily trading. These trades, which are completely or almost completely prearranged, are simply passed by the specialist's post to be recorded or sometimes rounded out with pending orders from the specialist's book.

Additionally, an NYSE electronic system instantly routes orders from member securities firms' offices to the specialists, automatically matching up and executing some of them and sending trade reports back to brokers' offices.

For more than a decade, as block trading and electronic technology mushroomed, their "upstairs" trader rivals in football-field–sized trading complexes at the big securities firms have insisted that specialists are mastodons. But, led by Phelan and Donny Stone, they and the system they represent refuse to die off.

Closely united and holding more than a third of the NYSE memberships, the nearly 500 specialist traders have formidable internal political clout. Like Donny, two of the three other floor directors are specialists. And Chairman John Phelan is both the son of a specialist and a former specialist himself. Yet in recent years at least, the specialists have been slow to flex their muscles at the exchange, some exchange officials say. With stock prices and trading volume soaring for the past five years, many have had all they could do to tend to their trading and count their money.

As Stone's car eases up to his building, there is but a single sign of the tumult that awaits: a Cable News Network live-telecast truck, which had also been at the exchange on Friday. Just ahead at Wall Street, where Broad Street ends and the narrower Nassau Street continues north, the early sun is already warming the huge bronze statue of George Washington and its plaque that says he first took the presidential oath of office here on April 30, 1789.

It is warming the white Georgia marble façade of the stock exchange building, a ponderous, neoclassic structure with six Corinthian-style columns holding a pediment dominated by the symbolic figure of integrity. In all, it is a pacific scene, as welcome to Donny Stone as it is rare here.

It's still too early today for the wild-eyed prophets who come to rail against the profit takers, or the candy and knish peddlers; still too early for the pickpockets and card scammers who work the crowds the others draw to the northwest corner of Broad and Wall. Too early for the phalanx of black limousines to crouch like napping cats along the curbs. Too early for the daily excoriation of the exchange and what it stands for.

Directly across Broad Street from the exchange building stands the financial fortress that J. Pierpont Morgan built. During the Panic of 1907, he personally arranged a $25 million bankers' fund to support stock prices, ending the panic and saving the New York Stock Exchange. "This was the last time," says an exchange historical brochure, "that one man could command the financial resources adequate to change the course of an unfavorable market."

Some saw no boon in the rescue during those early twentieth-century years filled with labor strife. Near noon on September 16, 1920, a horse-drawn wagon loaded with dynamite, nails, and other metal debris exploded in front of the bank, killing thirty-three people and sending three hundred wounded to the hospital. Neither the Bolsheviks nor the anarchist Wobblies took credit for the blast, although both were widely suspected.*

The New York Times used its front page and two other full pages to describe the bloodbath that took place that day. It will use the front page and four more full pages to describe the financial bloodbath that occurs here today.

The arithmetic is elementary. Stock prices tripled between mid-August 1982 and last Tuesday's close, making their owners $2 trillion richer. By today's close, $1 trillion of those gains will have vanished. Today's loss alone will be more than $500 billion, the value of all the work done and all the goods produced in America for a month and a half.

OCTOBER 19, 1987. ■ Miraflores Palace, Caracas, Venezuela, 9:00 A.M., EDT: He is a burly Connecticut milltown Irishman with the

---

*Over the years, suspects have been arrested, then freed as the case remains unsolved. Not long ago, some people at the Morgan Guaranty Trust Company ran into an old-timer who'd been a construction worker in the Wall Street area back then, and he theorizes it could have been an accident. "He believes a contractor could have been transporting dynamite illegally in the daytime along with other construction materials and was afraid to come forward after it blew up," says Morgan Guaranty spokesman Jack Morris. Whatever the truth may be, Morgan Guaranty never did repair the damage, and so passersby along Wall Street will find the bank's limestone façade still pockmarked with jagged holes, some the size of a fist.

ruddy face of a traffic cop in winter and the gut instincts of a plumber. But the Jesuits have taught him how to think, and Paul Volcker has taught him how to maneuver in the powerful, secretive world of central banking. So this morning, Eugene Gerald Corrigan, president of the Federal Reserve Bank of New York, is here at Miraflores, calling on Jaime Lusinchi, the president of Venezuela.

Lusinchi mentions the troubled U.S. stock market, but only in passing. Global economics, Third World debt, currency flows, these are the topics central bankers like Corrigan eat, sleep, and breathe, and they are the topics they pursue in meetings like this one.

Corrigan had come to Venezuela late Thursday night and he'll leave right after this meeting. Friday he'd addressed the Venezuelan chapter of the Interamerican Council on Business and Productivity at the western city of Maracaibo, on the channel separating the huge freshwater lake of that name from the Gulf of Venezuela on the Caribbean.

He'd known the Maracaibo talk would be sensitive. Public statements by any Federal Reserve officials are closely scrutinized by a small army of "Fed watchers," Wall Street bond-market analysts who are paid six-figure salaries to try to foresee the twists and turns of Federal Reserve Board policy that so deeply influence the levels of interest rates, the economy, and securities prices. And Corrigan isn't just any Federal Reserve official. He is paid $184,000 a year. Among federal bureaucrats, that is second only to President Reagan's pay of $250,000, and it is double Fed Chairman Alan Greenspan's $89,500 salary.

As chief executive of the largest and most influential of the twelve Federal Reserve Banks and, since the beginning of 1985, a member of the Federal Reserve's most influential policy committee, forty-six-year-old Jerry Corrigan already ranks among the most influential men on the American financial landscape.

As president of the New York Fed, he has a permanent seat on the policy group that Fed watchers scrutinize most closely, the Federal Open Market Committee. Its monthly deliberations determine how much money will be made available in America for bankers to lend and people to spend. The Fed keeps the minutes of the meetings secret for six weeks to discourage news of committee decisions from feeding short-term speculation in the $3.5 trillion of government, corporate, and municipal bonds in investors' hands.

The Latin American debt problem was another obviously sensitive issue, Corrigan knew. An incautious remark might confuse or further complicate the intricate Latin debt-restructuring negotiations that had been under way, more or less continuously, for five years. And the stakes were enormous. According to New York Fed staff estimates, financially strapped Latin American nations owed an overwhelming total of more than $425 billion to other countries at the end of the third quarter of 1987. They owed $290 billion to banks alone, mostly in the U.S., Europe, and Japan.

So the Maracaibo speech contained no nuggets from the latest FOMC meeting, no proposed revolutionary reforms, nothing to rock anyone's boat.

Instead, the Venezuelans got a generic speech written in longhand by Corrigan on a yellow legal pad. He had called for "underlying discipline" in all nations' management of money supply, taxation, and spending policies. He'd warned that "accelerating inflation is fundamentally in conflict with sustained economic prosperity," and urged that economies be "flexible and market driven." Nations "must maintain an environment of confidence" that encourages citizens to save and "must have safe, efficient, and impartial banking and financial systems," he'd told the Maracaibo audience.

Yet the speech might as easily have come from the mouth of Corrigan's longtime mentor, Paul Volcker. The thoughts were clearly compatible with Volcker's views on these subjects. Did he owe them to Volcker?

Corrigan, and his rivals at the Fed, knew he owed much else to the intellectually austere economist-banker who had headed the New York Fed from 1975 to 1979, and then the Federal Reserve Board through eight tumultuous years in Washington.

Not that Corrigan hadn't shown plenty of initiative before he ever met Volcker. He'd earned bachelor's and master's degrees in the mid-1960s at Fairfield University, not far from his hometown of Waterbury, Conn. His Ph.D. in economics came from another Jesuit school, Fordham, in New York City. Corrigan joined the New York Fed as a staff economist in August 1968, and when Volcker arrived seven years later, he found an ambitious, energetic young bureaucrat who'd already moved through a succession of staff jobs at the bank.

Volcker liked the rough-hewn young Irishman's mind and his skills with people. "He could go out and get things done," a high-ranking

Fed colleague later told a reporter. "He has the capacity to know whom to call up and how to yell at them if they have to be yelled at and how to stroke them if you gotta stroke them." Volcker told the reporter: "Wherever we had a problem, we sent Jerry Corrigan."

Thus Corrigan became Volcker's chief fireman of the 1980s. When the Hunt brothers' failed plot to corner the silver market threatened to bankrupt a string of banks and brokers, Volcker deputized Corrigan to sort out the mess. Ditto when government bond trader Drysdale Securities failed; again when Penn Square Bank collapsed, and when Chicago's big Continental Illinois Bank almost had to be liquidated.

Throughout there were reports of weekend fly-fishing trips and of late-night suppers, with Volcker and Corrigan chewing over monetary policy and home-cooked spaghetti. In 1977, Volcker created a senior-level job for Corrigan, running the bank's management and planning group. And when he went to Washington as Fed chairman in 1979, he tapped Corrigan as his executive assistant.

A year later, Corrigan, only thirty-nine, was named president of the Federal Reserve Bank of Minneapolis, a post he held for more than four years of constant travel and separation from his wife and two daughters, who had remained in New York. Volcker's patronage was widely attributed as decisive in landing him both jobs. Bankers speculate that without Volcker's backing, Corrigan's lack of international background would have denied him the New York post, since the New York Fed is the bank through which the U.S. central bank conducts its international dealings.

Notwithstanding his growing profile at congressional hearings, the jury had remained out on Corrigan. His test would come after Volcker handed Alan Greenspan the reins of a fairly junior Federal Reserve Board, on which Corrigan would be a grizzled veteran. That happened in August 1987; and sooner than anyone now dreamed, Corrigan would have to establish whether Volcker's faith in him had been well founded or whether he was clearly out of his depth.

OCTOBER 19, 1987. ■ New York Stock Exchange trading floor, Post 8, 10:45 A.M. Chaos quickly fills this huge space: With a 40-foot ceiling, 25,000 square feet of unvarnished oak floor, and a crowd of 2,500, the exchange could pass now for the world's biggest Gay Nineties saloon.

More than a dozen figure-eight–shaped counters resembling over-staffed cocktail bars are distributed throughout this immense room. Specialists' clerks are the "bartenders," standing every few feet behind the counters, processing orders. The steady "patrons" are the special-ists, who stand opposite their clerks at posts all along the outside of the "bar" throughout the session.

Floor traders operating from phone-equipped desks and booths along the walls spend their days getting orders from their firms' Wall Street trading desks over the phone, then carrying them to the specialists' posts to be executed.

Networks of six-inch metal pipe seem to grow like brass trees right out of the oak floor at the center of each figure-eight station. Cables hang down from the pipes holding a system of racks directly above the counter space. The racks contain as many as twenty-two large TV monitors with information on stocks traded at that station. The infor-mation includes the trading symbol, the prices at which sellers are offering and buyers are bidding each stock, and the last price—often midway between—at which a trade took place.

What usually matters most these days are those smaller monitors at the end of the two dozen hinged black pipes that extend outward like spider legs along the outer edge of the rack above each station. They are the monitors for Quotron, the electronic market-information ser-vice, which flash updated quotes on dozens of stock prices and market indexes throughout the trading day.

This morning, however, is anything but a usual morning here. Donny Stone at Post 8, like the specialists at all the other posts, has riveted his attention instead on the monitor for the stock exchange's Designated Order Turnaround system, a sort of electronic mailbox that accepts orders from all the member firms' trading desks. From well before the opening today, Stone has struggled with immense order imbalances.

There had been scores and scores of delayed openings. Although Donny and the other three floor directors have relaxed some of the administrative requirements that specialists must meet during trading delays, they and the sixteen floor governors had been swamped for over an hour anyway. "I felt like King Kong on the Empire State Building," Art Cashin will recall, "people coming at me from every direction."

Now many of the delayed stocks have finally been opened and the market is coming back a bit. A good time for Donny to rush upstairs and duck into Phelan's meeting with the moguls from the member firms.

Stone strides briskly across the oak floor that is already strewn with the paper flotsam and jetsam of trading. He acknowledges his colleagues' shouted greetings with waves or nods and whisks past them along the twenty-five-yard route to the main entrance at the northwest corner of the floor. From there, it is past the security station with its guards and across the narrow members' lobby that opens onto Wall Street to the elevator bank. The guards are armed in case any of the many threats the exchange receives are bona fide, but mostly their work involves shooing errant tourists and an occasional raving lunatic away from members' areas.

The six-floor journey to the senior executives' floor is as maddeningly slow as ever this morning. There are offices for trading operations, for market surveillance, where 250 staffers, who amount to house detectives, comb live and historical trading data, looking for cheats. A huge and slick fifty-member public-relations and communications staff. Personnel. Payroll offices. Everything now is done with computers and computer equipment. Computerizing this exchange was John Phelan's legacy and he has spent $200 million doing it over the past decade or so.

At last the elevator door opens onto the sixth floor, and Donny moves quickly across the lobby to the junction of the floor's two main corridor networks. If he turned right he would wind up at the huge board room with its ornate giltwork and heroic sculpture.

Instead, he heads through the doorway on the left, just a few steps down the hall that runs toward Broad Street, and into the executive suite lobby with its brace of big, comfortable couches. The vice-chairman's office, which Donny shares with Bill Schreyer of Merrill Lynch, is immediately off the executive lobby to the left. President Bob Birnbaum's office is kitty-cornered off the far right. But John Phelan's is thirty feet down the hall to Donny's immediate right, past a pair of small gray settees and the desk of John's executive secretary. A quick "Hello, Mary" and he walks into the tense minuet being played out in Phelan's office.

Phelan had ordered exchange operating staffers here before seven

A.M. today to open the electronic mailbox an hour early. It was clogged with "four or five times" the normal order flows, he remembers, almost all calling for sales. By 9:30, member firms had already loaded sell orders for 14 million shares, or half a billion dollars' worth of stock, into the exchange's electronic order delivery system. Another $475 million of sell orders would be loaded into the system by ten o'clock, and over the following hour, still another $1.1 billion of sell orders would be entered.

But far from the madness, some of the conferees are optimistic, some even insisting that there really doesn't seem to be massive selling pressure by either individual or institutional investor clients at their firms this morning.

"Well, if you gentlemen will come with me down to the post I just left," says Donny in the coldly polite tone that betrays his anger, "I'll be happy to show you the very substantial sell orders I have from your firms." There are no takers.

Phelan wants to know how badly the firms represented here were mauled in Friday's rout. Nothing they can't handle, he is assured. There is even talk for a while about getting up the $1 billion aid fund for the specialists, who are taking awesome losses this morning; it's already clear their trading capital will be strained today as never before.

But the specialist fund idea isn't pursued; discussion on the subject appeared to some attending the meeting as so vague as to be meaningless. Half a day hence, when more than a dozen of the specialist firms will desperately need an infusion of money, only one will get it, from exchange Vice-Chairman Bill Schreyer's firm, Merrill Lynch.

This is no cozy meeting of Wall Street's old boys' club. There is tension here. Some of the men bitterly complain about last week's news that the U.S. House Ways and Means Committee is moving forward with plans to tighten tax regulations on many takeovers. The news had sent the takeover stocks owned by their arbitrage departments down savagely. There is bitterness, too, about the Federal Reserve's current tightening of the nation's monetary policy that has been driving up interest rates since Labor Day. Phelan is urged to press their concerns on these matters in his role as the voice of the exchange.

"Considering what was at stake, I don't think it would be appropriate if that meeting had been chummy," recalls a participant. Yet a degree of tension between Phelan and some of these men long predates today's grim circumstances. In Phelan's view, over the past five years most of the firms represented here, particularly Salomon and Goldman Sachs, have been using stock trading strategies that amount to playing with fire.

Over that period, and particularly during the past three years, they have become deeply involved in several sophisticated, computer-assisted stock trading strategies loosely called "program trading," after the computer programs that trigger them. Since late 1984, and especially during 1987, program trading has become the hottest trend in the investment world.

Program traders use computers to instantaneously and simultaneously buy or sell whole portfolios containing from scores to hundreds of blue-chip stocks, with values from tens to hundreds of millions of dollars.

Program trading spread like brushfire because it offered professional money managers a way to rearrange the mix of their stock, bond, and cash holdings instantaneously and at big savings. Managers could dart in and out of the stock market to take advantage of rallies and to sidestep declines. Also, program trades could cost as little as two or three cents per share of stock, about one third the cost of conventional large trades without using computers.

The big Wall Street trading firms loved program trading. For one thing, clients using it tended to make up for the traders' lower commissions by trading more frequently. But there was another, stronger lure. Since 1984, the big trading firms had been using program trading strategies to produce a rapidly increasing stream of risk-free investment income for themselves.

But these strategies have a side effect that deeply worries Phelan and the exchange's specialists. The sudden tidal waves of programmed buy or sell orders sometimes produce wide swings in stock prices and inflict punishing losses on the specialists whose job is to minimize volatility.

After program trading was cited as a factor in a 86-point drop in the Dow on September 11, 1986, there had been a public outcry and a formal investigation by the Securities and Exchange Commission. On January 23, 1987, program trading explosions had sent the Dow on a frightening 115-point roller-coaster ride, all in about an hour. Phelan, and everyone else in his office, know that program trading was a factor in Friday's rout, too.

For more than a year, Phelan has been convinced that program trading eventually would turn a major market break into a crash. Beginning late in 1986, he had repeatedly and publicly said so, warning of an impending "financial meltdown," a "first-class catastrophe." Earlier in 1987 he had also confided his concern that these strategies might actually be manipulating the stock market.

The exchange chairman's attacks against one of their fastest-growing businesses had irked some of the men in this meeting who suggested Phelan's Chicken Little tactics might themselves precipitate the market meltdown he feared.

While Phelan's command of the exchange staff is unquestioned, he does serve at the pleasure of the 1,400 members. So these rumblings could be ominous. Some of the bigger members are clearly "more equal" than others, and the most equal among them are those here in this room whom Phelan has angered.

Furthermore, while Phelan is the highest-paid New York Stock Exchange chairman in history, earning over $1 million a year, he is an also-ran in the unofficial Wall Street power ranking based exclusively on dollars. Several of the men here earn multiples of Phelan's pay. Late in the year, even after Salomon Chairman John Gutfreund accepts a $2 million pay cut, he'll still be left with $1 million, plus investment income on whatever the $32 million Phibro paid him for his Salomon stock back in 1981 has grown into now. Yet even his $3 million regular pay package at Salomon wouldn't place him anywhere near the top of the Wall Street heap.

Years earlier, John Whitehead and John Weinberg, the co-chief executives of archrival Goldman Sachs, reportedly were paid more than $15 million a year, apiece. At Lazard Frères & Company, a secretive multinational investment bank little known outside Wall Street, Michel David-Weill, Lazard's senior partner who also has substantial interests in the firm's British and French affiliates, pocketed over $50 million.

A Mexican standoff on the issue of program trading had lasted since spring. Partly that reflected the heat Phelan was getting from the big program trading securities firms. And he had an internal split. Two of the largest NYSE specialist firms, Spear Leeds & Kellogg and Wagner, Stott & Company, were among the program traders.

So, "I determined we had to have somebody study this and the study had to be credible. We were too divided to do one internally," Phelan would recall late in 1987. Yet some believe the choice of that "some-body" spoke volumes about Phelan's private concerns. The designated investigator was Nicholas deB. Katzenbach, who in the mid-1960s had been the U.S. attorney general, the nation's top prosecutor.

Phelan won't press his program trading concerns before this group. Nor would the Wall Street executives be likely to give ground on the issue if he did. In recent years they'd sponsored or cooperated in dozens of studies, seminars, and reports on program trading's effects. Nearly all suggested these effects were highly transitory, not really dangerous.

And as the meeting breaks, prices on the trading floor below are trying to struggle up a bit. Perhaps Phelan's worst fears about program trading's impact today would prove to be excessive, unwarranted—as Salomon Brothers, Morgan Stanley & Company, Kidder Peabody & Company, and PaineWebber executives had been suggesting all along. After all, hadn't the Dow risen more than 800 points in the eight months after Phelan's meltdown warning, despite coincident record growth in program trading? No, Phelan shouldn't try to hold his breath this morning until he sees them squirm.

Still, after the meeting breaks and the limousines glide away from the exchange, Phelan will tell a visitor that what frightened him the most about this gathering was the securities firm executives' apparent lack of fear. "He said they didn't seem to have any inkling of how bad the situation really was," recalls Richard G. Ketchum, director of market regulation at the SEC.

To Phelan, what is left now is to confront the selling stampede below. Donny and the other specialists on the floor will just have to fight it through as best they can.

But Phelan knows it won't be pretty. He senses that the trading floor will become a financial abbatoir today and that the Dow might drop ". . . as much as 200 points."

OCTOBER 19, 1987. ■ Dow Jones Tower, World Financial Center, 10:15 A.M.: Paul E. Steiger, one of two deputy managing editors of *The Wall Street Journal*, picks up the telephone in his glass-walled office on the ninth floor, thirty yards down the south tier from Norman Pearlstine's.

The mellifluous but faint voice at the other end of the line is Pearlstine's. He is with Jean-Louis Servan-Schreiber in Paris now, reading the grim stock market reports spewing from the French publisher's AP-Dow Jones Economic Report printer. Looks like it could be another record drop, the two agree, as Steiger stares into the green glow of the Quotron screen behind his desk.

To the uninitiated, the screen is an alphanumeric alphabet soup, brimming with three-letter codes, two- and three-digit numbers, fractions and minus signs—minus signs everywhere. The key code has but four letters, INDU, followed by a single two-digit number, pointed off to two decimal places. INDU stands for the Dow Jones Industrial Average; −90.55 speaks for itself.

Steiger's already arranging a powwow on covering and packaging the story of any fresh market rout today, Pearlstine learns. He'll gather a small army of *Journal* editors, including Markets Group editor John Prestbo; Page One editor Glynn Mapes; National News editor Marty Schenker; Second Front Page editor Larry Rout, and John Geddes, the assistant managing editor who heads Graphics.

Steiger's office is only half the size of Norm's and hasn't much of a view. It is smaller, and farther from Norm's, than W. Stewart Pinkerton's office is. Stew, the other deputy managing editor, may be one of the best and most prolific front-page feature writers the paper has ever produced. He has a decade and a half of experience in management here, too.

But don't be fooled. Pinkerton's forte is features, not hard news, and he owes Pearlstine and *Journal* associate publisher Peter Kann nothing. Steiger, whose strengths are economics and market news, and the ability to package it effectively, owes Pearlstine and Kann everything. It's been clear since January of 1987, when he was handed responsibility for the National News desk and all domestic *Journal* news bureaus, that Steiger is Pearlstine's heir.*

When Steiger suddenly alit as a full-blown assistant managing editor four years before, few *Journal* staffers had known anything about the lanky young man in his early forties with the full head of brown hair, deep-set brown eyes, and square, Germanic jaw. He had been the

---

*The only significant part of the news operation not turned over to Steiger in January 1987 was the *Journal*'s network of foreign bureaus. They stayed under the control of Karen Elliot House, the paper's Pulitzer Prize-winning foreign editor and Peter Kann's wife.

business editor of the *Los Angeles Times*, Pearlstine's announcement memo to the staff had said. He had worked as a reporter in the *Journal*'s San Francisco and Los Angeles bureaus way back in the sixties. Before he was business editor at the *L.A. Times*, he'd been a senior economics writer for that paper in Washington, and so would focus on economic and financial coverage at the *Journal.*

With about that little to go on, a veteran *Journal* reporter in New York phoned a friend, Bob Dallos, a tough-minded, sometimes crusty senior business writer in the *L.A. Times*'s New York bureau. "I can only tell you three things about Paul," Dallos had said. "He's a genius, totally truthful, and the fairest human being I've ever met." So there it was. Steiger's return to the *Journal* was a second coming of sorts.

Pearlstine had gotten to know Steiger during the 1970s, and was mightily impressed. So was Barney Calame, the *Journal*'s Los Angeles bureau chief at the time. What if the *L.A. Times* didn't seem to be able to reach more than about 15% of the households in its circulation area. It was a damned good paper, and Steiger's business section was one of its strongest suits.

Pearlstine realized there were fundamental changes under way in the investment world. His experience in the Far East and in Europe had forcefully impressed on him the extraordinary growth in the sophistication and international orientation of investment institutions around the world. And he was determined that the *Journal*'s coverage under his leadership was going to reflect that.

Steiger saw it too, plus he had an unusually strong grasp of the domestic sociopolitical impact on investments and was a seasoned news manager. There were others at the *Journal* with a similar understanding of the evolving markets, and of the growing interconnection of politics and finance. And there were plenty of seasoned news managers around, too. But nobody had the whole package. So hiring Paul Steiger and giving him a mandate to direct and coordinate the *Journal*'s economic and financial coverage had been one of Pearlstine's first decisions as managing editor.

Four years later, as he speaks with Paul from Paris, Pearlstine is more convinced than ever he'd made a smart hire. And he decides the smartest course for him right now is to turn Steiger loose and get out of the way. But he promises to stay in touch.

While he was sometimes cautious and tentative about making decisions, Steiger was quick and facile in selling or enforcing them, typically overwhelming any opposition through a combination of enthusiasm and sheer persistence.

Four years into his tenure at the *Journal*, Steiger is memorable for a number of innovations of varying significance, but all perfectly in tune with the changing character of the *Journal*. Chief among them is the Markets Group—a squad of reporters covering the various markets and led by John Prestbo (also sometimes by Steiger himself) in regular story sessions that coordinate their coverage just as the world's increasingly sophisticated investment institutions are coordinating their investment strategies among various markets.

Another is the "Fast and Dirty" story involving "the usual suspects." "Fast and Dirty" was a term Steiger used to refer to stories he wanted to see in the paper quickly, and done as well and as thoroughly as possible—consistent with getting news to readers fast. Something major suddenly popping into the news required a Fast and Dirty response.

Typically, Paul would toss out such assignments in a meeting of editors, one of whom would press a reporter into service to do the piece. "Let's round up the usual suspects and do a Fast and Dirty story on . . . ," Paul would say; then he and the editors would add what elements ought to be covered in the story.

While nobody understood him to be asking for a shoddy job, the very concept of so aggressive an editorial approach shocked some old-timers at the *Journal*. For the implications are vast, and the course is nearly 180 degrees from past practice at the paper.

Pearlstine had made no bones about the fact that he wanted the *Journal*'s ability to "pounce" on a story to be honed and expanded on. He believed a cautious, deliberative approach to many stories was doomed to competitive failure, since readers would rather know whatever the paper knows about something *now*, while they are interested, than get a definitive story later, when their attention is elsewhere. Journalism is at least partly show biz, and the stuff of show biz is highly perishable.

To some of the veterans schooled under the earlier news-management system, Steiger's Fast and Dirty story symbolized the repudiation of everything they thought they knew about how the paper should work. Yet the new system was clearly more efficient and responsive to competition than the old, and it became increasingly entrenched in recent years as cost and competitive concerns mounted at the paper. With its circulation stuck around the 2 million level since the start of the decade, and national advertising coming under increasing pressure, the *Journal*'s profit contributions to Dow Jones in 1985, 1986, and 1987 all fell below the levels of a year earlier.

So it is a troubled ship whose rudder Steiger now holds during the gathering stock market whirlwind.

This Monday morning, Paul's wife, Heidi, is airborne, en route to Los Angeles on behalf of Neuberger & Berman, a nearly fifty-year-old Wall Street stockbrokerage and money management firm with thousands of clients and about $11 billion under management. Heidi is a managing director in charge of marketing, sales, and administration at the firm, and she plans to visit with some present and prospective clients there.

Steiger is scheduled to travel west tomorrow, too, on *Journal* business and to stay there for the remainder of the week. He plans to rendezvous with Heidi for a weekend at a country inn in California's wine district. Now he realizes that will be impossible, so he asks his secretary to call the Coast and cancel.

Later today, Defense Secretary Caspar Weinberger will steal an hour to hard-sell an overnight retaliatory attack on an Iranian oil platform in the Persian Gulf. There is a heated side discussion going on right now between the Foreign department, and the Washington bureau over whether a story on the attack is so important that it should be covered on tomorrow's front page.

Paul faces three editorial meetings with up to thirty editors, hours of checking and rechecking of the stories and charts to be produced, urgent conferences over delays at the printing plants. For him, Sunday had been a grueling marathon, too, directing the preparation of a huge package of stories and graphics on Friday's plunge for today's *Journal*. There was a front-page right-hand column story, a "right-hand leader" in *Journal* parlance, and four more stories and two big chart graphics on pages 14 and 15, as well as the regular look-ahead stock market column.

The New York Times, which publishes seven days a week, had covered the Friday decline in its Saturday editions. Hundreds of thousands of *Journal* readers—including Dow Jones top brass—read both papers, so the Monday *Journal*'s Page One story would have to offer readers more than just a blow-by-blow account of the Friday drop.

And today's *Journal* story did. However, the story about the market's prospects had been too bleak, using words like "meltdown," and it was bristling with devastatingly bearish quotes. That could make the *Journal* look silly if the market came roaring back on Monday.

So the story had been fixed. The word "meltdown" and some doleful quotes were excised. Steiger had Prestbo, also at work Sunday, put together three consecutive paragraphs of more optimistic material and insert them near the top of the story—the part that would appear on the front page before it continued on the inside. The insert section points out that the market weathered a decline nearly as bad as last week's 17.5% drubbing back in 1984 and came roaring back; the market is still 350 points above its level at the end of 1986; the economy is growing and without much inflation; and there's still a lot of investment capital sloshing around out there. If people were buying at 2700 on the Dow, imagine what a bargain 2246 must look like.

But no amount of tinkering would blunt the riveting thrust of a chart comparing stock prices in 1987 and 1929 that the Graphics department had prepared for Monday's package. It had an elaborate caption poohpoohing some concerns recently raised by academics, including Lester Thurow and John Kenneth Galbraith, that the United States was rushing headlong toward another 1920s-style crash.

Steiger had to wonder how many people were carefully reading the caption this terrifying morning. One ranting reader, who apparently hadn't, would phone the paper's New York offices tomorrow morning to charge that the *Journal*'s chart had caused the crash.

Repeating the 1920s?
Some Parallels but Some Contrasts
Tracking the DJIA

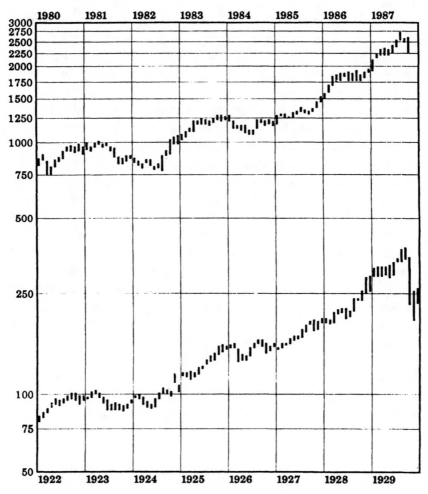

Market watchers have been fascinated for some time by a striking simi-
larity between stocks' surge this decade and their path 58 years ago.
Some academics, such as Lester Thurow and John Kenneth Galbraith, have
voiced concern that the U.S. may currently be repeating its unsustainable
boom of the 1920s. Wall Street analysts find the comparisons intriguing.
But they argue that much has changed in the intervening decades to make
the stock market—and the economy—more stable.

Moreover in percentage terms, last week's market moves are dwarfed
by market tumults in the past. Friday's drop falls well outside the top 10
daily percentage declines. On a week-to-week basis, last week's 9.6%
decline also doesn't make the top rankings of Monday-to-Friday downturns.

CHAPTER 4

AUGUST 25, 1987. ■ A storefront broker's office near Canal Street, 11:30 A.M.: Kathy wipes the tiny beads of sweat from her forehead and squints against the thin blue haze of pipe smoke.

The smoke comes from the knot of frail little men sitting on cane chairs up near the front window of this tiny hole-in-the-wall brokerage firm, founded eighteen months ago, when Kathy was just twenty-eight. This business is going to survive, and Kathy is president and one-third owner. Hey, it's even running in the black, with more than 700 accounts.

The firm is already something of a neighborhood asset, too, a community center of sorts, and a refuge from the hurly-burly of lower Manhattan's commercial district. Where else could Mr. Yee and her other retiree customers come to sit all day and smoke and drink strong coffee and brag about their stock market exploits like young men brag about their sexual conquests?

Much of the reason it all works is Kathy herself. After a couple of years each at Merrill Lynch and Drexel Burnham, she struck out on this venture. Chubby, well-scrubbed, and cheerful, Kathy projects a schoolgirl innocence that flatters the old men.

Every half hour or so, one of the men is dispatched to check the market on the Quotron at Kathy's desk. It has been programmed to continuously monitor and display the Dow, the volume, some other trading indicators, IBM and some other big trading stocks, and a couple of little stocks Kathy owns. Whoever shuffles over to check the market usually keys in and checks four or five of their favorites, too. But after that, it's usually five minutes or so of small talk, and Kathy has an idea that a little chat with a smiling young woman may be as big an attraction as the Quotron.

Not everything is perfect of course. Mr. Yee worries her a bit. His sophisticated and highly risky options plays don't seem too smart a strategy for a retiree. Every week or two she tells him so. But, as the patriarch of the Yee family, he makes all the investment decisions, he tells her. And he has done very well this year, thank you. So it has been made clear to Kathy that venerable Mr. Yee isn't at all eager to listen to advice from an American girl of thirty.

And why should he? He's made over $200,000 in the market this year and lords it over his more conservatively invested cribbage buddies. They're all doing well, Kathy knows. Everybody is. The floor traders she calls to enter her orders have been warning her to watch for a correction soon. It just can't keep going up like this: 800 points already this year. But at least everybody expects it. Nobody will be surprised, and so there should be time for Mr. Yee to pull in his horns when he needs to, she thinks.

After four o'clock, when the coffee klatch is finally over, it will be Mr. Yee's turn to check the Quotron again. "Another 20 points," he will tell Kathy with a smug little grin, and shuffle back to the window. The unremarkable gain will leave the Dow at a record 2722.42.

Ten months later, no one will know if Mr. Yee will live long enough to see it close that high again.

SEPTEMBER 20, 1987. ■ Connecticut Bank & Trust Building, Bridgeport, Conn., 2:00 P.M.: Whether he is presiding over his Wright Investors' Service like a stern father or traveling the world as a member of The Conference Board, John Winthrop Wright is worried.

The rotund and owlish seventy-five-year-old money manager's worries are legion: the horrendous budget deficit, the competitive failings of U.S. business, deficient ethics, the undisciplined stock-buying spree—all threaten the beneficiaries of the $4 billion of institutional money that Wright Investors' manages and the hundreds of pension funds, bank trust departments, and other investors the firm advises.

This Sunday John Wright is in his second and final day of struggle with a writing project on the stock market. A near life-size statue of an American Indian stands like a sentry in his bright office in the corner of a downtown Bridgeport building. Papers are strewn everywhere on his desk and nearby chairs. The purpose of this weekend's work is to warn clients about the puzzling and paradoxical five-year stock market rally that has defied virtually every investment principle that John Wright trusts and has now lifted stock prices to frighteningly high levels.

He doesn't believe that Wright Investors' should be influenced by investment fads. Accordingly, the firm doesn't even consider buying a stock until it has been on the market at least five years; it won't deal in futures or options, refuses to invest in baskets of stocks that mirror a broad stock market index, and won't borrow money to finance its stock positions.

Nor does Wright Investors' tinker with its blue-chip stock portfolios nearly as aggressively as many Wall Street money managers do. In 1986, for example, the total number of shares bought or sold for one of its typical large portfolios amounted to 30% of the stock held in the portfolio, with a significant portion of that "forced on us by takeovers of companies whose stocks we held," a Wright Investors' official says. Again mainly due to takeovers, the turnover ratio would rise to 40% in 1987. Meanwhile, New York Stock Exchange trading in 1986 amounted to 87% of the total number of shares listed on the exchange, and the ratio would rise above 100% in 1987, Columbia Law School professor Louis Lowenstein will note a few weeks after the crash.

Wright Investors' is far from alone, of course. Many, maybe even most of the pension funds in the United States, which these days hold a total of about $2.6 trillion, also pursue equally conservative investment strategies. Partly as a result of this, Wright Investors' is typical of a majority of U.S. money managers who have failed to match the performance of the major stock market indexes during the five-year bull market.

As John Wright sees it, investment advice is a grave responsibility, and investment decisions are not to be made without deep thought and analysis. Thus, clients receiving the firm's thirty-six- to forty-page weekly investment policy and analysis report find that Wright's investment policy rarely changes much. Indeed, it's hard to imagine a money management philosophy more hostile to the underpinnings of this bull market than John Winthrop Wright's.

Those underpinnings include the major Wall Street houses' and their investment institution clients' still-growing use of short-term, trading-oriented investment strategies that already account for a dominant share of stock market activity. Conversely, the reliance on fundamental investment research and analysis that has been Wright Investors' stock-in-trade for over a quarter century is fading fast.

Most of the seeds of investment change that have flowered in the eighties were planted in the seventies.

The 1974 Employee Retirement Income Security Act, ERISA, was widely interpreted to require the corporate and other private pension plans covering more than 50 million Americans to minimize risks by diversifying both their investment strategy and investment management. These changes meant switching around plan assets and managers. And they spurred trading.

Meanwhile, in May 1975, Wall Street completed an SEC-mandated phaseout of the fixed stock brokerage commission rates that had effectively precluded price competition among securities brokers. Discount brokers sprang up to snatch away many old-line brokers' individual clients. The discounted rates stimulated still more trading.

As the discounters chewed away great chunks of their retail businesses, the mainline brokerage firms fell into savage commission-rate competition for the growing institutional business that ERISA was spawning. Institutional commission rates plummeted from 26 to about 12 cents a share during the ensuing four years, the Brady Commission* will report, thus producing yet more trading.

At about the same time, "window dressing" became a force in institutional investment. A 1975 amendment to the Securities Act of 1934 required institutional investors with over $100 million of assets to disclose their holdings in public filings. With competition already surging among money managers, those whose stocks did well in the quarter took the process another step and mailed their quarter-end holdings to prospective clients. Ooops! Now everybody had to look smart at the end of the quarter or risk losing their clients.

No problem. The SEC filing didn't require you to say when you bought the stocks, only which ones you held at the end of the quarter

---

*The Presidential Task Force on Market Mechanisms, appointed in October 1987 to examine and report on the crash, it was chaired by Wall Street investment banker Nicholas F. Brady, and popularly referred to as the "Brady Commission."

and how much. Simple. You just waited till near the end of the quarter, bought the stocks that had done best, and dumped any big losers from your portfolio. From there on, it was just a matter of writing down the new portfolio structure and turning the filing in to the SEC. Investment pros appropriately named this little subterfuge "window dressing." And my, did it spur trading at the end of the quarter. Everybody stayed cool. Everybody looked smart. Everybody won. Especially Wall Street.

The way investment advisers are paid became a factor that drove trading, too. Typically, these advisers are paid a small, often fractional percentage of the value of the assets they manage. The bigger the pile of assets, the more the money manager earns in fees. The progression can be geometric. Smart portfolio picks meant the assets grew, and the money manager's fee with them. The growth, in turn, was recognized as superior performance, which attracted more investment by the client and new clients, too. But this meant constantly having to go after stocks that were hot and dumping those that were not. It meant more trading.

Inevitably the competition among the nation's more than 1,000 money management concerns came from investment performance measured not from decade to decade or year to year, but from quarter to quarter. The stock market basically went nowhere between 1976 and mid-1982, but the amount of stock trading grew sharply. NYSE volume surged to 11.85 billion shares, or an average 1,310 shares per transaction in 1981, from 4.69 billion in 1975, or 495 shares per trade.

The merger mania that gripped the nation beginning in the mid-1970s gave trading a double boost. When Wall Street firms joined Ivan Boesky in the immensely lucrative business of risk arbitrage, their money manager clients fell into step, too, opening a new frontier in institutional investment. Even otherwise conservative pension funds joined the move and by 1987, investment institutions other than the Wall Street securities firms accounted for well over half the $15 billion that Wall Street professionals estimated was invested in risk arbitrage. And, of course, the essence of risk arbitrage is a series of short-term investments acquired through active trading and then turned into cash in the takeovers or restructurings that follow.

Even institutions that eschewed risk arbitrage found themselves forced to trade. Long-term investments they held became takeover victims by the score. In the process, all their stock was bought up and the institutions found themselves holding cash and looking for another investment. By the mid-1980s, takeovers (and company stock buyback programs aimed at supporting the stock price to discourage takeovers) were liquidating stock in the United States faster than companies were creating it. Between the end of 1983 and June 30, 1987, the value of shares that U.S. corporations purchased exceeded that of the shares they issued by $274.3 billion, the Brady Commission task force would observe.

In the 1980s the Reagan administration's tax policy stimulated millions of Americans to pour hundreds of billions of dollars into tax-deferred Individual Retirement Accounts and Keogh plans. Some of this money went directly into the stock and bond markets and other investments. But most individual investors, befuddled by the growing price volatility and institutional domination of both markets, increasingly handed their money over to mutual funds. As a result, total mutual fund assets almost tripled between 1982 and the end of September 1987—to more than $827 billion. The more than $233 billion of that total invested in stocks represented a greater than fourfold increase since the end of 1982.

However, the dominant forces accelerating the trading explosion in the 1980s were the growth in packaging of stocks in tradable baskets, called "indexing," and, of course, John Phelan's bugaboo, program trading.

The two did not develop together. Indexing came first. Beginning in the early 1970s, investment professionals, and especially academics, began wondering what the institutions were really getting for their money management fees. And their answers were increasingly disconcerting. Statistically based studies of stock-price behavior led a growing influential group of academics to conclude that the stock market is a truly efficient mechanism for reflecting all the information that affects the stock values as soon as that information is available. And if that was true, then it was pointless to pay money managers to try to "beat" the stock market averages by actively selecting stocks.

Plus, if the efficient-market theorists were right, the best way to invest in stocks was to construct portfolios that mirrored broad market indexes, such as the S&P 500, the Dow, the S&P 100, and so on. The point was to come up with a portfolio that would do exactly what the stock market (at least as measured by these indexes) did. The way to do that was literally to replicate the index in your portfolio. In 1971, Wells Fargo Bank's investment advisory unit set up what is believed to have been the first of these so-called index funds for a client, Samsonite Corporation, using $100 million from the luggage maker's pension fund. Rather than being modeled after the S&P 500, as most "index" funds have subsequently been, the Samsonite fund was based on the gigantic New York Stock Exchange Composite Index.

Initially most professionals were bemused. Then, following the nearly 50% drop in stock prices that occurred in the 1973–1974 bear market, and the go-nowhere market of the late 1970s, more and more institutional clients began to resent the fees they were paying to their money managers, and indexing began to appeal as a way to cut investment costs.

In an index portfolio, trading would be more sedate and tied to overall shifts in investment strategy and from one major market to another. For those who switched, there would be no more window-dressing games with hyperactive trading (and hence trading costs) near the end of quarters. There would be no more research costs, using armies of securities analysts to look for superior stocks either.

And money management fees would be cut. Any money manager who resisted the idea of lower management fees for the immeasurably easier task of running an index portfolio could always be replaced by a money manager who wouldn't resist. Some institutions administered their index funds internally, eliminating management fees altogether.

There was also the matter of flexibility. Pensions, trusts, mutual funds, and other investment pools grew so bloated with profits in the 1980s that they effectively forced themselves to become index funds. By the end of 1986, about 800 institutions in the U.S. had stock portfolios worth more than $100 million. A prudently diversified portfolio of that size would necessarily hold scores of stocks—as many as are contained in a typical index fund, anyway—so why not just set up an index fund and reap the resulting research and money management costs savings?

By January 1987, according to a study by Greenwich, Conn., consultants Amen & Associates, 786 of the biggest money managers had stashed nearly 40% of the assets they were managing, or more than $500 billion, in index funds. The Amen report doesn't estimate the amount of assets in just those funds that were modeled on the S&P 500 index, but common belief on Wall Street would put the figure at perhaps as high as $400 billion, or 80% of the total.*

As the popularity of index funds grew, so did trading in the same big blue-chip stocks that account for all or most of the weight of the most popular market measures among index fund builders: the S&P 500, the S&P 100, and the American Stock Exchange's twenty-stock Major Market Index (MMI), which includes seventeen stocks from the Dow.

Thus was built the stock "leg" of the program trades to come. Meanwhile, the "synthetic" side of program trading had evolved from interest in the rapidly emerging public markets for stock options.

A stock option was a contract that entitled the holder to buy or sell 100 shares of the underlying stock at a stated price and at any time until the expiration of the option. A call option let him buy at a stated strike price and a put option let him sell at that price. Buyers of calls profited if the stock price rose above the strike price prior to expiration, and buyers of puts profited if the market price fell below the strike price. Sellers of puts and calls would profit under the opposite circumstances, or if the option expired with the market price of the underlying stock and the strike price of the option at the same level.

These features made options ideal instruments for money managers looking for ways to limit or "hedge" the market risk on their stock portfolios. Portfolio managers who were worried about stock price declines could buy put options (or sell call options) on many stocks in their portfolios. Then, if their fears proved justified, the gains (or income) they'd realize on the options transactions would at least partly offset declines in the value of their stocks. And given the nearly 50% drop in stock prices during the 1973–1974 bear market, the risk of stock price declines weighed heavily on money managers during the late 1970s.

Speculators and the risk arbitrageurs dealing in takeover stocks loved puts and calls, too, partly because their market prices were normally only a fraction of the stocks' prices. Also, options buyers could pay for

---

*Similarly, the remaining money would be allotted among funds designed to replicate movements of the S&P 100, the American Stock Exchange's Major Market Index (a mimic of the Dow), and such lesser-known broader indexes as the Value Line Index and New York Stock Exchange Composite Index. The $400 billion of S&P 500 index funds suggested by the Amen study is far greater than some estimates that will surface in the emotionally charged post-crash atmosphere. For instance, a Salomon Brothers study, publicized early in 1988, estimated that by June 1987 only $184 billion of assets were held in funds modeled on the S&P 500. See: Linda Sandler, *Wall Street Journal*, January 26, 1988, p. 54.

their options with borrowed money: up to 75% of the purchase price, compared with a 50% limit imposed by the Federal Reserve's margin requirement on stock purchases. So, stock options grew in popularity, until by the late 1970s, puts and calls on hundreds of mostly blue-chip stocks were trading briskly on stock and options exchanges around the country. To the extent that their portfolios were hedged, money managers felt they could prudently commit more assets to the stock market, and stock trading grew even more.

Initially, institutions were leery of the volatile young markets, where there were no track records and no objective yardsticks of value. But a growing torrent of tantalizing quantitative research at U.S. universities promised to provide those measures. Watershed studies in the 1970s at the University of California at Berkeley and the University of Chicago, among others, yielded a stream of objective formulas for evaluating options. Specifically, they provided ways to quantify the impact on the value of options of such varied factors as the cost of money and the cost and benefits of alternative investments. That, in turn, allowed for far more precise calculations on the most efficient ways to hedge stock portfolios with options, an exercise that soon evolved into a highly specialized financial services industry called "portfolio insurance."

The studies spurred intense interest by the Wall Street firms. Suddenly a rush was on to capitalize on the new knowledge. The lions of Wall Street began prowling the nation's top campuses in search of computer-literate mathematicians. When they found them, they offered them vastly more money than they would ever see in the groves of academe to refine and adapt the new formulas for direct use in trading. The new hires, dubbed "rocket scientists" or "quants" by their often anti-intellectual trader colleagues, helped veteran traders at the largest firms develop sophisticated strategies to capitalize on price discrepancies between options and their underlying stocks, or among various series of options. The quants, and their computers, began popping up as special trading departments, often close to the offices of trading department heads. The torrents of new trading and the geysers of profit these groups produced helped lift their trader bosses to the tops of their firms.

Yet more would have to happen to attract major institutional involvement, the Wall Street firms knew. The institutions were bulls in a china shop in the options market, whose 100-share equivalent contracts had been designed for individual investors. Large institutions that were really serious about hedging found it involved nightmarish administrative and trading headaches and commissions costs. If they could just deal in size—hedge the whole portfolio in a single trade, or a few trades—that would be different.

About the same time, in the late 1970s, speculators were hungering for a broader vehicle, too, a way to gamble on the whole stock market at once. "We had a big meeting on this," recalls Scott Serfling, who was a Merrill Lynch broker in Colorado Springs at the time. "Everyone knew even then that this would be the wave of the future." Indeed, "then and there" Scott decided that "whether a marketwide contract first surfaced as an option or a futures contract, I would go to wherever it was to trade it."

With the demand both strong and clearly identified among hedgers and speculators, the nation's futures and options markets raced each other to develop and win regulatory approval for the products to meet it. The big winner was the Chicago Mercantile Exchange (CME), whose innovative leader, Leo Melamed, during the 1970s had invented and successfully launched futures contracts on foreign currencies, Eurobonds, and U.S. Treasury bonds. Melamed's and the CME's winning entry, of course, was the S&P 500 futures contract that the exchange had introduced in April 1982. Most other index futures contracts and stock index options were launched the following year.

At the beginning, some wildly optimistic proponents of index futures contracts dared to hope that futures would literally replace stocks; that investment institutions could be persuaded to simply substitute the futures for the stocks in their portfolios, essentially making the stock market obsolete. After all, commissions were much lower in the futures markets than in the stock market, and the leverage (i.e., the amount of the investment that could be financed with borrowings) was much greater.

But it was no dice. Stocks were, after all, honest-to-God financial assets, paying cash dividends and giving their holders a voice in the management of a corporation. Futures contracts had none of these attributes. Besides, a good many institutions, especially pension funds, had neither the appetite nor the authorization of their sponsors to buy on margin. Still, the institutions did use the new futures to satisfy their hunger for a broad stock market hedging vehicle, specifically to hedge their burgeoning index funds in line with the portfolio insurers' formulas that were being rapidly refined during the 1982–1984 period.

Meanwhile, the quants on Wall Street stayed busy, helping their shrewd trader colleagues develop valuation models that would let them capitalize most efficiently on the obvious arbitrage potential offered by the price discrepancies between index futures contract prices in Chicago and stock prices in New York. These models proved immensely lucrative to a handful of Wall Street's largest firms, which used them in trading for their own accounts.

Portfolio insurance and index arbitrage, complementing one another and facilitated by the NYSE's enhanced capability to trade whole baskets of stock quickly, became awesome driving factors behind the stock market trading explosion of the 1980s. NYSE volume in 1986 hit almost 36 billion shares, more than double the 1982 total. Volume of all stock index futures contracts in 1986 would reach 26.5 million contracts, more than quintuple the 1982 level. Index options trading would grow almost tenfold from 1983 through 1986. And, reflecting the relentless advance of institutional trading, the NYSE block trades of 5,000 or more shares accounted for 49.9% of the total volume in 1986, up from 41% in 1982.

Given that John Winthrop Wright rejects the very investment strategies driving the boom, the big surprise isn't that Wright Investors' is underperforming the indexes, but that it is as close to them as it is. During the five-year bull market, the typical Wright Investors' portfolio has grown 14.3% a year versus 16.4% a year for the S&P 500. And with the performance gap widening to a sickening five full percentage points through the first three quarters of 1987, even some insiders are wondering whether their boss and their firm may be financial mastodons.

Yet John Wright and some other old-fashioned money managers around the country have seen the forest where the quants and the traders still are seeing trees. He isn't sure just why but Wright sees that by a number of tried and true relative-value measures, investors are paying more for stocks now than they did in 1929. And this is happening amid rising interest rates that are making bonds increasingly tempting to institutional investors. His resolve to share these insights with clients in a special edition of the firm's investment policy and analysis report is what has cost him this weekend.

In the ten days ahead, Wright Investors' staffers will get him to "tone down some of the 1929 stuff," says one, but it will go out to clients substantially as is, dated September 30, as the firm's only special report on the stock market this year. It will warn clients of an impending stock market correction of up to 20% or more and of "a considerable risk that a full-fledged bear market is in the offing."

Among the clients whose stocks Wright will sell off immediately is Jerry Corrigan's alma mater, Fairfield University. Later, a grateful Fairfield official will calculate that the move avoided a seven-figure, 30% drop in the value of the school's stock portfolio.

OCTOBER 19, 1987. ■ En route to the airport, Caracas, Venezuela, 11:45 A.M., EDT: On the whole, it has been a successful and enjoyable visit in Venezuela, but Corrigan is anxious to leave.

He phoned the office in New York just after the meeting with President Lusinchi. The news was bleak. The Dow had fallen about 200 points in the first hour and a half, but had struggled back about 75 points in the next half hour. Volume was practically blowing the roof off the stock exchange. The more that was traded, the more money would have to change hands and the greater the pressure on the banking system would be.

By now Corrigan ought to be inured to crises. God knows he'd been through enough of them in the past seven years, what with the Hunts' silver escapades, the Penn Square Bank and Continental Illinois Bank flaps. Now the great bull market of the 1980s—one of the few unabashedly wonderful things that had happened at least partly as a result of his work—was coming a cropper.

Not many people understand just exactly how much of the world economic fabric has been woven at the Federal Reserve since late 1979, when Jerry Corrigan, then in his late thirties, went to Washington as a special assistant to newly appointed Chairman Paul Volcker. Maybe the story would never be fully told or understood. But even as Corrigan steels himself for the ordeal back on Wall Street, the most ambitious attempt yet to tell that story is close to publication in New York. It is former *Washington Post* assistant managing editor William Greider's formidable *Secrets of the Temple.*

The book will show that within the first six weeks on the job, the Fed chairman had already decisively addressed the major mission of his eight-year tenure. As Volcker took office, the nation was agonizing under an inflation rate of 11.3%, a stubborn hangover of the guns-and-butter budget deficits run up during the Vietnam War. To Volcker, the mess clearly stemmed from a loss of financial discipline, and he determined to use monetary policy to restore that discipline.

The tool was monetarism, a theory long preached by arch conservative University of Chicago economist Milton Friedman. Monetarism revolves around the nation's money supply, literally the total amount of money in circulation, in individual and corporate bank accounts, money market funds, and the like. According to Friedman, if the Federal Reserve increased the nation's money supply too much, people would use the extra money to bid up the prices of goods and services, stoking inflation. Conversely, if the Fed supplied too little money to the economy, competition among borrowers eventually would send interest rates high enough to strangle economic activity and create a recession. As the monetarists saw it, the Fed's job was to set a rational target range for growth in the nation's money supply, then add or drain money from the system to keep the money supply within that range.*

With inflation at a double-digit rate at the turn of the eighties, the horse was already out of the barn. To bring inflation back under control, interest rates would have to climb high enough to throttle down the economy, maybe high enough to produce a recession. Everyone knew that, but nobody wanted to take the blame for allowing it. Greider's book will show that monetarism let Volcker and the Fed make the nation swallow the bitter pill of recession while escaping the political consequences. For, under monetarism, the needed interest rates surge could be demonstrated to be not the result of a Federal Reserve decree, but rather of foolish borrowers bidding up the price of the available supply of money.

---

*The Federal Reserve adjusts the money supply through its Treasury securities trading activities, centered at the Federal Reserve Bank of New York. When the Fed buys bonds, its payment is money injected into the economy, and when it sells them, the money it receives is in effect drained from the economy.

That is exactly what happened. Interest rates soared, and inflation fell away to barely measurable levels over the ensuing years. But exactly how it all came about had huge implications for stock and bond-market investors and for the broader segment of American society. Essentially, Greider will charge, Volcker's successful fight against inflation vastly benefited the richest people on earth at the direct expense of American farmers, workers, and the poor.

The early eighties' interest rate explosion that Volcker engineered delivered historic returns to American bond-market investors and other savers, and to a growing army of foreign investors. These returns helped them buy the $1.2 trillion of debt securities that the Treasury had to issue to finance the federal government budget deficits in fiscal 1981 through 1987. And there was enough investment capital left so that stock prices tripled the August 1982 levels over five years, and provided similar gains for bond investors and stoked even larger gains in other world financial markets.

But as the high rates drew hundreds of billions of dollars of foreign investment to the U.S. financial markets, conversion of their currencies to buy these dollar-denominated assets drove the value of the U.S. currency sharply higher. The strong dollar crushed U.S. agricultural and manufacturing exporters, contributing mightily to a deep thirty-three-month decline. Bitter regional and class resentments were stoked that will have some Americans fairly dancing with joy as the stock market collapses today.

Millions of other Americans were hurt, too. Greider will argue that, in a supreme irony, instead of pricing borrowers out of the market, the Fed's program to wipe out inflation instead helped spur the biggest borrowing binge in U.S. history.

Greider's harsh judgment notwithstanding, Volcker and the Fed were only partly to blame for the damage. Indeed, much of the trouble will arise from the deadly game of economic chicken that both the Fed and the Reagan administration will be pressed by their constituencies to play.

Cheering Volcker and the Fed on were the big banks and the bond investors, seeking what lenders always seek: higher interest rates, higher returns on their money. The Reagan administration answered to a broad coalition of right-wing antitax fanatics and millions of ordinary

middle-class wage earners disgusted by decades of carrying a dispropor-
tionate share of the nation's tax burden.

An unbroken string of massive budget deficits more than doubled
the American federal government's debt between 1979 and mid-1987;
foreigners would buy an estimated $400 billion of Treasury securities
by late 1987. And so the United States, which entered the decade being
owed more money than any nation on earth, by Black Monday already
has become the world's biggest debtor.

Yet, for the five years since mid-1982, it will seem that maybe neither
side will have to back off. For smack among the odious effects of the
Fed-White House stalemate will be two gloriously beneficent ones:
booming stock and bond markets.

The shrinkage of inflation at a faster rate than interest rates in the
early 1980s expanded real returns on bonds and drew crowds of avid
buyers into the bond market. Because yields on U.S. bonds were vastly
superior to those on their own, hordes of foreigners entered the market,
too. Moreover, foreign buying became a self-reinforcing cycle. The
rising dollar itself, by enhancing the yield on U.S. securities to foreign
investors, was an attraction. The strong dollar drew foreign investors,
which made it stronger still, and made it attract still more investors
from abroad.

By mid-1982, high real interest had nearly paralyzed the U.S. economy, and Fed analysts were having fits interpreting distorted money-
supply statistics, Greider's book will report. With inflation apparently
under control, a worried Fed board backed away from monetarism and
eased the credit reins. That was the signal for the stock market to roar
to life.

Pension funds and other investment institutions enjoying the historic triple and quadruple average returns from their bonds now reaped
another immense bonanza as the bond prices soared, too, in response
to declining interest rates. (Although the bonds they bought after late
1982 carried lower nominal interest rates, the sharp drop in inflation
kept real returns near unprecedented highs.) Many institutions took
those windfall profits by selling some of their bonds and plowed the
proceeds into the rising stock market.

To soak up the superabundance of investment capital, Wall Street
investment bankers will dream up or emphasize an endless supply of

financial exotica. High-yielding, low-rated "junk" bonds will flourish, as will securities backed by mortgages, accounts receivable, even auto loans.*

The mountains of money seeking to make new money helped reshape the global markets' landscape, too. Especially after the dollar peaked early in 1985, a growing group of internationally oriented mutual funds and other U.S. institutional investors began seriously investing in high-quality foreign stocks and bonds.

In 1986 and early 1987, these institutions, crowding into the smaller foreign markets alongside local investors whose own pockets are bulging with U.S. investment profits, drove up prices in those markets even faster and further than in the United States. In turn, even more foreign investment was lured to the U.S. stock market, where stock prices seemed to be bargains compared with those in their home markets. In 1986, for example, foreign investors dealt in a record $277.6 billion of U.S. stocks, while Americans dealt in $102 billion of foreign stocks.

After abandoning monetarism, Volcker and the Fed continued to keep a sharp eye out for signs of inflation. So while they allowed interest rates to fall, they didn't consciously drive them down to stimulate the economy following the long recession. However, in 1982 some of the stimulative effects of the Reagan administration's deficit budgeting began to seep through to the economy, propelling a tepid but continuous economic expansion since then.

It was nonetheless an expansion and, after a thirty-three-month recession, the stock market roared ahead as if it were a bona fide boom. The president and his men gladly took credit for the improved economy and the bull market, blamed the Democratic-controlled congress for the woes of agriculture and manufacturing, and privately puzzled with the rest of Americans over just what it all meant.

SEPTEMBER 11, 1986. ■ The Blue Room, New York Stock Exchange trading floor, 4:05 P.M.: An exhausted Art Cashin, who could be the

---

*All these have the effect of transferring at least some of the credit risk for the underlying loans to the holders of the loan-backed securities. Since they could shift the risk to others, the originators of the loans would get more and more daring. By the fall of 1987, ads for some car dealers in the East will be promising "no money down, no credit check."

actor Art Carney's double, stands in front of PaineWebber, Inc.'s, trading desk in this blue-walled annex to the trading floor, grateful it is over.

Neither Cashin nor anybody else has seen the stock market jerked around like this before. The Dow: down 86.61 at the close, more points than it has ever fallen in a day and its worst percentage decline in decades. Trading volume: a record 237.6 million shares. The press will be howling that program trading did this and also the further 34-point decline in the Dow that will occur on volume of 240.5 million shares tomorrow.

The press will be right, although the SEC will never fully concede it. In a report on the October 1987 "market break," the SEC will say that this financial bloodbath "appeared to reflect" investors' fears of higher interest rates and that program trading "may have condensed the time period" in which investors adjusted to those fears.

By late 1986, nobody here is mystified about what program trading is doing to the market. The sudden spurts of trading, the odd price behavior, with the Dow sometimes rushing up or down 20 or 30 points in a matter of an hour or less, all this had puzzled even many veteran traders before 1984 but it is now understood. It's fairly well known outside the exchange, too, at least in the institutional investment community.

A lot of that understanding is thanks to Arthur D. Cashin, Jr., one of the sixteen NYSE floor governors, and one of the rare program traders who is both able and willing to explain the strategy. PaineWebber is one of twenty-six securities firms involved in program trading, according to the Katzenbach study commissioned by the NYSE in March 1987.*

Back in 1984, when the stock exchange began to accommodate program traders' orders in its automated order system, the strategy had really taken off. Cashin found himself inundated with questions about

*Other firms identified in the Katzenbach report as being involved in program trading, either on their own or on their clients' behalf are: Salomon Brothers, Kidder Peabody, Goldman Sachs, Merrill Lynch, Shearson Lehman Brothers, Bear Stearns, Drexel Burnham Lambert, First Boston, Donaldson Lufkin Jenrette (and its Pershing division), Oppenheimer, who are among the best known on Wall Street; plus BT Brokerage, Cowan & Company, Fossett Corporation, Gold Securities, Gruntal, Intervest, Mabon Nuget, Manko, Nomura Securities, Revcon Associates, Rosenblatt, Susquehanna, and two big NYSE specialists, Spear Leeds & Kellogg, and Wagner Stott. Apparently overlooked—Morgan Stanley, a major rival of Salomon in the S&P 500 pit.

program trading. People here on the stock exchange floor asked him, and so did PaineWebber brokers and other executives who were being queried by the firm's clients about it. Just what the hell is program trading? How does it work? What is it doing to the stock market?

Finally Cashin decided to write down what he knew before he was driven crazy by such endless repetitive questioning. So in December 1984, he circulated copies of a 1,500-word, plain-English explanation both here and back at PaineWebber's headquarters offices. The mini-treatise, "A Layman's Guide to Stock Programs," is mistitled; few laymen ever saw it. But hundreds of stock market professionals did. By Cashin's own immodest estimate, it was "the most copied document on Wall Street for four months."

Part of the confusion about program trading is historical and semantic. "Programs" back in the days of Wall Street B.C.—before the computer—were the extended trading campaigns large institutions had to use in order to get into and out of their hefty stock positions without moving the market in ways that would hurt their own investment objectives. By the example in Cashin's little treatise, a pension fund seeking 500,000 shares of a stock might well decide that only about 20,000 could be bought on a normal day without unduly moving up the price, which would in effect force the institution to pay more than it should for the shares. The process of patiently accumulating the 500,000 shares to avoid that is a stock program, specifically, a buy program.

Later, but still B.C., the word "programs" took on another meaning. The pension fund might receive a $500 million contribution from its sponsor in the second quarter, but not be convinced the time is ripe for investing that money in the stock market. So the money is temporarily "parked" by being invested in Treasury bills, which can be sold in an instant, while the fund's managers study the outlook. Some weeks later, after it's been decided the time is ripe, the pension adviser designs a diversified portfolio of industrial stocks. The fund's managers want to make a quick, clean switch from the T-bills to the stocks so they won't lose income on the $500 million between investments. They contact several brokerage firms and ask them to bid on the job of lining up the needed blocks of stock, with all switches to take place on the same day. This is a *buy program*, too. Similarly, if the fund managers later decide to pull the $500 million out of the stock market and put it into bonds, they'll arrange a *sell program.*

Enter the computer, used increasingly in investment research and trading since the mid-1970s. By the early 1980s, powerful personal computers could now complement the work of some of the rocket scientists and other quants being hired by Wall Street firms. One fertile area of work was designing and refining the structure of the index funds—those baskets of stocks whose value rose and fell with the market index they were based upon.

The computer simplified designing the funds and confirming their performance. In 1984 the most popular index funds are portfolios containing from 330 to 390 S&P 500 stocks that are worth, in aggregate, about $10 million, Cashin says. Beyond selecting the right stocks, the design job involved determining just how much of each stock should be in the basket. For, unlike the Dow Jones Industrial Average or the Amex's Major Market Index (MMI), the S&P index doesn't give equal weight to the price of each component stock. Instead, weighting is determined by the total dollar value of all the shares of each company's stock. (For example, IBM stock alone accounts for more than 5% of the value of the S&P 500.) The hundreds of stockholdings in the typical S&P 500 index fund range in size from as little as 200 shares to as many as 5,000 shares, notes Cashin in his 1984 explanation. In contrast, Cashin adds, an MMI fund contains an identical number of shares of each of the twenty component stocks, "These [index funds], too, were called 'programs,' although 'baskets' would be more closely descriptive," says Cashin in his treatise.

Soon program trading evolved to yet another stage—incorporating concurrent dealings in certain publicly traded futures and options contracts that didn't even exist before 1982 and 1983: those based on the S&P 500 and other popular stock indexes—stock index futures and options.

Brokerage firms with large inventories of stock also began to use the futures right along with speculators, who loved them because they were a gamble on the stock market (except that the margin deposits required in the futures and options markets were far smaller and the brokerage commissions lower). Investment bankers got involved, too, because over a brief period they had to own the millions of shares of stocks they underwrote and distributed to the public.* Both the brokers and invest-ment bankers were seeking hedges, reasonably priced protection against cataclysms. "What if they blockade the Straits of Hormuz tomorrow? What if there is an international incident? What if some nut shoots the president? Even Lloyd's of London doesn't sell insur-ance to cover all of those," Cashin poses these questions in the program trading paper. His answer: "But if you sell enough futures you are insured," even if this "insurance" works to deny you the fruits of pleasant market surprises.†

By 1984, hedgers and speculators together had already made the Chicago Merc's S&P 500 futures pit a vibrant and highly liquid market, and a two-year-old, cross-markets trading strategy would soon dominate the stock market scene—stock index arbitrage. Indeed, in late 1986, stock index arbitrage is what Art Cashin and most of the other pros mean by "program trading," although the explosive growth of portfolio insurance has influenced a growing number of people to lump it with index arbitrage under this umbrella term.

The index arbitrageur aims to profit on divergences in value between a basket of S&P 500 stocks on the one hand and a comparable-sized holding of S&P 500 futures on the other. Theoretically, in perfectly efficient markets, each holding would be worth exactly the same, for example, the $10 to $20 million that Cashin says is a common design size for program trades. But the stocks and futures are traded in differ-ent markets, whose participants, trading objectives, and trading costs differ. And so in the ebb and flow of trading, value discrepancies that the arbs can capitalize on are bound to occur.

When the basket of stocks is worth sufficiently less than the stock index futures, the index arb can turn a profit by selling the futures at the CME pit and buying the cheaper basket in New York. Conversely, if the basket fetches sufficiently more than the futures to offset the arb's costs, he can profitably reverse the process by buying the futures and selling the stocks. No risk, only reward, it would seem.

Of course, it's not quite so simple in practice. For not all the costs

---

*Normally major underwriters pay the whole amount of the financing (less a modest underwriting fee) to the company issuing the stock. They then get their money back by selling the shares to the public.
†Index futures prices go down with the index. This lets the seller profit by the difference between what he was paid for the contracts sold and the smaller amount he now has to pay to buy back the contracts that will close out his futures position.

of pushing around $10 million stock and futures positions are easy to quantify. The easy ones to determine are: brokers' commissions; interest on money borrowed to help buy the $10 million of stocks or futures; or, if no borrowed money is used, the return on, say, Treasury bills that the index arbitrageur is foregoing. But how do you ascertain and reflect the dividends that are likely to be paid to the holder of stocks during an arbitrage play but not to the holder of the futures? What about trading vagaries that prevent the purchase or sale of some stocks at exactly the prices anticipated?

Wall Street's quants have figured formulas to reflect all these costs and more. The costs are programmed into computers to adjust continually to passage of time, price changes and other variables. The formulas yield a figure that everybody has decided to call the "fair value" of the futures contracts.

The fair value varies from day to day with changes in varied costs and time frames. Also the amount of the premium or discount cushion beyond fair value that is needed before index arbitrageurs swing into action varies from player to player, based on the exact construction of each one's basket of stock, and on their differing costs and investment objectives.* But late in 1986, it is normally about 1 point.† So, assuming the S&P 500 index is at 170.00, the futures price will have to be above 171.00 or below 169.00 before index arbitrage could theoretically yield any profit at all.

As a practical matter, Salomon Brothers, Goldman Sachs, Morgan Stanley, and others don't wheel $10 to $20 million positions back and forth between the stock and futures market for nickels and dimes. Their exact expectations vary with their costs and strategies, but as a rule of thumb in late 1986, they usually won't aggressively launch program trades unless the contract's price premium or discount exceeds the fair value by at least another 75 basis points or so.

Therefore, if the futures price spikes to, say, 171.75, or a premium

---

*One fairly obvious difference, for example, is that a Wall Street firm, trading at cost for its own account, can profitably execute program trades on slimmer premiums or discounts than its clients, who must pay the firm commissions for the trades.

†This is oversimplified to avoid bogging the reader down in detail. But when futures traders and other professional investors use the term "points," they mean $1/100$ of a full point on the indexes (or index futures prices). That's because, except for the cataclysmic trading that will surround Black Monday, the prices in the index futures pit rarely change more than a full point from trade to trade. Indeed, the change is commonly as little as $1/10$ of a full point—or "10 points" in traders' parlance.

of 1.75 points over the index itself, then look for the index arbitrageur to sell futures in Chicago and buy stocks in New York. Or if it drops to 168.25 or less, look for buying in Chicago and program selling on the NYSE. Assuming the full-point fair-value estimate does in fact reflect all the costs of such trades, the index arb's profit is a bit over $44,000 on a $10 million position. That may not seem eye-popping, but what if the arb could do that every day? A $44,000-a-day return over 250 trading days is more than $11 million, or a low-risk return on investment above 110% of the $10 million of capital being risked.

From the start, the big Wall Street trading houses were the major players in index arbitrage. And because their costs and objectives don't radically differ, index arbitrage trading tends to come in concentrated waves that make prices bounce or dip as much as 2% or more in minutes. In late 1986, no market on earth is big enough or active enough yet to absorb a half dozen or so $20 million waves of buying or selling in a half hour or an hour without stock prices gyrating in response. While the programs involve less than 20% of the stocks listed on the NYSE, these stocks are the biggest and most visible blue-chip issues, components of the S&P 500 (and of the Dow). So, when more than 300 of them pop all at once—or when they plummet in response to heavy program selling by index arbs, as happened today, September 11—it seems like the whole stock market is going mad.

In the remaining months of 1986 and through most of 1987, Wall Street firms will become more and more aggressive in their index arbitrage, and more and more of their clients will ask to get on the bandwagon. So the program trading waves will grow larger and more frequent. The trend will also be driven by another evolving program trading strategy, "dynamic hedging," more widely known by the misnomer "portfolio insurance."*

You don't buy an insurance policy on your portfolio the way you do on a house or car. Instead, portfolio insurance is based on the incredibly

---

*The strategy of "index substitution" will also come into use in 1985 and 1986, but fade away before Black Monday. Users of this strategy answer index futures backers' original prayers by treating the futures and baskets of stock as investment equivalents. They invest in whichever market is cheaper, flip-flopping from market to market, pocketing the savings much like an arbitrage profit. Some observers believe that the strategy faded because institutions using it feared their trades were being handled poorly by the major Wall Street houses. In 1985 and 1986, as new Wall Street players poured into index arbitrage, major institutional clients demanded to be in on the game, too. Most index substituters were relative small fry in this collision of interests and may have been swept aside.

obvious notion that it's smart to own more stock when the market is going up and less when it's going down. You simply add to your stock holdings as the market goes up and reduce them as it goes down.

The idea would have been just an academic exercise in the sixties or much of the seventies, when big institutions took weeks or months to trade their way into or out of their major stock positions. But in the eighties, the only really tricky part is coming up with a realistic game plan. Given the cost of trading and the cost of money, just what are prudent gains enhancement or loss protection objectives? Exactly how much stock do you buy or sell to reach those objectives, and under what circumstances do you buy or sell it? The gurus of portfolio insurance were Hayne Leland and Mark Rubenstein, two Cal Berkeley professors who in the late seventies developed formulas to answer those questions. The company they formed, Leland O'Brien Rubenstein Associates (LOR), is the cornerstone and leader of a new investment advisory industry that really began to come of age in 1984.

As LOR and its competitors spread the portfolio insurance gospel, converts began to elect to protect (or enhance) from 20% to about 65% of the value of their stock portfolios. And the typical portfolio insurance game plan would call for minor adjustments each time the S&P 500 moves 3%.

Program selling or buying on the NYSE easily accommodates the rapid adjustments called for by portfolio insurance. Until mid-1984, Leland O'Brien Rubenstein was recommending that clients make their portfolio adjustments this way. That is, it told them to execute buy programs on the NYSE for each 3% gain in the S&P, and to execute sell programs for each 3% decline. But from that point forward, LOR advised clients to use the synthetic markets in Chicago, rather than the real stock market, to make their portfolio insurance adjustments.

The change reflected the LOR partners' conclusion that the S&P 500 futures market had grown big enough and liquid enough to accommodate the institutions, and that index futures really could substitute for stocks, at least for short-term trading purposes. That decided, futures are now the hands-down choice, since using the CME is vastly simpler and cheaper than using the NYSE. You can do with a single trade in the CME's S&P 500 pit what takes more than 300 trades on the NYSE floor. And not only is the brokerage commission rate a lot lower in Chicago, but the CME's clearinghouse requires just a 5%

security on S&P 500 futures positions, or $7,500 on a $150,000 contract. That compares with the 50% margin deposit the Federal Reserve requires of investors who buy stocks on credit and the 25% specialists and broker-dealers have to put down when they finance their own stock inventories.

As 1984 came to a close, the heyday of portfolio insurance lay ahead. By the time the stock market peaks in August 1987, the paltry $200 million of assets then being managed with the help of portfolio insurance would explode to more than $60 billion, the SEC's study will estimate, noting that some put the figure at as high as $90 billion.

Thus, the program trading that Art Cashin has seen dominate the stock market on this September day in 1986 is just one strategy, index arbitrage, being practiced by the largest Wall Street trading houses. Index arbitrage had been a significant force in the stock market for only about six months in late 1984, when Cashin wrote his little treatise on it, and it involved only about half as many Wall Street firms as were actively involved in late 1986. It is remarkable that even back in late 1984, Cashin wrote that program trades "seem to disproportionately influence or control the market." Cashin's insight was deadly accurate. Three years later, blue-ribbon commissions will be blaming program trading for the catastrophe of Black Monday.

But what few will understand in 1987, and no one will say, is that the same program trading strategies that will make Black Monday so black will also drive the incredible stock market rally that precedes it. Feverishly pursued in markets dominated by a trading mentality and awash in overabundant investment capital, program trading would be the flywheel of the engine that doubled stock prices between 1984 and 1987.

The problem is one of perspective. You can't fully see the phenomenon on the New York Stock Exchange floor. Nor is it totally clear when viewed from the S&P 500 pit. But if you look at what both Donny Stone in New York and Scott Serfling in Chicago see, you will understand.

CHAPTER 5

EARLY IN 1987. ■ Chicago Mercantile Exchange trading floor, a typical moment at midsession early in 1987: Salomon's floor trader puts down his phone and raises both arms in the air, gesturing like a parking lot attendant warning a customer to stop. He wants to sell.

The Salomon man and all the other traders along Scott Serfling's bank take orders from their firms' trading desks on the phone and relay them via coded hand signals to the independent brokers they have chosen to execute them in the noisy S&P 500 pit below.

When it gets busy, the codes usually are ditched in favor of the universal sign language of the pit. Upraised arms with palms inward signals a buy, palms outward, like the Salomon trader's, mean a sale. They convey price and quantity information with their fingers, fists, and foreheads.

It has been busy for three years now, so Serfling can usually tell just what any of the biggest players is up to by glancing down the trading station, or at his own broker in the pit. The only major power in the pit that isn't trading from Serfling's station is Kidder Peabody, and Kidder uses the same broker Serfling uses to execute orders in the pit.

It's impossible to overstate the value of Serfling's trading desk perch near the S&P 500 pit. Beyond a commanding view of pit itself, there are the other "tenants" along this fifteen-foot bank of trading desks that resembles a bank of pay phones at an airport. From left to right, the space is leased to Salomon Brothers, Goldman Sachs, Morgan Stanley, E. F. Hutton, Shearson Lehman, Scott Serfling, and Refco Group, Ltd., a big Chicago-based diversified futures trading concern.

Serfling's station is rumor central, too. There the market rumors flow in all day from the huge Solly, Goldy, Morgan, and other trading desks in New York, and from Refco's desk, which covers all Chicago markets. Several of Serfling's three dozen clients are highly sophisticated investors with their own well-developed information networks.

For years now, Salomon Brothers has been easily the most powerful force in the pit, trading more often and in bigger lots than anyone else here. Solly's trader on the phone just ten feet away is a tall, handsome young chap in his late twenties. Several clerks a few years his junior rush about at his direction. He uses any of three brokers to execute Solly's orders in the pit, but mainly his choice falls on a bearded man in a bright green blazer who stands out from the other, red-jacketed traders and brokers.

Serfling doesn't remember whether he first saw Solly's trader in late 1983 or in early '84, but he has never lost sight of him since. In Scott's mind, a local trader's success, even survival, in the pit depends on watching the Solly trader like a card counter watches a dealer in a Las Vegas. How many has he bought or sold? At what prices? What is his net position now?

One of the oddities of the pit is that everybody calls contracts "cars." Until Leo Melamed began introducing oddball financial futures contracts in Chicago in the early 1970s—contracts on foreign currencies, Eurodollar bonds, U.S. Treasury bonds, and the like—the CME was a market for futures on agricultural commodities, the kind moved around in railroad cars. An agricultural contract usually involved about as much meat or grain as it took to fill a freight car, and so traders thought of and spoke of the contracts as carload quantity lots, or "cars." The young men trading in this pit haven't been around the exchange that long. But to defer to the old-timers who built this place (and to use the jargon of the insider), they call the S&P contracts "cars," too. These days Serfling watches the Solly trader routinely buy and sell whole freight trains; hundreds and hundreds of cars a day, almost always the "near" contract, the one that expires soonest.

Other savvy locals in the pit watch him, too, for the Solly trader's muscle in this pit can make a local rich or crush him like a bug— the Solly trader doesn't care which. For three years now, between fifty and seventy-five of the locals have managed to take out $300,000 to $750,000 a year from this pit each year, Serfling estimates. A few make in the low millions a year.

Most of the winners have done it with one eye always on the Solly trader, scampering ahead when they can see his direction, staying away when they can't. When he's buying big, they buy. When his buying slows, or they smell a reversal, smart locals think about taking profits and stepping aside.

However, the Solly trader and his fast young competitors from Morgan Stanley and Kidder Peabody can saddle an inattentive or incautious trader with punishing losses in the blink of an eye. Serfling has seen Solly chew up more than its share of 85% of the locals who lose all their money and leave the pit within three years. Many simply don't watch Solly carefully enough or read what they see correctly.

Day after day, month after month, Serfling peers down the bank of trading desks or down into the pit, watching the pattern develop, moving with the flow. Solly buys fifty cars. Serfling buys a couple of cars and the other locals pick up maybe fifty or sixty among them. Solly may buy another fifty.

The cumulative buying pushes the contract price up to a smart premium over the S&P index itself. The price posted on the wall near the S&P pit is starting to creep up now. So, more locals buy another fifty cars. Solly also buys another fifty. The premium keeps growing, and it nears everybody's estimate of the day's fair value. It will probably have to expand three quarters of a point or so more before index arbitrage starts.

With luck, a speculator might ride the contract price up another 1 to 2 points or more before the rally fizzles or the premium gets fat enough for the arbitrage reversal. Serfling and the other savvy locals quickly check the electronic bulletin boards around all the walls for the quotes on all the markets trading here and the relevant markets elsewhere. If the dollar is steady or higher, the bond market looks okay, and Solly is standing pat, Scott may pick up three more cars and the rest of the locals another eighty or one hundred.

Now if Solly wades in to buy an additional 50 or 100 cars, the locals will go berserk and snap up hundreds more, driving the price premium well into index arbitrage territory. But Scott won't chase it from here. He'll shed his three-car lot at a profit of maybe a full point, or $1,500 in all. He'll hold on to the two cars he bought at a lower price since his already bigger paper profit on them gives him the speculative leeway to hang in a little longer and see what develops. Other locals start lightening their positions, too.

Ultimately, unless the premium shrivels too quickly, Solly, or Morgan or Kidder, or Goldy—maybe all of them—suddenly dump 300 or 400 or even 500 contracts into the pit as they pull the trigger on $15 million to $20 million buy programs on the NYSE floor. (By Black Monday, Salomon's trading baskets will have grown to $30 million.) Most of the locals would be hard-pressed to make the margin requirement needed to hold their positions overnight. The risk entailed in sticking with the position seems unbearable. So Serfling and the other locals sell, too, and the premium quickly falls back out of arbitrage territory.

Scott's remaining two cars may fetch a profit of, say, 125 points, or $1,250, giving him $2,750 in profits over the past half hour and eliminating his position in the market. Odds are he'll just watch the rest of the action today. For Scott's profit so far is right in line with the $650,000 he will take out of the pit this year, and he has a thing about walking away ahead of the game.

The index arbs' and locals' selling spurt, often when the S&P 500 index itself is still rising, creates some opportunities for bargain hunters. Typically, they've been big brokerage houses like Shearson, Hutton, or Merrill Lynch. Especially in 1986 and before, when the number of contracts involved wasn't huge, these big wirehouses,* often soaked up the bargain-priced positions at such turns without much problem. And lately, as the bull market heads toward its fifth anniversary, their small institutional clients and even a few high-rolling individuals are becoming more active speculators in the pit. Refco is a major trader in behalf of institutions seeking to hedge their stock portfolios. Because of this, it is often active in mopping up the contracts dumped during an arbitrage reversal.

Hedging is also becoming a tremendously potent factor in helping drive the game this year, particularly the hedging done by the portfolio insurers. Many of their game plans call for the purchase of S&P 500 futures when the market advances 3% and for their sale when it declines 3%. This year, the market will rise or fall more than 3% on twenty-one days prior to the crash. In the first week of January, "they

---

*The big retail stockbrokers, named "wirehouses" for the teletype networks that long ago linked their thousands of branch offices with Wall Street's vast branch offices.

plowed money into the pit like I'd never seen it plowed in before,"
Serfling says. The buying spree touched off a surge of index arbitrage
and related stock market buy programs that drove up the Dow about
75 points in the first three trading days of the year.

The volatility, and the portfolio insurers' game plans, will contribute
to an undocumented explosion in index arbitrage in 1987. Neither
NYSE nor CME trading statistics include it, but "my distinct impression is that index arbitrage was pursued far more actively in 1987 than
in prior years," says Robert Mnuchin, Goldman Sachs's top stock
trading official. "The movement of stock prices through the year pre-
sented a great many opportunities for it."

The portfolio insurers' and the index arbitrageurs' interests mesh
perfectly. Like any other institutional investor clients, portfolio insurers
want to sell at the highest price available and buy at the lowest.
Meanwhile, one of the few constraints on the index arbitrage strategy
being pursued by the big Wall Street brokers and investment bankers
is liquidity in the pit when they want to reverse gears.

There's no way Serfling and the locals can be persuaded to buy when
a Salomon or a Morgan or a Kidder is a major seller. Nor can they be
persuaded to sell when the big fish are buying heavily. At those times
the liquidity burden is squarely on the shoulders of the wirehouses and
the larger speculators. As a practical matter then, the size of the
programs is limited by the depth of speculation in the pit rather than
by the liquidity of the stock market.

The index arbs and portfolio insurers are made for each other. When
does a portfolio insurer want to buy contracts? When the market is
rising. What makes the market rise? Buy programs. When can the
lowest price in a rising market usually be found in the pit? When
arbitrageurs sell there while unleasing their buy programs in the stock
market. Conversely, when the market plunges 3% or more, and portfolio insurers want to sell contracts, the best price they are likely to get
for them will be from the index arbitrageurs aggressively buying futures
as they pull the trigger on their stock selling programs.

This year the army of portfolio insurers has grown so large that their
buying pressure in the pit sometimes offsets the selling, even those sales
explosions that occur at arbitrage turns. Over and over again this year
Serfling will see this buying pressure holding the premium of the S&P

contract price above the index, squarely in arbitrage territory, while the index arbs repeatedly dump contracts and pull the trigger on wave upon wave of stock buying programs.

Sometimes the process works in reverse, with portfolio insurance sold in the pit maintaining the discount, even as arbitrageurs aggressively buy while they sell basket after basket of stocks in New York. But of the twenty-one stock market price moves greater than 3% prior to the crash, fourteen will be advances.

The downside seemed to be limited in other ways, too. An index arb doing buy programs could keep going until he ran out of money for stocks, while apparently one doing sell programs would be finished when he ran out of stock.* And these days, there is a whole lot more money around than stock.

In early 1987 it seems unimportant that both index arbitrage and portfolio insurance are "price insensitive" strategies. This fact is perhaps the ultimate expression of the trading mania that will overtake Wall Street. For as 1987 begins, portfolio insurers and index arbitrageurs routinely deal in billions upon billions of dollars' worth of stocks and futures contracts, literally without regard to price.

EARLY IN 1987. ■ New York Stock Exchange trading floor, Post 8, midsession: For Donny Stone and his colleague specialists in blue-chip stocks, the most important tool here often is that TV monitor at the end of the hinged black tube that reaches out from the rack above like a giant spider leg.

This is the monitor for Quotron, the electronic market information service. It can be programmed to update quotes on dozens of stock prices and market indexes continuously throughout the trading day. And that's exactly how the specialists use it.

---

*Theoretically, the arb could keep borrowing and selling stock indefinitely. But under the SEC's long-standing "uptick rule," any such sales would have to take place at a price higher than the immediate prior trade, hardly a likely occurrence in a plunging market. On December 17, 1986, the SEC told Merrill Lynch it could sidestep the uptick rule in some program selling situations without fear of enforcement sanctions. The ruling was communicated by private letter to Merrill's lawyers, and so is not yet generally known in the securities industry. Also, the kind of nasty market break that would allow aggressive use of the exemption has not occurred yet, and Merrill is believed to be loath to use it aggressively anyway.

Because the Quotron monitors are suspended out away from the trading stations, the specialists can keep one eye on them while staying alert for approaching floor traders. Five years ago it was more important for Donny Stone and the other specialists to watch out for the floor traders. Now it's more critical to stay current with the Quotron, or at least with two of the numbers that are programmed one above the other on virtually every Quotron screen in this place: the S&P 500 index and the "near" S&P 500 futures contract price.

The Quotron has become the specialists' radar. For many specialists, staying attuned to the direction and size of the spread between those two numbers—and moving fast when the spread opens far enough for index arbitrage—has increasingly been the price of success. Donny Stone and his colleagues stare transfixed up into the Quotron's green glow through much of their workday.

Once the specialists ruled this floor like feudal lords and, indirectly, the world of investments. If you approach a specialist's post, you had better be ready to open your order book. If you did manage to chisel him in a trade, you could expect stinging losses the next time he spotted you at his post.

Nowadays the specialist is likely to show you his book. For he is but one vendor of a trading service in a competitive world where you have the choice to trade in London or Tokyo, on another U.S. exchange or over-the-counter after hours. These days his performance rating by the exchange—and hence his chances of being assigned newly listed issues—partly depends on whether his service pleases the floor traders who do approach him. And if he is a specialist in one or more of the nearly 400 "program" stocks, his performance under the extreme pressure of program trading will be scrutinized by the flinty-eyed men who run the equity trading desks at Salomon Brothers, Morgan Stanley, Kidder Peabody, Merrill Lynch, Shearson, Hutton, and so on down the line.

Donny Stone and a few others are under even more intense scrutiny, for they handle stocks that, like Johnson & Johnson, are included not just in the S&P program trading baskets, but also in the basket assembled by index arbitrageurs using the Major Market Index future traded at the Chicago Board of Trade.

Until late 1984 and early 1985, most of the program trades on the NYSE were done "by hand," that is, without using the exchange's automated order system. Some still are. They begin with a phone command from a member firm's trading desk to its floor booth. Responding, the floor director unseals an envelope previously sent from the firm's offices and removes a stack of playing-card–sized individual stock orders, aptly called a "deck."

If the trade is to be an S&P 500 program, the deck will have 330 to 390 "cards" calling for the purchase or sale of varying amounts of stock "at the market," that is, wherever the stock is trading when the order reaches the specialist's post.* The floor director parcels out the orders among the firm's floor traders and clerks, whom he may augment with independent floor traders. The floor traders then scurry to the appropriate specialists' posts to get the orders executed. Within five or ten minutes, it should all be over. An MMI program should go even faster, since there are only twenty cards in the deck, all calling for the sale of an easy-to-trade lot, say, 2,000 shares.

Meanwhile, however, "some [risk] arbs got into their pants," says one risk arbitrageur. "For fifty dollars, you could arrange to get a call from the floor when they opened the envelope and a minute or so head start to get your orders in ahead of them," he says. "But the big houses went nuts and made the exchange fix up the DOT system for program trades."

The DOT system, or Designated Order Turnaround system, is the exchange's electronic mailbox and more. These days, most program trading orders come in and are executed by the system. DOT has been around since 1976, when it was introduced to give specialists a way to handle small orders (initially under 200 shares) more efficiently and to relieve floor traders to concentrate on bigger orders. Member firm traders away from the exchange could just press a button on a computer terminal in their offices and transmit the orders directly to the NYSE electronic message switch, where they were instantly routed to the

---

*An order to "buy 5,000 J&J at the market" tells Donny Stone to execute the purchase for whatever price Johnson & Johnson is trading at when the order arrives at Donny's post. Acquiring the stock is a primary goal, the exact price paid for it is secondary. This contrasts with the "limit order," which is conditioned on a stated price, and is widely used by professional investors for nearly all other trades but program trades. A limit order to buy J&J at, say, 70 tells Donny to buy it, provided it can be had for $70 or less. If the price is higher when the order arrives, Donny is to hold it until the price comes down enough to execute it. Unexecuted limit orders expire at the end of the trading day.

appropriate specialist's post. He then matched the order among those already at the post, completed the trade, and confirmed it on his own DOT terminal.

Urged on by the largest Wall Street member firms—the major players in index arbitrage—the NYSE in 1984 introduced important changes in DOT and renamed it Super DOT. One of its new features is "automatic" trading, which is actually something a bit less than that. Provided the buyers' bid price and the sellers' asking price at the specialist's post are no more than ⅛ (12.5 cents) per share apart, an income "market" order will be marked with a reference price based on that current market price and, unless the specialist personally executes it within three minutes, it will automatically be confirmed back to the sender as executed at the reference price.

The NYSE also lifted the size limit on the DOT market orders to 1,099 shares from 599. By October 1987, it will rise to 2,099 shares. The exchange further paved the way for program traders in 1984 by modifying the DOT system to accept whole lists of program trade stocks together instead of one after the other.

Automatic trading means that most program trades can now be handled five times faster through the DOT system than by hand. The reduced trading time cuts the risk of price slippage for stock index arbitrageurs, and is one of the reasons that "fair value" on the S&P 500 contracts is usually closer to 80 points today than the approximately 100 points prevalent in late 1984.

Already in early 1987, Super DOT can routinely automatically execute wave upon wave of program trades, each typically involving a $20 million basket of S&P 500 stocks. DOT's speed makes it all the more important that Donny and the other specialists in the popular program stocks stay alert to a widening of the S&P futures/index premium or discount into arbitrage territory. So typically these days, when Scott Serfling and the other locals in Chicago react to a decisive Solly purchase by driving up the futures price, Donny Stone needs to judge immediately whether he has enough sellers in his book to meet a possible buy program at or not much above current prices. Other sharp traders have seen the premium opening up on their Quotron screens and are already starting to buy the Johnson & Johnson shares they hope to ride up on the crest of a program.

Should Donny start buying stock to have it ready, or will the rally in the pit fizzle and leave him up to his ears in J&J stock? If the buy programs begin and he doesn't have enough sellers in his book and not enough Johnson & Johnson shares of his own to accommodate them, Donny will be under pressure to borrow stock in order to sell it to program traders—hardly a comforting prospect as the stock price begins edging upward. The stock borrowed and sold to the index arbs must of course eventually be purchased in the market and paid back. If Donny has to pay more for it than he was paid by the program traders, the difference will be his loss.

Early in 1988 the SEC's Division of Market Regulation will starkly summarize months of analysis of the October 1987 trading records from Chicago and New York, and hundreds of interviews conducted with virtually every major participant in both markets:

> . . . stock index futures have supplemented and often replaced the secondary stock market as the primary price discovery mechanism for stocks . . . availability of the futures market has spawned institutional trading strategies that have greatly increased the velocity and concentration of stock trading . . . [and] the resulting increase in index arbitrage and portfolio insurance trading in the stock market has increased the risks incurred by stock specialists and at times exceeded their ability to provide liquidity to the stock market.

Stone and his colleagues will have nowhere to hide as the portfolio insurers turn up the buying pressure in the CME pit during 1987. Their voracious buying will give the index arbitrageurs countless opportunities for risk-free gain as they lock in the premium in the pit and relentlessly transfer all the buying pressure onto the Big Board floor. Their buy programs in New York will send the stock market soaring and the portfolio insurers scampering back into the pit to trigger the whole mutually reinforcing cycle again and again. This year alone, the Dow will rise nearly 850 points, or 43.5%, to its August 25 peak.

At the center of it all, demonstrably doing nothing but being seen in public doing its job, will be Salomon Brothers, the powerhouse of the S&P 500 pit; the King of Wall Street.

THE SUMMER OF 1987. ■ Like millions of other finance professionals, Phelan, Serfling, Stone, Corrigan, and Steiger have drifted down the 1980s from success to success like canoeists on a sleepy river who are unaware of the whirlpool around the next bend.

There have been signs of impending trouble since the decade began, signs that their worlds were slipping out of focus, out of control. But those signs have been subtle and difficult to read, like a clutch of willow leaves drifting to starboard instead of straight down the channel.

All the while, the forces that will suck them into the vortex have been growing unrecognized around them, around all Americans. Some have been unwittingly unleashed by earnest men clashing over public policy, each doing what felt so right that he knew it just had to be right. On one side, an eloquent president promised vast new growth that could trickle down to heal a sick underclass without a tax-enforced redistribution of wealth. On the other, a powerful and dedicated Federal Reserve Board chairman was determined to crush the inflationary spiral that was punishing savers, rewarding spendthrifts, and undermining the U.S. dollar and America's control of its own destiny.

The administration's policies and the Fed's were mutually exclusive, and when neither would back off, a deadly game of financial chicken ensued. The Fed spurred huge new investments in stocks and bonds with an anti-inflationary policy that prevented the Reagan administration's deficit budgets from stimulating the level of growth necessary to justify those investments.

By mid-1987, driven by the trading mentality ruling Wall Street, by mountains of investment capital, and by the interaction of the breathtaking new stock and futures trading strategies, the stock market was riding the crest of the longest and strongest rally in its history. And yet the vast majority of American investors and money managers neither understood nor trusted what their eyes told them was happening. Like John Winthrop Wright, they did nothing to drive the rally. Indeed, during 1987 the anxiety level among American investors seemed to rise with the Dow. All through the summer, Connecticut commuters to New York were overheard agonizing with fellow commuters over whether to sell their stock or mutual fund shares and run, or stay in what they realized was becoming an increasingly unstable market.

The very rise itself produced some of the anxiety. The higher the stock prices rose, the lower the yield on dividends became for investors who paid those high prices. Too low a dividend yield, compared with the yield on high-grade bonds, has traditionally diminished the appeal of stocks and enhanced the appeal of bonds to money managers like John Winthrop Wright and a majority of other U.S. money management professionals. And with the market above 2700 in late August, stock yields were near historic lows in comparison with bond yields.

Just before Labor Day, newly installed Federal Reserve Board Chairman Alan Greenspan will exacerbate the disparity by getting the board to raise a key Fed interest rate by ½ of 1%. The increase will immediately transmit upward pressure to most other interest rates. The move will be variously interpreted as a preemptive strike by Greenspan against budding inflationary expectations, as a shot across the bow of currency market speculators against the dollar, or as a warning to the Reagan administration not to assume that, ignoring economic conditions, he'll open a spigot of cheap money to stimulate the economy and buy a Republican White House victory in 1988.

Whatever its motivation, the import of the Fed action will be chillingly clear. With stocks already looking too expensive relative to bonds, the Fed will have suddenly and substantially enhanced the allure of bonds. Scores of conventional institutional money managers will begin cautiously edging out of their stock positions ahead of the feared imminent correction, like revelers at an orgy who expect a raid.

The selling will begin like a spring rain, softly, gradually, drop by drop, then build steadily into a downpour amid the flow of unsettling news developments in the week before Black Monday.

Late-breaking news on Tuesday, October 13, will confirm the rumors that for days have been unnerving Wall Street risk arbitrageurs: The House Ways and Means Committee is seriously at work on a bill that would effectively eliminate the tax benefits associated with the heavily debt-financed "leveraged buyout" takeovers, a mainstay of the deals business. Takeover target stocks, which will already have fallen 5% since October 9 in response to these rumors, now will plunge as much as an additional 45%, in a few cases, by the end of Black Monday.

By Wednesday morning, the conventional views of value-oriented investors—that stock prices are far higher (and yields far lower) than they should be relative to bond prices and yields—will get serious attention on Wall Street. But few will closely focus on the impending announcement of U.S. balance of trade figures by the Commerce Department. And at 8:30, when the news crosses the wires, investors will be stunned to learn that the August trade deficit was $15.7 billion, more than $1 billion above widely held expectations on the Street.

Instantly, the dollar will plunge more than 1% against the Japanese yen, and U.S. Treasury bond prices will break by ⅝ of a point, or a paper loss of $13.75 billion on the total number of T-bonds outstanding, and push the thirty-year Treasury bond's yield above 10% for the first time since November 1985, the Brady Commission will note. And when the day ends, the Dow will have lost a record 95 points despite unremarkable volume of 207 million shares. Portfolio insurers, just warming to their task, will sell about $250 million worth of S&P 500 contracts in Chicago, according to the Brady Commission study. Index arbs will transfer the portfolio insurers' selling pressure, and a lot of other sellers' pressure from the Chicago pit straight into New York; they will dump $1.4 billion of stocks in program selling, accounting for more than one sixth of the total market activity, as the Brady task force will find.

On Thursday morning, with the dollar threatening to break below the level against the German mark that seven major Western economies had agreed in early 1987 to defend, rumors will surge through the bond market that the Federal Reserve will imminently raise interest rates once again to help defend the dollar. Wall Street's fear is that if the dollar cracks, foreign investors will liquidate their U.S. stocks and bonds and convert the funds back into their own strengthening currencies. Given the level of foreign holdings, such a wholesale selling would crush both markets, the pros believe.

Corrigan's New York Fed will ride briefly to the rescue by announcing that it has been injecting funds into the economy, a move consistent with downward rather than upward pressure on rates. In response, bonds will firm, and the Dow will rise to an approximately 20-point gain at midday.

But other news will discourage investors. Chemical Bank will raise its prime lending rate, the bedrock rate from which many of its con-

sumer and commercial loan rates scale upward, to 9¾% from 9¼%.*
About midday, too, the administration will bring more sellers rushing
into the market by stating that there'll be no special action taken to
trim the budget deficit further.

Even so, the Dow will be down only 4 points with a half hour to
go on Thursday, before collapsing another 53 to close at 2355.09,
down 57.61 points. Portfolio insurance selling on Thursday will exceed
3,600 contracts worth more than half a billion dollars, the SEC will
report.

The Friday, October 16, horrors will start with eight A.M. news
reports of an Iranian attack against a U.S.-flagged oil tanker, followed
by an announcement that the president and national security officials
are weighing a response. The Brady Commission will report that "the
growing tension in the Persian Gulf added to the general feeling of
uncertainty and at times there were rumors of war between the U.S.
and Iran."

Nevertheless, the Dow will be down just 7 points at eleven o'clock,
before an hour of market pyrotechnics will give a jolting glimpse at the
mayhem that is to come on Black Monday. The SEC will report that
index arbitrageurs will snap up most of a thunderous $265 million
sell-off of S&P 500 futures by three portfolio insurers, and then execute
$183 million of sell programs on the NYSE, or 18% of the Big Board
volume between 11:00 and 11:30, as the Dow reels down a further 30
points.

Suddenly, the index arbs will reverse their field and power an eleven-
thirty-to-noon rally that will trim the Dow's decline to 15 points. Then
ordinary institutional investors will join the index arbs in selling and
mercilessly pound the market until the Dow breaks down 70 points, to
about 2270, by two o'clock. Chart-watcher traders, responding to the
widely held belief that the correction should end at 2280 to 2300 on
the Dow, will lead an ill-starred rally to carry the Dow up to 2311, the
SEC will report. Meanwhile, in Chicago the discount between the
S&P 500 futures and the index itself will widen to its greatest point
of the day by 2:30, and the index arbitrageurs will strike again with a

---

*Marine Midland and RepublicBank in Dallas will follow suit on Friday, but other banks will
stand pat, probably averting a public-relations disaster for the industry. Chemical, Marine Midland, and RepublicBank will all have swallowed their pride, and their rate increases, by the close
on Tuesday, October 20.

program selling bloodbath in the final hour and a half that will drive the Dow down a record 108.35 points to 2246.74.

For the day, portfolio insurers' sales will total more than 9,000 S&P 500 contracts worth about $1.3 billion and at least $151 million of stock directly in New York. In the meantime, the SEC will find, index arbitrageurs' sell programs will total $1.37 billion. By 3:50 P.M., the Dow will be down 130 points from Thursday's close before recovering 22 points in the final ten minutes, presenting the odd spectacle of a market full of people relieved that the Dow is only down 108 points. The program traders will account for a stunning 43% of the NYSE's total volume in the final half hour, the SEC will learn.

Yet the savviest professionals will walk away from Friday's massacre knowing it could have been—should have been—far worse. According to formulas that are common knowledge on Wall Street trading desks, the portfolio insurers will have sold far fewer contracts during the week than their models called for.

Among insiders there is no question that the market will plunge on the coming Monday. But how far, and at what cost to investors and the system?

CHAPTER

6

Finally, there came the awful day of reckoning for the bulls and the optimists and the wishful thinkers and those vast hordes that, dreading the pain of small loss at the beginning, were now about to suffer total amputation—without anesthetics.

— E D W I N L E F E B R E , J R . ,
on the crash of 1907*

OCTOBER 19, 1987. ■ Chicago Mercantile Exchange trading floor, 9:27 A.M., EDT: Three hundred fifty brokers and locals surge and sway in the pit, whose tiered contours act like a megaphone for their shouts. "Fifty at sixty-aaaight!" . . . "Two hundred at sixty-six!" . . . "Sixty for seventy!" . . . "Sixty-one for fifty!"

A dozen yellow-jacketed clerks rush breathlessly back and forth through the crush of 200 other locals and brokers pressing in around the rim. Outgoing clerks carry reports of the quotes to their bosses at stations across the trading floor and clerks who arrive bring orders. Mostly they are sell orders at this most tumultuous opening call in the brief history of the S&P 500 futures contract.†

What's happening isn't trading . . . yet. None of the bid and offered prices being shouted below can be accepted until after the opening bell, three minutes hence. There is a $25,000 fine for trading before the opening bell or after the closing bell.

After Friday's selling stampede, the CME sought to discourage

---

*From his book *Reminiscences of a Stock Operator,* reprinted 1980, Fraser Management Associates, Burlington, Vt. The book's main character, a "Mr. Livingston," is believed to have been the notorious speculator Jesse Livermore. Some believe Edwin LeFebre is himself actually Livermore. Livermore made $1 million by 1921, when he was thirty years old, but lost this fortune and three others. On Thanksgiving Eve, 1940, again penniless and deeply in debt, he put a gun to his head in the checkroom of New York's Sherry Netherland Hotel and pulled the trigger.
†Technically, futures markets don't have an opening call. That term normally is applied to the pretrading information exchange in the options markets. No matter what term is applied to it, the process is real each morning. Serfling refers to it as the "opening call."

financially weak traders from wading into the market by lifting the margin deposits required to maintain S&P 500 futures positions to $7,500 today from $5,000 on Friday. Margin deposits on the futures contracts (as opposed to those on stock) are essentially security posted against any possible default on the promises involved in the futures contract by either party to it. In a futures trade, both buyer and seller must post margin, called "initial margin." In addition, both must stand ready to post additional amounts of security. Each day the security is perfected according to the movements of the market. This is done by assessing another margin called "variation margin" (after the variation in prices that causes it to be imposed). Unlike initial margin, variation margin is assessed against only the seller or the buyer, whoever is adversely affected by the prior day's price movement of the contract. And the variation margin taken from one side is posted to the account of the other. Therefore, depending on the position taken, each morning the buyer or seller will either have to meet a variation margin call or will be credited with a variation margin payment. In the stock market, margin serves two functions. In most cases it is a payment requirement—the 50% a buyer must put up himself before he can borrow from his broker to finance the rest of a stock purchase. However, margin must be posted, too, by short sellers—those who sell borrowed stock. And in the latter case, segregating part of the sale proceeds as margin effectively imposes a security deposit against the short seller's walking away if the price goes up instead of buying the stock he needs to settle the debt insured in selling short.

But the move has done nothing to thin the crowd in the pit, which is even a shade larger today than on Friday, CME figures will show. All the bellowing isn't just an academic exercise, either. The opening call gives all the traders an idea of the range of bid and offered prices and the type of orders brokers have been given to start the day. That lets the locals and the major Wall Street players decide whether and how to participate in the opening market. For any bids and offers well inside of the range they are hearing now will probably result in an immediate trade once the bell rings.

As the opening call continues, the trading officials at their desks across the floor can't believe the numbers they are hearing from their clerks. Many are sent hustling back to the pit for confirmation. Scott Serfling, seeing and hearing it from his trading desk above the pit, has never felt quite so alone. His stomach churns and he tries to swallow what feels like a fistful of cotton in his throat. Sellers at 268? 266? Buyers down at 261 and 262?

My God, the contract settled Friday above 282! Twenty minutes or so before that, when he bought his 2 cars and saw Solly buy 240 cars, it had been at 287. Solly hadn't unloaded by the Friday bell, either. And if Solly doesn't know what's going on in the pit, who does? This just can't be true. Surely whatever has caused this temporary insanity will pass once trading begins. Surely they'll come to their senses.

But even as he has this thought, Serfling knows better. The MMI futures opened at the Board of Trade down 14 points, equivalent to the Dow opening down 70 points. Ten minutes ago, the word made the rounds near the pit that Big Board specialists will be among the aggressive sellers on the opening. The specialists have been looking at early order flows on their stocks for at least an hour by now. They know about where stock prices are going to open, and they're big sellers. No, the odds are good that it could get even worse for a while. Also how long can he afford to wait for the turn?

There is less than one minute to decide now. Or should he wait and see just what the bids are on the opening? Maybe some of these brokers around the rim are standing there with a fistful of buy orders, playing possum. Dealing with trading gains or losses ranging from hundreds of dollars up to a few thousand dollars over a trading day was one thing. But tens of thousands on a single trade was quite another. After all, by the time he'd paid all the bills for his fledgling company in 1986, there was only a bit over $100,000 left. Even with his firm's losses continuing at around $300,000 this year, he should do several times better than that, yet . . .

No, he'd already made one big mistake by walking out the door with the two contracts on Friday. He won't tempt fate again. If the market looks healthier, he can always open a new position and trade it today. So Scott signals his broker in the pit to sell both contracts at whatever price he can get on the opening.

The bell rings. More shouting and jostling. Then, it's over. Scott's two contracts sell at 264.00, down 1825 basis points from Friday's close.

The $23,000 loss is more than he paid for the fishing boat he bought for his retired dad in Pompano Beach, Fla., out of last year's earnings.

It's more than the new Cadillac he bought for his mother early this year. If only Serfling could figure out what is happening, really happening here. He carefully reviews his recollections of the past several weeks in the pit.

From a trading standpoint, as Scott sees it now, Solly unleashed this Frankenstein by aggressive selling, which recently drove the S&P contract's price down through an important support area. Just a few weeks ago, as the S&P index slipped from 335 to 330, "quite a number of major firms" took short positions in the pit; that is, they sold contracts. "Most of them" then bought contracts to cancel out their short positions "about 10 points lower, at around 320," Scott will recall. "But Solly didn't."

Thursday, October 8, had been crucial. The correction had picked up steam in the stock market in late September and early October.* The S&P began the day just above 318.50 and "a lot of people thought that if we didn't break 320 on a rally later we were headed lower. I told my clients that if we don't make 320, you should be out or short, but if we got as low as 308 you had to be short.† I knew a lot of portfolio insurance plans called for sales of contracts around the low 300s."

But the rally failed to materialize and "the S&P was at around 317, and in the last five minutes of trading Solly sold 1,000 cars and drove it to 314. Solly was the one that aggressively whacked it. That's when I knew Solly was going to stay short for a while."

Now the trading is beginning in the pit below and Serfling sees that Solly buys 200 cars. The trade is hard to read, hardly assertive for a firm that in the past has bought 500 or more cars at a crack without batting

---

*On October 6 the Dow had fallen almost 92 points, exceeding the 86-point blowout that had kicked off a two-day, 120-point market break in an avalanche of index-arbitrage–related sell programs back on September 11–12, 1986. The SEC studied the trading and, in a public report, blamed the break on market reaction to bad economic news, accelerated by index arbitrage. It found no evidence that portfolio insurance, then being used to help manage less than $10 billion of pension fund stock portfolios, was a big enough factor yet to have figured in the decline. In its massive study of the October 1987 market crash, the SEC will be silent on any part it believes portfolio insurance played on January 23, 1987. At that time the Dow roared ahead more than 64 points by 1:39 P.M., only to drop back 115 points, or 5.2%, in a little over an hour. The SEC's probe of the January 23 trading wasn't made public. (See: SEC, *The October 1987 Market Break*, pp. 1–9.)

†In futures, unlike stocks, any open position of a seller is called a "short position." In the stock market, a short sale is the sale of borrowed stock, from which the seller hopes to profit by replacing the borrowed shares later at a lower price. Futures markets short sellers also hope to profit by paying less for the contracts they buy to cancel out their positions than they were paid for those sold in establishing them.

an eye. Solly could be starting an index arbitrage, or closing out such a position. It depends on what happens next.

But Scott will not see Solly do anything in the pit for the next fifteen minutes. There's nothing he can do now but watch and wait and, oh yes, warn clients. So, he picks up the telephone and starts down the list of Serfling & Associates' three dozen clients. He tells them to "stay out of this market; things are going on here that I don't understand." He will later refuse to execute any client trades in this pit until December 1.

Yet in the course of this morning, even before he reaches all his clients, Serfling will go against his own advice and buy $650,000 worth of the December contracts.

OCTOBER 19, 1987. ■ New York Stock Exchange trading floor, Post 8, 9:32 A.M.: Setting opening prices in a volatile market is a bit like giving someone a garden hose that's still running water. It's usually a whole lot better to hand it over slowly than to toss it.

At times like these, the specialist's goal is an opening "equilibrium price," as John Phelan puts it; "a price that will hold a while" instead of shoot all over the place in the trading immediately following the opening. As the Big Board chairman sees it: "The way to make sure stocks open well" in volatile markets is "don't open them too quickly. Give the buyers and sellers some time to think instead of pressuring them into acting mostly on emotion."

And today is going to be a lulu of a volatile market, Donny Stone realizes, as he looks up at the Quotron screen above Post 8. The S&P 500 futures in Chicago are 12 full points below the index itself. In order for the stock market to be at that level, the Dow would have to be down 85 to 90 points, Donny knows.

He realizes the S&P index itself is grossly misleading. With so many stocks not yet trading, "calculations of most major stock indexes [are] next to impossible," the SEC will observe later. But 12 points! That's more than double the biggest discount Donny has ever seen in the futures price. The fair-value adjustment on the December contract is only about 1 point today. Donny doesn't want to even think about the avalanche of sell programs such a discount is likely to unleash. Even if an index arbitrageur could capture only half the discount that Donny sees on the screen above, he'll still pocket $3,000 each on contracts on which he'll only have to put up about a $7,500 margin deposit to hold.

The Quotron's stark numbers confirm the decision Phelan and Donny and the other three floor directors made earlier this morning to switch to an emergency operating plan, a "prearranged package of things we do when there's pressure," Phelan calls it. There'll be closer scrutiny of specialists' financial condition by NYSE staffers.

But the heart of the plan is trading delays. Just past the market's 9:30 opening, hundreds of stocks are not trading yet, and many of them will remain halted due to order imbalances late into the morning. Also the specialists handling these stocks are being allowed to wait up to a half hour to post preliminary price indications on them.

The delays will help specialists both to solicit needed buyers and to get a clearer reading of market forces. They'll need the latter to help determine opening prices that reflect instead of go against the market forces that will take over soon after the trading begins. An opening price that doesn't truly reflect these forces will increase rather than dampen price volatility, Donny and Phelan know. They also know that would frighten away precisely those sober, long-term investors so desperately needed now.

Normally, specialists are required to post price indications on delayed stocks—specifically, the bid and offered prices then in hand—promptly at the opening of the trading session. The idea is to call attention to any delays—in effect, advertising for buyers or sellers—as needed to help specialists bridge the price gaps.

But in a selling panic like this one, the sight of hundreds of trading delays scrolling by on the Dow Jones broadtape or Reuters will only worsen the chaos, quite probably worsening the order imbalances, too.

Prices alone can't convey the magnitude of these imbalances and might even amount to inviting prospective buyers to their own funerals. For buyers would find whatever price they paid would be clearly above the market within minutes. Their potential losses could grow practically trade by trade, until the selling fury was finally spent. However, delaying the indications emphasizes the massive nature of the order imbalances. In effect, it says: "This is how far apart buyers and sellers are now, even after the specialist has worked on closing the gap for half an hour."

Some program traders will privately suspect other motives are involved, since the delays will have a surprising impact on the index arbs later this morning.

By ten o'clock, ninety-five of the S&P 500 stocks, representing 30% of the index's value, will still not be opened. At 10:30, a total of 175 NYSE stocks, including IBM, Sears, Exxon, and eight others among the thirty industrials, won't be trading.

However, the delayed openings will have a major, unintentionally harmful effect on the futures pit. Scott Serfling and the other locals in Chicago don't realize the NYSE foot-dragging at the opening is so purposeful. They read the delays as a sign of the impossibility, rather than inadvisability, of opening the stocks.

Their misreading, and the widespread knowledge of the short-selling by specialists in the pit, will heighten the fear in Chicago. By 10:15, New York time, the December S&P 500 futures price will be about 32 full points below Friday's close, a plunge equivalent to a 224-point drop in the Dow. The discount to the index itself will be a horrifying 17 full points.* All the while, the fearsome figures will be relayed around the world in the green glow of trading terminals everywhere.

OCTOBER 19, 1987. ■ Financial Square, Thomson McKinnon Securities, Inc., 9:50 A.M.: She had done the obvious thing, the right thing,

---

*The fright is over index arbitrage. As noted earlier, each point of an S&P contract's cost is determined by multiplying the "price" by 500. Therefore, each point of the price of an S&P 500 futures contract is equal to $500. Even after subtracting today's fair-value estimate of 1 point, that leaves an unbelievably fat differential between the stock and futures markets (and therefore, potential profit for an index arb) of 16 points, or $8,000 per contract. Considering it costs only $7,500 of initial margin to own a contract these days, this means a potential profit of more than 100% on each trade. Of course, the chaos in the markets today will prevent any index arbs from achieving so good a result, because by the time their orders to sell the stock are executed, stock prices will be lower (and their profits will be less) than they've planned. But when Donny Stone sees a 16-point potential profit sitting there for the index arb, he knows there will be a feeding frenzy among these arbs today. If the S&P futures price was just 17 points higher than the index, there would be huge selling in Chicago and buying in New York. Since it is the other way around, the selling explosion will occur here, Donny realizes. Professional traders like Donny also have a rough gauge of just how much selling pressure or buying pressure a premium or discount in the S&P futures price (to the index itself) will have. The traders' rule of thumb is that each point of the S&P 500 index is equivalent to 7 or 7½ points on the Dow Jones Industrial Average. A 17-point discount (and today's 1-point fair value of the contract) tells him the Dow will have to fall (or the S&P rise, or some combination of the two) the equivalent of 16 S&P 500 points, or 112 to 120 points on the Dow, before the pressure for index arbitrage selling in the stock market abates.

but she had still been wrong. Perhaps she had acted too soon. Well, she was out now, with a loss of just a few thousand dollars.

So Ruth Barrons Roosevelt, futures trader and broker, artist and eccentric ex-wife of FDR's grandson William, leaves her desk on the Thomson McKinnon trading floor to get a cup of coffee. The fear in the trading room is "palpable, I've never felt anything like it," she will recall later.

Ruth passes by the traders, whose faces are "perfectly still and their eyes [are] open a bit wider than usual." She mumbles to the coffee vendor in the little room across the hall that he should be happy he is out here instead of in there. He chuckles, without comprehending.

Blond and fine-featured, with a son out of college, Ruth must be more seasoned than she looks. She specializes in particularly interest-sensitive futures like those on bonds, stock indexes, currencies, and precious metals.

She has long known that what happened at this morning's opening was a classic trader's buying signal. If you consulted a computer-updated chart of recent trading in the NYSE Composite Index futures contract for December, the big gap between Friday's close of 158.80 and this morning's opening price of 151.00 would make anyone's mouth water. Ruth had noticed that huge gap and had bought one of the $75,000 contracts twenty minutes ago.

"Good traders tend to buy a gap down opening," Ruth will explain later. "When there's that big a drop in perceived value from the majority of the trading all through the previous day, you should expect at least a partial recovery." The larger the gap, the bigger that price bounce should be. And the December NYSE Composite futures price opened down a huge 5% from Friday's close.

It was soon clear to Ruth that something was terribly wrong with today's market. Rather than bouncing out of the starting blocks, the NYSE Composite futures price continued to deteriorate rapidly. So she'd sold a few minutes ago and taken her loss.

Later, Ruth will get on the phone and warn her clients to steer clear of the markets today, just as Scott Serfling is warning his clients in Chicago. But also like Serfling and thousands of other trading professionals around the world, she will be a buyer again this morning and will lose still more money in the ersatz rally that is to come.

Today's tab for Ruth Roosevelt will be $7,000, but she will take it in stride. Just last Friday, she had managed to dodge a much larger bullet by selling off all the stocks in her Keogh plan "at a substantial profit" and putting the proceeds in a money market fund.

Later this morning, she will phone her close friend and precious-metals guru Julian Snyder in Switzerland. She'll compliment the international investment adviser for having warned his clients in August to get out of stocks and for his subsequent advice to take short positions in S&P 500 futures. "He told me this is just the beginning" of a world financial cataclysm, Ruth will recall almost six months later. "He said to guard my fort."

She will enjoy the guard duty. Less than a month hence, Ruth will entertain clients and friends at a "Crash party" in her spacious Wall Street loft hung with her own wall-size paintings. They show blond women who resemble Ruth, but are nude and riding powerful horses at breakneck speed in deep forests. Big-time Wall Street money managers, corporate executives, and brokers will mingle and chatter near a life-sized wooden statue of a monk in whose hand she has impishly placed a wineglass, and a thirteenth-century statue of John the Baptist hidden in a jungle of potted plants. The hostess will laughingly greet her guests in a black Betsy Johnson dress that she has torn into rags for the occasion.

OCTOBER 19, 1987. ■ Chicago Mercantile Exchange trading floor, 10:20 A.M., EDT: Following the purchase of 200 contracts on the opening, Serfling hasn't seen Solly's trader make any move at all for fifteen minutes. He guesses that maybe the firm's top trading officials in New York might be in an emergency strategy session because of the chaos. But Solly has been wearing a white hat ever since, and Scott cannot help but occasionally interrupt his conversations with clients to watch the unfolding drama.

About every three minutes for over half an hour, against an avalanche of portfolio insurers and big speculators' selling that has driven the December contract price steadily lower, Serfling has seen the Solly trader buy a couple of hundred cars. The SEC's report on today's trading will suggest later that the total was at least 2,600 December contracts.

At the average prices prevailing in the pit over that half-hour span, Solly has so far plowed about $350 million into the pit, about evenly divided between purchases for its own account and those for clients, as the SEC report will indicate. The trading records contained in the report will show that the purchases were made in connection with stock index arbitrage; that each 200-contract purchase at CME resulted in an offsetting sale of a basket of S&P stocks on the NYSE. The baskets were designed to have a value of $30 million each, but with stock prices dropping fast, Solly is probably getting less than $27.5 million for them.*

Theoretically, such continued index arbitrage should firm the price in this pit even as it depresses the prices of stocks in New York, until the price here and in New York, as indicated by the S&P index itself, are virtually the same. There is however, so much other selling here that even Solly's and a few other index arbs' aggressive buying aren't pushing the contract price up. Indeed, the price has fallen nearly 20 points during the half hour that ended at 10:15.

Yet the Solly trader didn't flinch, just kept grinding out the buy orders every few minutes. Surely, Scott figures, if the chaos were too great in New York to get the baskets of stock sold, Solly couldn't have continued buying here against the tide. Now, in just the last five minutes, the tide has begun to turn. The futures price is actually moving up, narrowing the gap with the still-falling S&P index itself. An unnamed foreign buyer is committing $218 million to the pits to reap its profits by closing out the short positions it took earlier, the Brady Commission will report later. A trickle of locals has begun bidding alongside Solly, too.

Some of the selling pressure is about to ease, also, as Wells Fargo Investment Advisers begins diverting some of its massive portfolio insurance selling to the stock market in New York. The Brady Commission will report that today, between 10:30 and two o'clock, New York time, one institution will augment the 14,000 contracts, or $2 billion,

*Assume that neither the Dow nor the S&P index itself is a reliable gauge of value on the NYSE floor at this hour. (Due to massive trading delays, both indexes are still being computed on the basis of many Friday prices.) Therefore, the December S&P 500 contract price, averaging about 8.5% below Friday's close through this period, is probably a more realistic measure of what the sale of a basket of S&P stocks will bring at this moment. Presuming the $30 million design value of the baskets was based on the most recent available hard price data (Friday's closing prices), an 8.5% decline in their value would make them now worth a bit less than $27.5 million each.

of futures it sells for pension fund clients in the pit here with $1.1 billion of direct stock sales on the NYSE floor in thirteen approximately equal sell programs. That institution later will be identified in the press as Wells Fargo.

The fast-moving "hedge funds" are about to turn, too. Hedge funds are largely unrestricted investment pools seeded with money from adventurous, superrich individuals—the "smart money" crowd—and a tiny portion of conventional institutional investment assets earmarked for aggressive investment plays. Unlike big pension funds and most other conventional institutional investors, the "hedgies" frequently use short selling as an investment tactic in the stock, options, and futures markets. Early today, they had been actively opening short positions, running ahead of the portfolio insurers they were sure would be out in force. The lower the price sinks here, the more they'll make.

But Solly's relentless buying, now spreading to some locals, has the hedge-fund traders nervously thinking about taking profits now. To do that, they will cancel out their earlier sales by making offsetting purchases at prices as much as $9,000 lower per contract than they have been paid early in the session. In other words, they will join the emerging wave of buying.

More and more locals will jump on the bandwagon. A half hour from now, after a nasty jolt from some NYSE specialists, the index arbs will suddenly double up on their buying here, too. And just before eleven o'clock in New York, the futures price will actually struggle to a premium over the S&P 500 index itself. Even though the Dow will be down 206 points by then, some on the NYSE floor will dare to hope that the stock index futures turnaround signals the end of today's mayhem.

Although he is tempted to buy December contracts now, Serfling remains puzzled and worried. For the moment, he will wait.

OCTOBER 19, 1987. ■ The storefront broker's office in downtown New York, 10:30 A.M.: "I really think you should do it . . . 36 is not so bad," says Carol to the worried-looking Chinese man sitting in the chair beside her desk.

"But I only say 35. I lose too much at 36," protests a gentleman we'll call Mr. Yee.

"Remember what I told you Friday, Mr. Yee? If we have a market where you shouldn't be taking positions, then you should be thinking about closing out your existing positions, too," Carol says earnestly. "And that goes double today," she adds, lifting her eyebrows for emphasis. "If you're serious about holding that position in this market, you have to put another $200,000 in the account right away."

"Two hundred thousand dollars? But you say $100,000 Friday."

"But look what's happened to the price already today, Mr. Yee," Carol says, looking at the Quotron screen. "See, you're up to $200,000. I'll need a bank check."

"Don't put up the margin, you stubborn old fool! Close out your position before it's too late! Take the trade at 36!" Carol wants to shout. But she doesn't. Mr. Yee nods assent to her demand for the margin deposit and shuffles out the door to make arrangements to post it. Carol grabs the phone and quickly dials the Amex floor to resell the option contracts she has bought in the trade that Mr. Yee has just renounced.

Mr. Yee is one of Carol's major problems today. The stubborn patriarch of the Yee family, a retired shopkeeper, is in far over his head. Several weeks ago he'd made a risky bet in the options market that the stock market would hold or go higher rather than go down.

Specifically, he had sold forty "November 450" put options on the American Stock Exchange's Major Market Index—the twenty-stock index developed to mimic the Dow after Dow Jones refused to allow the Chicago Board of Trade to offer a futures contract based on the Dow Jones Industrial Average. At expiration, on the third Friday of November, these particular options entitle their owners to be paid an amount equal to 100 times any shortfall of the MMI below the 450 level. If the MMI isn't below 450 at expiration, the buyer's bet will be lost and the put will expire worthless. That leaves the seller free to walk away with everything the buyer paid him for the contracts (less broker's commissions) as profit. In Mr. Yee's case, he would get to pocket the $40,000 ($1,000 per contract) that he was paid for the put options with the Dow at above 2500. That is the kind of options market game that Mr. Yee has been playing, and winning, all through the year.

Time and time again during most of the past five years, buyers of puts wound up losers as the market raced up. But buyers of the MMI's November 450 puts are in the catbird seat now. The index itself plunged nearly 25 points on Friday, closing at 441.73, and the closing market price of the option itself was 22. Just in today's first hour, the index is off even more, and the price of the November 450 put is exploding. This is precisely Mr. Yee's and Carol's problem. The price Mr. Yee got for his puts was 10.

Mr. Yee's choices now are like those of a futures trader who has gone short. He can cancel out his position by buying forty puts to offset those he sold. Of course, that means incurring an immediate, six-figure loss because that's how much more it will cost to buy the forty put options he needs to close out his position than he was paid for the puts he sold some weeks back.

Alternatively, he can tough it out, wait and see if he'll actually have to pay the holders of the forty contracts anything on the third Friday of November; or perhaps the stock market will rally and push the price back to 450 or better by that date.

But, as in the futures market, the holder of an options position that is adversely affected by price movements cannot wait for a turn in the market without suffering other consequences. On the contrary, he must increase his or her margin deposit to reflect any adverse price movements on the very next business day after they occur. The margin system in the options and futures markets is designed to insure that come expiration day, if Mr. Yee's is a losing bet, the owners of the puts will not have to come looking for him to collect their money. What they are owed will already be on deposit at the clearinghouse in the form of the margin that has been collected daily from Mr. Yee and from all the other losing investors, in accordance with the prior day's price changes.

Carol had thought the huge margin call would bring him to his senses, that it would force him to consider doing the most rational thing. For openers, today Mr. Yee is required to post margin of about $2,500 per contract, or $100,000, to reflect Friday's price surge in the puts, whose price has risen that much again in less than an hour's trading this morning. Technically, this second $100,000 won't have to be posted until tomorrow morning (assuming the market situation, and thus the amount, don't change by the end of the day). However, the $200,000 margin addition Carol seeks truly reflects where Mr. Yee's risky options play stands at this moment.

After Friday's close, Carol had convinced Mr. Yee to "cover," or close out, his position by buying forty puts, if their price ran up much higher. Specifically, he had agreed that 35 was the price at which he would give in and cover. At that price the forty puts would cost him $3,500 each, or $140,000, which would nearly wipe out the Yee nest egg. Just minutes before Mr. Yee came in, the thirty-five price had already looked imminent and so Carol had phoned her Amex floor broker to buy the forty puts.

However, the market was already running away from Mr. Yee and he had had to pay 36. Now that Mr. Yee has rejected the trade at 36 as unauthorized, he has forced Carol into a panic resale that narrowly avoids a big trading loss for her tiny firm.

As Carol well knows, Mr. Yee is far from being alone in his plight. Both the SEC and state securities authorities probing the causes of the crash will find a surprisingly high incidence of senior-citizen investors losing big money in similarly sophisticated, risky stock index options speculations.

"This all started way back in the late 1970s and early 1980s, when interest rates were rising so fast that old people started putting their savings into money market funds," she will explain after the crash. "Everybody was getting two things: huge returns on their money, and a brokerage firm's statement each month."

But then after Paul Volcker's Fed eased the credit reins amid a deep recession during mid-1982, the lofty interest rates came down. While inflation had come down even more, that didn't console many retirees who had become accustomed to getting a third or more of their income from a money market fund that had paid 16% interest last year and suddenly was paying only 8%, Carol says.

Searching ever more desperately for ways to keep their incomes up, elderly investors began talking with the bright young people at the brokerage firms sending them their monthly statements with the now glum news on their clients' money funds.

The bright young people had some bright ideas, Carol says. "The market was dead in the early eighties, so Merrill Lynch and other brokerage firms—I trained at Drexel on this—suggested they could get additional income in the options market."

The idea was this: Many retirees held stock in the companies they had retired from. The stock market was going nowhere, so the retirees had a good shot at selling to other investors call options on their company shares, exercisable at prices above the current market. Each call option let the buyer acquire 100 shares at a specified strike price during the term of the option. If the market price went above that price, the seller of the call could reasonably assume that the buyer would exercise and pocket the difference as a profit. If the market price of the stock didn't exceed the option strike price by the expiration date, the call option expired worthless, and the seller pocketed what he was paid for it as a profit.

During the deadly dull stock market that prevailed between 1976 and 1982, selling call options usually amounted to having your cake and eating it, too. In any event, the worst calamity that could befall an investor selling calls against his stock would be if the stock were called away at a price lower than he could get in the stock market. Still, that price would be higher than the stock market price at the time he sold the option.

It was a powerful idea. As an example, say a retiree from General Motors has 1,000 shares of GM stock selling at 70 and paying an annual dividend of $5 a share, or $5,000 on all his stock. Twice a year he can sell 10 six-month call options with a strike price of 75. Typically, such options would sell for around $2.50 per optioned share. That price, times the 100 shares covered by each option, gives the seller $250 per contract, or a total of $2,500 for all ten contracts sold. If the seller is right, and GM doesn't make 75 all year, he makes $2,500 profit every six months. And the additional $5,000 he takes in each year through this strategy doubles his annual earnings on his GM stock to $10,000, and its yield to 14.2%.

It was true that being cleared to trade options took additional paperwork, and investors had to be warned, under the securities laws, about the extra risks involved in some options strategies. But with stories like the one above spreading among retirees like wildfire, the extra regulatory niceties proved only a minor annoyance. Besides, the extra warnings, and the investors' acknowledgment of those warnings, strengthened the hand of the securities industry in case any flaps did develop over options losses.

However, beginning with the bull market in 1982, the call-option strategy didn't work well anymore, stocks began shooting up through the option-strike prices, and the options increasingly were exercised.

But the brokers had a ready answer for this problem. If selling calls against your stock doesn't work in a rising market, selling puts against the stock would. The put option just reverses the call. Instead of the right to buy 100 shares from you at the strike price, as in a call option, the buyer of the put has the right to sell you the stock at the strike price. So if the price falls below the strike price, he can force you to buy the 100 shares from him at that price.

"That worked fine, too, but then the stock index options came along and there was the chance to make really big money," Carol recalls. These options settled in cash, not stock, and so it was a pure and simple bet. Except it was immeasurably riskier, since almost none of the smaller investors using the options markets actually owned a basket of the various stocks in the index their options were based upon. If they did own such stocks, a losing bet would involve in effect selling them and handing the winner the money. However, not owning the stocks, the investor is essentially naked against the risk of the position going against him.

That is where Mr. Yee and thousands like him come in. Even though such "naked" options strategies were extremely risky, odds were good that any brokers who advised senior-citizen clients to use them would not be called on the carpet by the legal compliance officials of their firms for endorsing inappropriately chancy investments. "They could just show the compliance people the signed risk disclosure forms, and often a five-year history by that investor of trading in options, too," Carol will explain.

"The market prognosticators all figured the bull market would hold up until there was excessive speculation among individual investors and they saw no evidence of that in the stock market," she adds. "But it was there—in the options market—all along."

Mr. Yee's refusal this morning to yield, and eat a big loss in front of the circle of friends to whom he has been bragging for months, will cost him dearly. By late in today's session, when he will finally allow Carol to cover his position, his losses will be awesome. The first ten contracts will be bought at 90, around three o'clock. The rest, bought in ten-contract lots amid escalating chaos, will cost 110, 120, and 130. In the end, it will take $450,000 to settle the bet Mr. Yee was paid $40,000 to make. If the additional $310,000 needed to settle the trade isn't provided, the firm will have to pay. It could put them under.

Mr. Yee won't be able to pay, but his three grown children will have to reach into their savings and borrow money to bring the Yee accounts up to zero. Mr. Yee will lose face. And he will not be seen at the firm in coming months.

Nor is Mr. Yee's the only tragedy at Carol's firm today. A troubled new client steps up to her desk now, half knowing what she will say. She has been pestering him for a week. He is stoop-shouldered, defeated. "How much money? How much time?" he asks. "A half hour, and another $10,000, or I'll have to sell it out," comes the reply.

The client first walked into the office in August, near the market peak, with a list of undistinguished smaller stocks. He said he wanted to invest $100,000 and had done exactly that, buying $200,000 worth of the stocks on margin. But their prices had been sliding virtually nonstop since the day he bought them. Now the account was down to only $108,000, and sinking fast.

She isn't prepared for what he tells her next. "Please don't sell it. It'll come back. The money wasn't mine. It's from my daughter's accident." The truth quickly emerges. The $100,000 is the insurance settlement from an auto accident that had disfigured his teenage daughter. She was to have received the money when she reached twenty-one, still a few years hence. Meanwhile, he would roll the dice in the market and skim any profits before handing over the $100,000 to her.

"I'm sorry," Carol says, "but it's still a half hour." He shakes his head and heads for the door without a word. He will not return. Carol will wait a half hour, then another half hour before she finally sells.

By then she will get only $98,000 for the stocks—$10,000 less than if he had authorized her to liquidate the account on the spot. Instead of walking away with $8,000 of the $100,000 in his pocket, he will owe the little brokerage $2,000 that it will take "four telegrams and two nasty letters" to collect.

OCTOBER 19, 1987. ■ Dow Jones Tower, World Financial Center, 10:45 A.M.: Paul Steiger huddles with a group of a dozen or so key *Journal* editors and writers in the large ninth-floor conference room twenty yards from his office.

Page One editor Glynn Mapes and his deputy and designated heir,

Lewis D'Vorkin, are present. So are Marty Schenker, the National News editor, Second Front Page editor Larry Rout, and Money Group editor Dick Rustin, whose reporters' beats include the securities, banking, and insurance industries.

And of course Markets editor John Prestbo is here. Prestbo had literally built the Markets Group with Steiger, arriving on the paper as both Markets editor and deputy to Steiger in January 1984, three months after Steiger had come from Los Angeles. Prestbo had been running a nascent electronic market and business news monitoring project that Dow Jones had decided to fold. With nearly two decades of experience at the *Journal*, including stints as Commodities editor, a bureau chief, and assistant managing editor, Prestbo was the perfect deputy to aid a green Paul Steiger in learning the ropes. Competent, unassuming, and fiercely loyal, he can often anticipate Steiger's reactions. When Steiger moved up to the deputy managing editor's chair, Prestbo's powers as Markets editor expanded. And the two men have functioned hand in glove ever since.

The glass-walled room, decorated predominantly in black, is equipped like a Pentagon war room. The wood-paneled wall behind Steiger hides an expensive VCR-video monitor tandem as well as projection equipment and movable briefing boards. The editors sit in soft black-leather swivel chairs around a twelve- by fifteen-foot black conference table that staff wags call the "carrier deck." Careers can crash on the carrier deck if too many of Pearlstine's or Steiger's questions at the noon or 4:30 meetings go unanswered or poorly answered over time. But this is not the noon meeting or the 4:30 meeting. This is a coverage session that is pulling all the participants away from other places where they need to be, and it is all business, no posturing, no politics.

The mission, as Steiger defines it, is to be certain that: (1) the Markets Group was right on top of developments not only in the stock market, but in all the financial markets as the day rolled on, and had the manpower it needed to handle the extra explanatory and reaction stories; (2) all seventeen domestic *Journal* bureaus were transmitted a list of suggested questions for a massive roundup of individual investors' reactions to seeing their stock market investments go down the toilet; (3) any related leads were followed up, especially rumors of financial emergencies in the banking or brokerage industries.

With the *Journal* reporting and interpreting Friday's market debacle in a Page One story, and there being a related package of stories on the inside pages, and because the stock market has been showing some signs of life recently, nobody knows yet just how much the paper will be carrying on the market tonight, or where. The story could require another all-out Page One effort if the picture worsens drastically or completely reverses and roars to a historic gain. If neither happens, perhaps one of Prestbo's Markets Group staffers will wind up doing an "up-front markets wrap" for the main inside news spot, Page Three.

The Markets Group as a discrete coverage unit and the up-front markets wrap are among Steiger's more significant innovations at the *Journal*, both dating back to 1984. The Markets Group came first. Steiger, then in charge only of the Markets and finance staffers, began calling regular weekly meetings to jaw about story ideas, complemented by *ad hoc* huddles in periods of market turbulence.

Suddenly and consistently, the reporters covering the stock market, the bond market, the futures markets, corporate finance, international finance, venture capital, and so on were confronted with the fact that there was interaction among the markets and activities they were covering. The weekly Markets Group sessions were followed by informal consultations with Steiger and, soon, among the group's reporters during their daily reporting and writing chores.

With Markets group consultations in place, the markets wrap story was a natural development. When one or more markets convulsed enough to make news, the idea was to get a story for Page Three that would summarize and broadly interpret the market action, while referring readers to the respective market columns for further details.

Like many other changes at *The Wall Street Journal*, the evolution of the up-front markets story was slow and sometimes frustrating. And it underscores the numbingly banal chain of decisions that occupy much of a senior editor's time and make his job far less glamorous than many people outside the business suspect. The chain was often built like this:

If, say, bond prices skyrocketed 2% or 3% late in a day's trading, there should be a story about it up on Page Three.

So, have somebody write one.

Who? The people who know what happened, the bond-market reporters, are busy writing it up for today's Credit Markets column. Everybody else is covering their own thing, and probably couldn't get up to speed fast enough to do a credible job for Page Three anyway.

In days gone by, the solution was simple. Just splice a one- or two-paragraph summary of the bond action, distilled by a Credit Markets editor, into whatever other major story of the day led to the bond-market fireworks. Ah, but in this age of the traders running rampant on Wall Street, market movements result more and more often from the trading process itself, or from other purely market-related concerns, than from fundamental news. So, how dumb do you want to look to your readers on the days when this is true?

What seemed a better solution was to pull the Credit Markets column out of its space deep in the second section and run it up on Page Three. Oh, but if you did that, the column wouldn't be back "where it belongs," in the view of the many *Journal* bond column readers, who do not rank among America's most flexible people.

Alternatively, how about starting the Credit Markets column on Page Three and continuing, or "jumping," it to the regular Credit Markets space in the second section?

Sorry. *The New York Times* jumps some stories from the first section to the back, but that's a no-no here at the *Journal*. As some see it, intersectional story jumps would only call readers' attention to the inconvenience they've had to endure since the paper added a second section in 1980.*

Oh, all right. Sometimes Paul and Nancy Cardwell would bite the bullet and yank the column up front in its entirety, but to guide market fanatics who read the *Journal* starting at the back (or those who read only the back), they put a little squib of type surrounded by black lines back on the Credit Markets' usual page to tell readers the column was on Page Three that day.

Ultimately, as the up-front markets genre developed, the solution was to shanghai a generalist in the Markets Group to do a broadly interpretative up-front story that left most of the juicy details to the columnists, who would focus on the nitty-gritty in their usual spaces that night.

---

*The decision was arguably the biggest hurdle faced in expanding the *Journal*. But it was unavoidable. The folding equipment at the *Journal*'s printing plants won't handle a section fatter than forty-eight pages. In the spring of 1988, top management authorized the *Journal* to proceed with plans to add a third section as early as September. Facilitating the increasing move toward compartmentalization, rather than conforming to size requirements, underlies management's approval of the third section to contain the *Journal*'s markets and investments coverage.

A decision to do that was sometimes made as late as at the top editors' 4:30 huddle. When this happened, Prestbo would then rush to the Markets Group section and try to drop a net over a broadly experienced and quick staffer like George Anders or Randy Smith, or a similarly gifted news editor in the group such as John Andrew. If all of them escaped, Prestbo would pass some of his own editorial chores to another news editor and do the story himself.

Initially, the annointed writer's task involved butting in on a handful of other *Journal* writers, all crunching to meet deadlines phased between five P.M. and six P.M. There would be a series of thirty-second huddles with, say, Tom Herman or Ed Foldessy (or, later, Matt Winkler) on Credit Markets, with Bea Garcia on the Abreast of the Market column, Chuck Stevens on the currencies trading column, and with whoever in New York or Chicago was writing the main or lead item in that night's commodities market report.

If these consultations answered all the major questions about how and why the markets moved in relation to one another that day, there might be time for a frantic phone call or two to an appropriate market professional for further elucidation. Meanwhile, copies of all the markets' reports for that night's edition would be rushed to the writer's desk, page by page, as they were produced.

Very soon—usually within a half hour of getting the assignment—the first page of the Page Three story needed to be complete, or nearly complete. Hitting the SEND button on the computer keyboard sent the story into the *Journal*'s reporting computer network, where it was then available to be called up on Prestbo's or Andrew's (later, Anders's) computer screen for rough editing and any rephrasing needed for clarification.

From the Markets Group editor's terminal, the page was transmitted into a separate *Journal* computer network, where it came up on the screens at the National News desk staff, located in a basketball-court–sized room, one story below the Markets Group's office.

There the story was logged in, assigned a headline code chosen by deputy National News editor Cathy Panagoulias to conform with her Page Three design for that night's edition, and then transmitted to the slot man (or woman) supervising the copy editors. The slot then assigned the story to one of sixty National News copy editors who would read it carefully several times, on several levels, and make appropriate revisions.

Did the story make sense? Read smoothly? Were there any obvious errors of fact? Grammatical errors? Were people's and companies' names spelled correctly? Were the abbreviations, titles, prices, and other numbers expressed in accordance with the *Journal*'s uniform style. The copy editor's questions were phoned immediately, as they arose, to the Markets Group editor or to the writer if the editor wasn't immediately available. So close to deadline, these questions had to be dealt with immediately, regardless of what else the writer or editor was doing.

Also near deadline, when all markets stories are produced, the copy editor had to stop work after editing the first page in order to write the story's headline and move it on to the master printing plant at Chicopee, Mass. Page by page, headline by headline, the slot did the final inspection and granted final approval of the copy editor's work. The slot's SEND button sent the page or headline into the nearby wire room and on to automatic typesetting equipment at the Chicopee plant, duplicated in its entirety at South Brunswick, N.J., in case of a power failure, fire, or other disaster.

Composing-room staffers in Chicopee assembled full-size page mock-ups using Panagoulias's inside-page layouts, the advertising department layouts (with which Panagoulias has coordinated hers), and layouts provided by other editors for Page One, the Second Front Page, and the Editorial, Op-Ed, and Leisure and Arts pages. Meanwhile, yet final editing and proofreading was under way, with last-minute changes typeset on the spot and spliced into the page mock-ups with a razor blade.

As the mock-ups cleared final inspection, each page was photographed, and its full-size image transferred onto a photosensitized aluminum-alloy sheet, which was then attached in the proper place to one of the cylinders on the plant's huge offset press.

In the process that the *Journal* pioneered, the same full-page images that were transferred onto offset printing plates at Chicopee (and in the redundant operation at South Brunswick) were also transmitted, via satellite, to plate-making equipment at the *Journal*'s fifteen other printing plants in the United States.

Finally, all the plates were strapped onto the presses at all the printing plants, around 7:30 P.M., New York time. Everything backed up from that time, which was about the latest the presses could start to roll if the first, or "two-star," editions were to reach post offices around the country soon enough to make the morning mail for approximately 1 million subscribers in small cities and outlying areas.

Considering the time required for various tasks along the route to publication, the writer of the up-front markets wrap, amid frequent interruptions, had no more than two hours, and often as little as an hour and a quarter, to produce a 650- to 850-word interpretative report.

Increasingly, as 1985 and 1986 wore on, there no longer had to be a big move in the dollar or a jolt in the economic statistics issued from Washington to touch off an explosion in the markets—especially in the stock market. Market factors themselves, which frustrated market writers frequently referred to simply as "technical factors," increasingly became the shadowy explanation behind major moves.

By mid-1986, Bea Garcia was being told almost routinely that the 30-point rise in the Dow during the final hour of trading began with a sharp jump in the bond futures pit, which excited a buying flurry in stock index futures, which led to index arbitrage and buy programs in the stock market. It was as if the world had gone insane.

While the conferees around the big black table don't yet know just how, today's cataclysm too is being market-driven by technical factors. Nor do they yet know how far beyond the realm of the up-front markets wrap it will be driven.

OCTOBER 19, 1987. ■ New York Stock Exchange trading floor, Post 8, 10:50 A.M.: Suddenly, the futures discount on the screen above Donny Stone is only about 7 points and narrowing fast. Could the market be pulling out of its nosedive at last?

"Don't believe it," Donny tells a visitor, the SEC's market regulations division head, Richard G. Ketchum. "I'm still a seller here. This isn't over at all. This market is going down another 200 points anyway."

Besides, Lasker Stone needs to do some selling after a bruising opening. Donny had to buy tens of thousands of shares to get Johnson & Johnson open by 9:52, and it was still down 4 points, or 5% below

Friday's close on the first trade. Lasker Stone's Coca-Cola specialist opened trading at 9:53, down 3½ points, or almost 9%. The Lasker Stone specialist trader bought 88,000 of the 273,700 Coke shares trading at the opening.*

As Donny sees it, the specialist's first need in a market like this is to "get liquid whenever the market gives you an opportunity, because you never know when it won't," Donny will observe later. "You can't make markets without capital and the way to raise capital is to sell stock."

He will dramatically prove his point today. While suffering heavy losses in the budding rally by selling aggressively at prices below what he paid for them during the first half hour of trading, Donny will manage to rebuild his capital and keep a reasonable market going in his stocks. For example, Johnson & Johnson, the stock he personally trades, will end down 14½ points, a decline of a bit over 18%, or not much more than three quarters of the Dow's 22.4% decline today.

Meanwhile, the managing partner of A. B. Tompane & Company, Warren R. (Pete) Haas, a forty-year veteran specialist who handles USX (formerly U.S. Steel) Corporation stock at Post 12, is taking another path. The sell imbalance in USX stock had been 125,000 shares at 9:25, but Pete Haas, an ex-marine veteran of the Korean War, stood against the wind and opened right on schedule at 9:30. Although he is awash in USX stock, Haas will eschew selling in the hour ahead partly because he believes in the rally and partly because he doesn't want to sell from his inventory at a loss, as he will tell a magazine writer later.

By day's end, however, USX's stock will close down 38% from Friday, and by three o'clock tomorrow morning, Haas will shake hands on a distress sale of A. B. Tompane—which survived even the 1929 crash as an independent firm—to Merrill Lynch.

Stone's view and Lasker Stone's performance are consistent with the pattern the SEC will find in a detailed analysis of specialist trading in

---

*Large volume on the opening is typical for actively traded stocks, especially after a trading delay. It represents the number of shares that are actually bought (and sold) after the specialist matches all buy and sell orders that can be executed at the opening price that he determines. The specialist himself enters the opening as a buyer or seller, as needed, to match up exactly the shares being bought with those for sale. The bigger the imbalance of such orders, the more stock the specialist buys or sells on the opening, which is reported as a single trade involving a number of shares, and is the sum of its many parts.

sixty-seven mostly heavily traded blue-chip stocks, including Coca-Cola. In addition to all the Coca-Cola shares it bought in the opening, Lasker Stone will acquire additional 87,000 over the next seven minutes, the SEC will find. The SEC study will add that thereafter, until about three P.M., the firm will be in the market for Coke shares "primarily as a seller. . . . During the last hour the stock dropped five points to 30; the specialist bought 84,000 shares, but sold 81,000. For the day, the specialist was a net seller of 5,700 shares."

This hit-and-run, in-and-out activity will be a hallmark of most specialists' performance today. However, most of them have stocks that are less actively traded than Johnson & Johnson or Coke, and many will wind up adding to rather than reducing their bulging inventories today. Despite their aggregate buying power being only about 7% of the value of today's purchases and sales, the SEC will discover that the specialists will account for 17.5% of them. That's half again more deeply involved than they were on an average day during the first nine months of 1987.

Donny's firm will stretch its $22 million of capital to trade in just under a billion dollars' worth of stock this week. Yet it will take Lasker Stone two weeks to trade its way out of excess inventories that had accumulated during the period October 14–20 in the least actively traded of its twenty-five stocks.

Meanwhile, there is a futures rally just getting under way in Chicago that has bizarre roots here. Minutes ago, three stocks that were prominently represented in S&P program trading baskets finally opened. And they opened at prices that gave the index arbs a nasty surprise. IBM's specialist began trading the stock five minutes earlier at 125, down 10 points, or 7.4%. Three minutes later, both Merck and Exxon opened, down 14% and 8%, respectively.

Professional traders know that the S&P index itself, plus the Dow and other market measures, all looked stronger earlier than they really were. In calculating these measures, the most recent closing price is used for those stocks that have not yet opened. So while the continuing price decline of those stocks that have been trading has been continuously reflected in recalculating the market indexes, the prices being used for those issues that are still delayed don't change. The net effect has been to make the indexes appear to be falling less rapidly than trading circumstances warrant. In effect, the major indexes have consistently been understating the severity of this morning's plunge here.

None of the index arbs who are furiously shoving sell programs into the market this morning believes that the prices he or she will get for those stocks (and therefore the profits received from the arbitrage) are actually as large as the S&P index reading suggests.

But they had expected at least some opportunity for profit. Few were ready for this. Simply by living up to their responsibilities to make the "fair and orderly markets" that the exchange requires, the specialists have opened these crucial issues at prices that are too low to allow any profit from index arbitrage! And the situation is actually even brighter. Not only have the beleaguered specialists confronted the index arb bully boys with a stone wall, but they are forcing them to turn and run for their lives, sparking sudden rallies in Chicago and here.

The index arbs have already committed themselves and are now over a barrel. Instead of waiting for IBM and Exxon and Merck to open before pulling the trigger on their sell programs, many just loaded them into the DOT system as "market orders" early this morning. And by the time they see the Merck and Exxon and IBM opening prices, it is already too late to pull their program sell orders back—they were executed in the very trades that established the opening prices "at the market," that is, at the prices the specialists chose.

Moreover, some of the index arbs haven't yet completed their arbitrage trades by purchasing the presumed "cheaper" S&P futures they'll hold in place of the stocks they've sold and, with futures prices soaring, there's now a threat they can't be obtained at a profitable discount to prices in the stock market. What's worse, some have actually sold borrowed stock, and are now exposed to the risk of having to replace it in what may soon become a runaway buying surge in New York. The SEC's report will show that one unnamed firm launched nine such "short-selling" programs, involving $116 million worth of stock, in the first hour of trading.*

---

*As indicated, short selling in the stock market involves borrowed shares. The underlying investment judgment is that prices will fall after the sale and that the borrowed shares may be replaced for less than the short seller received in the sale, with the difference being his or her profit. In the futures or options market, a short position is simply a seller's open position, although here the investment judgment—speculation on a price decline—is the same as for the stock market. Short sellers in the stock market must declare themselves as such, and sales may be executed only following an uptick in price. The SEC adopted this "uptick rule" during the 1930s to prevent short sellers from ganging up on stocks whose prices were already falling, causing a further price decline from which they plan to profit.

There was only one rational way out—buy back the stock—and they would have to move quickly. However, since baskets of real stock here and S&P 500 futures contracts in Chicago are functionally identical, the stocks could be bought back in either exchange. Both trading costs and margin requirements are lower in Chicago than in New York, so the arbs will decide to buy back the stock in Chicago. "Starting about 10:50 A.M., [index] arbitrageurs rushed to cover their positions through purchases of futures," the Brady Commission will report. "The result," coupled with other buying already under way, "was an immediate rise in the futures market. By 11 A.M., futures were at a premium, and the stock market, in turn, began an hour-long rally."

By 11:40, the December S&P contracts will be selling about 16 full points above their morning low, but still a few points shy of the nearly 270 price that some overoptimistic bargain hunters paid a few minutes after the opening. The Dow will be more than 60 points higher, but still about 135 below Friday's close. And portfolio insurers will seize the opportunity afforded by the newly buoyant demand and will sell more than 5,000 S&P 500 futures between now and noon, and will also launch sell programs on the NYSE floor involving nearly 12 million shares.

Yet, the rally will be a bluff. General Custer is charging the Sioux. Months hence, Dick Ketchum, the boyish-looking SEC official watching Donny Stone use this rally to rebuild capital, will marvel that during the hour he spent at Post 8 this morning, "I really learned how Donny survived on the floor all these years."

OCTOBER 19, 1987. ■ Chicago Mercantile Exchange trading floor, 11:15 A.M., EDT: Until this moment, Serfling has been too shell-shocked to join the buying parade. But he has watched the December contract trade higher and higher through most of the past hour despite heavy selling by portfolio insurers. He is impressed. Beginning an hour ago, the price rose steadily from 250 to 258 during a stretch of twenty to twenty-five minutes. Then it had begun to fall back to around 253. Then it had taken off again and is nearing 260 now. This fresh run is what impresses Scott.

He gets his broker's attention in the pit and signals him to buy five cars. Seconds later, the trade is executed at just under 260. Only fifteen minutes from now, the price will have risen another 6 points, giving Serfling a paper profit of $15,000.

However, he lost $23,000 at the opening, and now it looks to him like this market can run far higher. He cannot know that this is the ill-starred rally, by the New York specialists' lowball opening prices forced on the index arbs. Ultimately this development will be overwhelmed by the portfolio insurance sellers it attracts.

Scott will hold onto the contracts for now.

OCTOBER 19, 1987. ■ The Mayflower Hotel, Washington, D.C., 11:30 A.M.: David Ruder, chairman of the Securities and Exchange Commission for less than three months, has finished a midmorning speech to an American Stock Exchange–sponsored overseas investors' conference.

Amex Chairman Arthur Levitt, Jr., who arrived during the speech, had to press past a mob of reporters standing out in the hall, turning aside their requests for comments on the crisis. "I didn't really know the extent of the carnage [in New York] and all that flashed through my mind was a recollection of what was said and done in 1929—and how fatuous, self-serving, and incredible the statements of support for the market had been then," he will tell *Washington Post* reporter Steve Coll.

Ruder tells Levitt that he is anxious to get back to his office and monitor the unfolding crisis, but that

. . . he understood the press was anxious to talk with him. So we went out to see the press.
The first question he responded to was one concerning a possible trading halt. I was surprised to hear him say he had been in touch with John Phelan and had given consideration to it. From that point on the topic took up the rest of the press conference and he [Ruder] was on the defensive.

By 11:41, the first wire story hits: SEC HAS DISCUSSED TRADING HALT. NOT NOW. Thirteen minutes later: RUDER ON HALT: ANYTHING POSSIBLE.

By 11:45, the December S&P contract price slips below the level of the index itself. Less than five minutes later, the Dow is heading south as traders immediately react to the discount now flashing on the specialists' Quotron screens.

The reaction is in some ways surprising, since Ruder has essentially reiterated what he was quoted saying in a national newsmagazine the previous week—that one obvious thing the SEC would think about if a market meltdown began was some brief trading halt. But national newsmagazines aren't required reading on trading desks, and, in this environment, such thoughts are incendiary.

Moving quickly now, index arbs leap at the newly established discount to open new arbitrage positions. Simultaneously, they will ram home 6.5 million shares of sell programs on the Big Board floor between noon and one o'clock. Portfolio insurers, also knowing that a trading halt would put them out of business for the day, accelerate their selling to the eager index arbs and on the Big Board floor. They will sell more than 2,000 contracts in the S&P 500 pit between 11:49 and 12:10. And they will sell 9 million shares in New York between noon and one o'clock.

Then it will get worse.

At 11:30, the Dow Jones News Service passes up the story its reporter has furnished on Ruder's remarks. Everett Groseclose, the Dow Jones executive in charge of the ticker, will explain later: "The market was recovering then, so there was a question about whether it was still relevant and I felt the headline might be unduly alarming."

But nearly an hour and a half hence, with the market deteriorating rapidly, Groseclose will decide the story should run and will put it on the wire at 1:04, quoting Ruder as saying, "There is a point at which I would be interested in talking with the New York Stock Exchange about a temporary, very temporary, halt in trading. I don't know at what point that is."

The delay makes some traders think Ruder has brought up the topic of a market closing for the second time in an hour and a half, and the SEC's hastily issued denial that it is considering a halt adds still more fuel to the fire at 1:24. By 1:30, the Dow will again be down more than 200 points.

CHAPTER
7

OCTOBER 19, 1987. ■ Paris, Hotel Plaza-Athénée, cocktail lounge, noon EDT: The Dow is down more than 143 points, and Norm Pearlstine knows the noon editors' meeting is just convening at *Journal* headquarters in New York.

Ruefully he recalls his two-decade professional journey to this place and time. Having finally attained the best position in business journalism, with the financial story of a lifetime breaking like a tidal wave, Pearlstine finds himself on the sidelines. There are no flights to the United States until tomorrow morning.

Pearlstine knows that Steiger is in a position to see the facts and make the calls that need to be made today. And he knows that Steiger is frantically busy. So he has kept both of his calls to his deputy brief and has resisted the urge to armchair-quarterback.

Well, mostly. He has suggested that if Steiger thinks tonight's story merits it, he'd support running it under the first multicolumn headline on the *Journal*'s front page in over thirty-five years.

What has brought Norm to the Plaza-Athénée is the AP-Dow Jones Economic Report wire-service machine clacking out market news in the hallway just outside the entrance to the lounge. A couple of times during the past hour or so, Pearlstine has shuffled out to read the latest, shuffled back, settled heavily on the barstool, and had another drink.

Only Norm and a Lebanese businessman in the bar seem very interested in market news, for there is a clothing-industry convention at the hotel this week, and "nearly everybody in the bar was talking about hemlines going up, not the market going down," Pearlstine will recall later.

Today's negotiations with Jean-Louis Servan-Schreiber about the *Journal* sharing news with *La Tribune de l' Économie* had gone well. And in three hours, Norm will attend a dinner party at Servan-Schreiber's luxurious Paris apartment. Whether he is at the table or on the telephone to New York, Pearlstine's conversations tonight will be dominated by the market. As the party begins, the Dow will be down almost 300 points.

OCTOBER 19, 1987. ■ Dow Jones Tower, World Financial Center, noon: "What about a business leaders roundup?" someone asks the assembled editors. "Aren't they likely to be just as confused as we are?" asks someone else.

After all, the Dow plunged to more than a 200-point decline an hour ago, but has since recovered about a third of the lost ground. Quite a few market professionals and financial journalists thought last week's blowoff was the climax of the correction that began early in September. And some people at the *Journal* are clearly upset that it hasn't worked out that way. Dow Jones employees don't have guaranteed pensions, but they do have a generous profit-sharing retirement plan. And for years many *Journal* employees have opted to have most of their plan assets invested in a balanced fund weighted toward stocks.*

"I think maybe we should wait a day or so and give them some time to absorb what's happening," says Paul Steiger, who's running the meeting. "I think we should stay focused on the market action itself and the reaction of investors, large and small."

In some ways it resembles a town meeting, this regular noon huddle

*The plan allows employees to decide periodically how to allot their retirement assets between the balanced investment pool (Fund A) and a guaranteed fixed-return investment pool (Fund B). With the market roaring for the past five years, many have heavily invested in Fund A. At least a half dozen today are making what Dow Jones Public-Relations Director Larry Armour will term "hostile and abusive" phone calls to Armour, trying to learn Fund A's plight. In fact, the young Bank of New York money manager assigned to Fund A has been nervously withdrawing funds from the stock market and 60% of the fund's assets are now in cash. Nonetheless, there will be significant losses. For example, the author's profit-sharing plan assets, invested 100% in Fund A, declined by a shade under $50,000 in October 1987.

of top editors and about two dozen news department middle managers who supervise the *Journal*'s more than 150 reporters, editors, and artists in New York.

But what Steiger thinks matters most. There are never any votes called for.

When Pearlstine is here, he runs the noon meeting, and another much smaller gathering of top editors at 4:30 each afternoon. The most basic task of the noon meeting is to let everybody review lists of the pending major stories. The U.S. and Canadian bureau managers, plus the Page One, Second Front, Editorial Page, and Foreign departments, are asked to submit a list, briefly describing all major stories for the next day's edition, in time to be compiled and duplicated for the noon meeting. After the meeting, which rarely lasts more than twenty minutes, the list is sent to all *Journal* bureau managers, in effect, extending the results of the noon consultation around the world.

Sometimes, the meeting affords a sounding board for management ideas, or an opportunity to announce major policy or operating changes. For this reason, attendance is highly prized by the paper's foremost newsroom gossips.

There are inner and outer circles at the noon meeting. Those whose jobs or counsel are of greatest importance sit around the huge black conference table, where Steiger and up to twenty-one others all sit in soft black leather swivel chairs. Only about fifteen seats at the conference table are universally understood to be reserved. The remainder can go to early arrivers, who may then array themselves among the elite. There is a small but adamant band of early arrivers.

Lesser luminaries fill more black-leather swivel chairs, which are lined up around the three floor-to-ceiling glass walls of the room. On truly busy days, a few people even get stuck and have to stand.

Steiger briefs everyone on special coverage arrangements that are under way to get the full market cataclysm story to the *Journal*'s readers the next morning. Sue Shellenbarger, the Chicago bureau chief, has already dispatched reporters to the floors of both the Chicago Merc and the Chicago Board Options Exchange, where popular options on the S&P 100, also called "OEX options," are traded.

On the other hand, New York won't be able to get anyone onto the Big Board floor. Rich Torrenzano, the NYSE public-relations vice-president, and his predecessors have always barred the press from the trading floor except for limited visits, and then they must always be accompanied by an exchange official. Today no press is being allowed on the floor for any reason, although the Cable News Network TV camera eye is continuing to stare down on the action from the press gallery, a 100-foot-long, 5-foot-wide catwalk over the trading floor.

To Torrenzano and others at the Big Board, the pace and crowding on the floor at times like these are so extreme that any visitors, the press or otherwise, will be a disruptive presence; the specialists and floor traders down there have quite enough trouble without having added disruption. Journalists, on the other hand, have long wondered whether the Big Board's tightness about access to the floor is aimed at preventing them from discovering and reporting on trading abuses there.

No one should rule out the possibility of an up market today either, Steiger believes. The Dow has been roaring back and has about halved its losses in the past hour. Who knows what might happen from here? But whatever does happen, the paper has touched all the right bases to deal with it, Steiger feels as he breaks the meeting.

He had talked to editors in Washington earlier about doing a story on what the Reagan administration might be expected to do to ease any stock market disaster effects. Washington reporter Tom Ricks, following up on last week's market rout, had already learned that, given its free-markets stance and the practical realities of the situation, there was little the Reagan administration felt it could or should do to intervene. Steiger wants Washington to keep poking around for an angle anyway. When a national event occurs on this scale, you'd like to believe there is some role the government might play.

But the fact is, many in the administration have other fish to fry today.

James Baker, the Treasury secretary, is secretly huddling at an airport in West Germany with officials of the Bonn government, winning a tiny concession on German interest rates that he hopes will be a start toward a German economic stimulus that would help boost U.S. exports and narrow the abysmal American trade deficit.

Meanwhile, President Reagan's thoughts are divided between his wife, Nancy, recovering from breast-cancer surgery just two days ago, and the world reaction to the U.S. air strike against Iranian oil platforms in the Persian Gulf in retaliation for the Iranians' Friday attack on U.S.-protected shipping in Kuwait's waters. White House Chief of

Staff Howard Baker has been briefly in touch with John Phelan at the stock exchange, Salomon's John Gutfreund, and Merrill Lynch Chairman Bill Schreyer as well as with some congressional leaders, but Iran has a big place on his agenda today, too, and White House information on the disintegrating stock market is coming largely from periodic phone calls to Merrill Lynch.

The retaliation against Iran's attack is a *cause célèbre* of sorts here at the *Journal*. By a happy accident of prior scheduling, Defense Secretary Caspar Weinberger is due to visit with a group of editorial-page writers and editors in their ninth-floor offices at about 2:30. Top editors from the news side, including Steiger and foreign editor Karen Elliot House, are also invited.

In the meantime, Karen is pushing for a Page One story on the raid. And when Karen pushes, she has all the muscle she needs. Karen is one of the paper's five active Pulitzer Prize winners; another, associate publisher Peter Kann, is her husband. Both powerfully manipulative and quintessentially feminine, she is referred to by some *Journal* wags (who stay judiciously out of earshot) as the "Dragon Lady."

The Washington bureau produces a story that carefully describes the air strike as "tightly focused and limited."

To Karen, the raid is big news because it represents "the U.S. throwing off the stigma of Vietnam and showing itself ready to assert itself in the world arena, even if it means using force as a policy tool."

In Washington, the deputy bureau chief, June Kronholz—who's the boss here in the absence of Al Hunt, who's on vacation—and Features editor Kenneth H. Bacon discuss Karen's proposal with Pentagon reporter Tim Carrington and White House reporter Gerald F. Seib.

Carrington and Seib are aghast. They note that the United States had attacked an unarmed target, after carefully warning the Iranians to evacuate the oil platforms so no one would be hurt. They believe Karen's view amounts to a gross overreading of the situation. Washington recommends that there be no front-page story, but rather a straightforward news report for Page Three, the main news page inside the *Journal.*

But when the noon schedule arrives in Washington, the Iran retaliation story is scheduled for Page One.

And at the afternoon session with Caspar Weinberger, the Defense secretary, will be asked about a radical Iran-Iraq peace plan recently proposed to influential Americans by Saudi Arabia's former oil minister, Ahmed Zaki Yamani. The United States, Yamani urged, should bomb Iran's huge Kharg Island oil-processing and transportation complex to cut off its ability to export oil. Yamani's theory is that, denied oil, Iran will no longer be able to pay for the war and will have to accept peace. Such a plan might well drive the Iranians into the arms of the Russians before it would bring peace with Iraq, Weinberger believes.

Karen's realization that these key issues are even being discussed will make her all the more convinced that the raid on the Iranian oil platforms is a bigger story than the mere event suggests. But, true to their understanding of the facts, Carrington and Seib will produce a tightly focused description of the U.S. attack and a cautiously written, conservative view of its likely consequences.

Karen will find that the piece is "too mushy," and will propose a new beginning, or lead, to give it "more breadth and sweep," and inserts several quotes from the meeting with Weinberger to help support it. The new top of the story "flatly stated her interpretation of what the raid meant," Carrington will recall. It says that the attack on the Iranian oil platforms was a seminal event, showing that the United States had finally shaken off the aftereffects of the Vietnam defeat and was signaling that it was ready, willing, and able to fight what would be a popular war.

Carrington and Seib will feel so strongly about the proposed change that they ask that their names be removed from the story if it is to run that way. Karen will decide the broadened lead is not worth the struggle, will withdraw some of the Weinberger quotes, and so leave Page One with the tamer, Carrington-Seib version. Thus the *Journal*'s readers will be spared a breakfast with Black Monday and the prospect of imminent war with Iran over the same cup of coffee.

OCTOBER 19, 1987. ■ New York Stock Exchange, Chairman John Phelan's office, 1:15 P.M.: Rich Torrenzano takes a seat in a chair that is turned sideways just in front of Phelan's desk. "I think we should have a full press conference here, right after the market close today," Torrenzano tells his boss. There is a long pause as the Big Board chairman stares at his young public-relations chief, "as if I was crazy," Torrenzano will recall.

Where Phelan's and the New York Stock Exchange's public image is concerned, Torrenzano sometimes does seem to be a little crazy. He had shown that aspect late last year, (1986) when the Boesky scandal broke.

Phelan had just finished a week in China at the invitation of Deng Xiaoping, leading a seminar for Chinese financial executives on raising capital in America.

When SEC Chairman John R. Shad had called the NYSE with the Boesky news, it was about an hour before market close on Friday, November 14, 1986, and Phelan was still in China, taking up Deng's invitation to stay an extra week and see something of the country. So exchange President Bob Birnbaum had taken the call and urgently sought to reach Phelan. Rich had then awakened John at 3:30 in the morning at his hotel in Xian to answer Birnbaum's call. An announcement would be made right after the market close that Boesky would be cited for insider trading, had settled with the government, would pay $100 million, and get out of the risk arbitrage business, Phelan was told.

Would there be a selling deluge by investors fearing the impact of a forced sale of Boesky's $2.3 billion portfolio?* Possibly.

A reluctant Birnbaum was instructed to go ahead and appear on TV news shows Friday evening, where he pooh-poohed fears of a market break. The NYSE traded over $6 billion of stock per day. And although

---

*In fact, the SEC had already allowed Boesky to liquidate a substantial portion of his huge holdings, but it didn't disclose that fact when making the settlement announcement. Later, after the SEC admitted that it had known of and approved the early sales, Boesky's bitter rivals in the arbitrage business were furious. In their view, the SEC had in effect preempted Ivan and his investors from the very sell-off that news of his criminal activity could precipitate.

The question would be very much on Paul Steiger's mind that afternoon, too. Also unaware of Boesky's early sales, he'd focused instead on one sentence in the settlement announcement that noted that Boesky would be given a grace period of more than a year to wind down his arbitrage business. "We've got to put this in perspective, or there'll be a big stock market sell-off on Monday!" he'd said in a meeting with reporters and editors called shortly after the Boesky announcement.

While the Boesky news was cited among factors contributing to a market blip the following week, the initially feared major market break never materialized. SEC staffers would later argue that this was proof of the wisdom of allowing the early Boesky sales. In fact, many market pros already had seen evidence of extensive Boesky selling in the fall of 1986, and they put two and two together when the settlement was announced.

stock prices sagged in the following days, fears of a full-fledged market break proved unfounded.

On Monday, at a press conference in China, Phelan commented on the Boesky affair and the wires carried the statement. The press coverage wasn't memorable, but it had the distinct disadvantage of pointing out to the world that while Rome was burning, or at least threatening to burn, Phelan was touring China.

In any event, "I thought it important to have Phelan seen in the U.S. in a high-profile public-affairs forum. We picked Brinkley [David Brinkley's *Journal*]," Torrenzano will recall. But Rich realized that Phelan would first have to finish his China tour (to avoid offending Deng), and he was due in Paris the following Monday to chair a meeting of the President's Council on Private Sector Initiatives.

To achieve those ends meant flying Phelan and his wife from Hong Kong to Frankfurt to Paris, then on to New York via the Concorde, and from there to Washington—all on Saturday. Phelan would stay overnight in Washington, appear on David Brinkley's *Journal* Sunday morning, fly from Washington to London again via Concorde, stay at an airport hotel overnight, fly to Paris at seven A.M. Monday and walk right into the meeting. Anything but insensitive to public opinion, John Phelan had done just that.

So Phelan doesn't brush aside Torrenzano's proposal now. They had huddled briefly just as this morning's Wall Street summit meeting was breaking up, agreeing that communication was vital, that as much information as possible should get to as many people as possible as soon as possible.

The strategy would earn points with the news media even as it helped the exchange manage their coverage. With CNN beaming hourly live reports around the world, the Financial News Network running the rapidly deteriorating numbers on TV screens throughout the U.S., and the news wires smoking with market bulletins, the market panic had become a dominant world news event.

Torrenzano realized that in such a situation the facts themselves, no matter how distressing they might be, would never be as alarming as what people would imagine and speculate about in the absence of the facts. The speculation content in the media had to be reduced. In the presence of hard factual answers, there would be little room for speculation.

In the midst of the emergency, Torrenzano quadrupled the thirteen-member media-relations staff by assigning the entire remaining professional staff of his big PR department to servicing press inquiries.

Still, that's essentially a reactive stance, and with the market breaking down so quickly now, Rich wants to go on the offense—to project an aura of calm and control at the exchange. A full-dress press conference is a must, he argues.

Phelan asks Dick Shinn, executive vice-chairman of the exchange and former chief executive of Metropolitan Life, to react to Torrenzano's proposal. Shinn agrees with Rich, and the latter gets a green light for a press conference right up on the sixth floor immediately after the close.

The high-profile strategy will turn out to be the single shrewdest decision Phelan makes today. As a result, he will come off in the press as a cool, calm leader, and in later Senate hearings as a hero.

While the reporters at this afternoon's press conference will never guess from his self-assured demeanor that he felt the need to do it, Phelan now prepares to conduct a test he'd learned as a marine sergeant in combat. He'll descend to the trading floor on the first of "four or five" brief walking tours this afternoon "to get the feel of the place," he will say later. "To look in people's faces—to see if they were all right."

OCTOBER 19, 1987. ■ A broker's office in a northern suburb of New York, 1:45 P.M.: The sales manager's idea was inspired, the stockbroker had to admit, and he can't believe his luck. The customer sitting here at his desk, signing the letter, doesn't know, he actually doesn't know what's happening in the market! Turning the Quotron that sits on a lazy Susan at his desk a little out of the customer's line of sight had been a worthwhile exercise after all.

At a luncheon meeting weeks hence, the broker and his sales manager will recount the scene to New York State Assemblyman Peter M. Sullivan, himself a registered stockbroker. Sullivan, withholding the identity of his informants and their firm, will repeat their story:

The customer at the broker's office is a senior gentleman with a modest portfolio ("I think around $100,000 or a little less," says Sullivan). He's complained for weeks of wanting to take his stock market profits, but the broker keeps finding reasons not to sell. After last week's debacle, the sales manager had suggested that the broker quickly arrange a session with his customer to get him to sign a "hold harmless" letter.

Such letters formally attest to the customer's rather than to the broker's responsibility for the account. They purport to hold the broker harmless from responsibility for any investment losses in the account, other than those resulting from outright fraud. While their legal force is far from certain, such letters are coveted by managers in case customer complaints eventually lead to an internal or regulatory investigation. It provides the kind of defense that goes: "What? He's complaining that we lost his money? Why, I have a letter here he signed only three weeks ago taking responsibility for the losses himself."

The customer has said little during the brief, postlunch huddle. But now he asks the killer question: "How is the market doing today?"

The broker doesn't reply, but he slowly turns the Quotron machine until his customer is looking straight at the screen. The customer says nothing, either. He bolts to his feet, a gurgling noise rising from deep in his throat, then falls to the floor, unconscious.

It isn't a heart attack. The customer has simply fainted, and he will recover quickly once the ambulance gets him to the emergency room of a nearby hospital. However, nobody yet knows there'll be a happy ending. As the stricken investor is carried away on a stretcher, the concerned sales manager approaches his broker and fixes him with a panicky stare.

"Don't worry," the broker tells him. "He's already signed."

OCTOBER 19, 1987. ■ New York Stock Exchange trading floor, Post 8, 2:00 P.M.: This post is Fort Apache now, as the floor brokers charge. "Five thousand to sell, what's your market, Donny?" asks one. "Seventy and a half/five eighths, 2,000, 20,000," comes the reply (70½ bid, for 2,000 shares, 70⅝ being asked by holders of 20,000). The DOT system keeps spewing out the sell orders. Donny Stone has never seen selling pressure like this. No one has.

This morning had begun with an avalanche of index arbitrage and mutual fund sell programs. Then came the portfolio insurers. One group at a time. The rally slowed the selling a bit until about noon, and then buyers hung in to slug it out with them until about one o'clock, when the S&P 500 discount started widening again. But since one o'clock, the index arbs and portfolio insurers have all piled onto to the floor, shoulder to shoulder, dumping massive amounts of stock.

The selling has been out of hand for the past half hour, with the S&P 500 futures' price falling from 7½ points below the value of the index itself at 1:30 to about 22 points now, a half hour later. Even as the index arbs were buying contracts heavily in Chicago during the past half hour, they and the portfolio insurers have dumped stock here with abandon. Together they've sold almost 12½ million shares since 1:30. The SEC will find this amount of sold stock exceeds total selling during any other half hour this day by almost 3½ million shares.

Donny hangs in and keeps buying Johnson & Johnson, but his modest purchases can only slow, not stop its now relentless decline. The buyers, as they have been doing all day, are bargain hunting for institutional investors.

Between 2:00 and 2:45, the value investors will lead another ersatz rally, but it will be feeble—only about 25 points on the Dow, and more the result of a confused lull in the program traders' selling than any real strength in buying. Meanwhile, the seeds of a far worse slide are being planted.

The options markets are in disarray because individual stock prices and stock index levels have been changing so rapidly that option-strike prices continue to be made obsolete virtually as fast as they are established. The biggest casualty is trading volume. On the Chicago Board Options Exchange (OEX), for example, today's volume in the S&P 100, will be just 35% of Friday's level, the Brady Commission will note. As a result, frustrated institutional investors are increasingly trying to hedge their plunging portfolios in the CME's S&P 500 pit instead.

Back here on the NYSE floor, there are rapidly worsening problems with the DOT system. The biggest problem is with the Universal Floor Device Controller (UFDC), which feeds data into all the order printers on the floor.

Although it will be replaced with a much faster updated version in less than six months, UFDC here today is an old system that doesn't automatically arrange backups of data into electronic lines or "queues." Instead, it must be fed data manually, a piece at a time. And to keep the floor controller from "going down" and crashing the whole system, NYSE computer technicians will "intentionally create queues in the other systems," as one of them will later explain.*

That, in turn, is leading to mounting frustration, confusion, and, ultimately, fear among investors, who see the market plunging and realize it will be some time before the orders they have entered can even be executed. In response, many will send new instructions, changing price limits on their previous orders, thereby contributing even more to the developing snarl.

Nor are all the DOT troubles related to the inflow of orders. In a particularly frightening snafu, the electronic messages confirming the specialists' execution of between 5,000 and 9,000 trades will never get to the member firms that originated them. Instead, they will disappear from the NYSE computers' memory banks without a trace, and the originating firms won't know for days whether they were executed or not.†

Exchange officials and member firm trading executives alike begin to worry that some of the busiest companies are now in effect trading blind—without reliable information on just what their positions are. This raises the chilling possibility that when the trade confirmations are sorted out at the Big Board clearinghouse three days from now, some major participants might learn that they are insolvent. "If we were going to lose somebody [big], it was going to show up in clearance and settlement," an NYSE official will later say. "And it's a miracle we didn't lose one of the big firms."

The DOT troubles here are compounding the woes in the S&P pit in Chicago, where the main buyers are of course the index arbs. But beginning about two P.M., the arbs will rapidly pull back from trying to execute their sell programs because they won't be able to estimate

---

*The term "DOT," Designated Order Turnaround system—the computerized order-processing system—is broadly applied to the exchange's whole network of interconnected trading information systems, including the slower and older Universal Floor Device Controller.
†The mess will be sorted out three days later as the NYSE's clearinghouse compares its members' unmatched trades. The snafu is suspected of having provided many would-be losers in those trades with just the opportunity they needed to wash their hands of them and walk away unscathed.

what the baskets of stocks they dump here will bring them. And having pulled the plug at the New York end of their arbitrage, they will naturally stop buying in Chicago, too.

Meanwhile, the army of portfolio insurance sellers in Chicago is being reinforced by other frustrated market players who would prefer to use the options market but can't. So a CME pit that is already burdened with too many sellers will get still more of them, even as it begins to lose buyers. The resulting relentlessly deepening discount of the December S&P 500 futures price to the index itself—displayed in the eerie green glow of Quotron screens everywhere—will inspire rising panic through the remainder of the day.

Confusion over the DOT problems in New York and in Chicago, as investors who are abandoning the options markets wade into the S&P 500 futures pit to sell, will buy the market three quarters of an hour of seeming stability before the final devastation begins.

Amid the late pandemonium, the top floor-trading executive at one firm will plead in vain with Donny to close the exchange. Stone refuses to discuss the encounter, but another NYSE official, familiar with the incident, will say that the trading executive "told Donny they'd lost control of their book"—literally, that they did not know anymore what they owned and what they had sold and therefore were in the position of a prizefighter who has been blinded in the middle of a round.

OCTOBER 19, 1987. ■ Chicago Mercantile Exchange trading floor, 2:30 P.M., EDT: "I'm going to get some money and get out of here, Scott," says a strapping youth as he mounts the three steps up to Serfling's trading desk. "Coming?"

"What do you mean?" Scott asks, without diverting his gaze from the pit where the day's penultimate rally is already fizzling at the ripe old age of ten minutes.

"You know," says the big, open-faced lad. "This. It's over. I'm pulling out some major money and cutting out. Can I use your phone?" Scott shrugs obligingly. The red-coated trader punches seven buttons and waits a few seconds.

"Marsh? Bill. I'm going home early and I want to take some cash . . .

"Eighty thousand dollars in $100s . . .

"That's right, $80,000 . . .

"No, I DON'T think I could get by with $50,000 . . .

"God damn it, Marsh, $80,000! . . .

"Look, Marsh, you've got a choice. I either get a bag with $80,000 in $100s in ten minutes, or I'll withdraw all of it and close the account . . .

"Now you're talking, Marsh. Right. Ten minutes." He hangs up.

"What do you want with all that cash?" Scott asks.

"I don't know. I just want it. Now, c'mon, you coming or not? There's nothing here for us anymore."

"No, I'm going to watch what happens. You go ahead," Scott replies. "Don't spend it all in one place."

Bill starts down the steps, then turns in midstride. "God damn it, Scott. I don't think you realize what we're into."

Serfling laughs and shoos him on his way, but Bill isn't the last or the richest refugee from the pit Scott will see today. Later he will go downstairs for a snack and find another colleague emerging from the bank branch in the main lobby with a bulging canvas sack that he will be told contains $250,000. "He just took it down to the parking garage and tossed it in his Porsche," Serfling will recall. "Then he roared up the ramp and disappeared."

Eight others are taking even more extreme action, selling their trading memberships for the pit. "One guy came down from the membership office [where seat sales are recorded] and said they were practically handing out numbers," Serfling will remember. Another fifty seats will be sold in the remaining third of the month, one at just $90,500, barely more than half the going price when October began.*

Scott had held the five December contracts he bought this morning for a couple of hours—far too long. When he finally tossed in the hand over an hour ago, he was down $8,800. From up $15,000 to down $9,000 in less than two hours. He had never felt like such a fool. And it made him both sick and angry to realize that the $31,000 he had lost here today was more than the top salary his father had ever made in fifty-one years as a high-school teacher and guidance counselor.

Scott's father, Arthur, had supplemented the family's income as

---

*Figures are from the seat-sale log kept in the CME membership office.

high-school basketball, football, and track coach, and by refereeing college basketball games for as little as $35 apiece. Scott had seemed to head in his direction early on. An excellent athlete in high school, he had played two years on the football team, three on the basketball team, and four on both the golf and track teams. Then he'd decided to parlay an interest in horses and other large animals into a career, and got a veterinary-medicine degree at Colorado State in the early seventies.

Yet all the while, Serfling was actually moving toward playing the hand his mother had urged on his father. Fresh out of veterinary school, while looking for a job at a horse- or dog-racing track, he decided to pass the time until he found one by being a stockbroker. Soon the market was his passion, and he moved from broker jobs at Merrill Lynch and E. F. Hutton in Colorado Springs to manage the Smith Barney, Harris Upham & Company branch in that city. Finally Serfling had realized there would be gold in the S&P 500 pit and back in 1982 had gathered every cent he could raise into a $100,000 grubstake to come to Chicago to mine it.

Scott shares important similarities with his younger colleagues in the pit. All but a handful are men, many of them athletes, including even ex-Chicago Cubs baseball players and Chicago Bears football players. For in the lightning-fast pace of the pit and through a grueling six and a half hours of uninterrupted trading, superior hand-eye coordination and stamina are all but prerequisites for survival.

Donny Stone needs plenty of stamina to stand down at his post on the Big Board floor for six and a half hours each day. But working in the pit presents an added obstacle—the pressure of thinking, acting, plotting, always amid shoving and unceasing din. Eventually, this takes its toll on almost everyone, and it is one key reason why Serfling operates up at his trading desk rather than down in the midst of the fray.

"The saying here is that after three years in the pit, you'll either be rich and crazy, or broke and crazy," Serfling says. "Either way, you should count on being crazy."

As his conversation with Bill suggests, Scott's differences from his younger colleagues are significant. For one thing, most of them live a whole lot harder. After work, many of the more successful ones "have their limos pick them up and take them to a health club or condo pool, or they drive their Mercedeses or BMWs there," Scott says. He takes a $4 cab ride home to his North Side apartment.

"Something funny happens to a young guy earning $30,000 or $40,000 a year who suddenly finds himself in the S&P pit earning sometimes as much as $30,000 or $40,000 in a day," says Serfling. These guys get enormous egos, ditch their wives—if they're married—or stay single and date five or ten girls. You can carouse all night here. There are bars that don't close until five in the morning, or there's drugs for a lot of them. If they don't feel good the next day, they just don't come in," he says.

"Or if they want to take off for Jamaica for a week, they just get on an airplane and go. They're besieged by women. Look at all those good-looking young women clerks. They're not here out of love for trading. They're here to nab a man—a rich man."

Sometimes it's the other way around. Take the case of the relatively unsupervised trader for a New York firm who had worked out hand signals with his girlfriend—also on the floor—to tip her in advance of large orders he made for his firm. She would then trade for her own account ahead of him, a practice called "front-running" that is barred by the CME.

It worked like this: If the guy had been given, say, a big buy order by his firm, instead of executing it right away, he would signal his girlfriend so that she could buy ahead of him, then profit later when his large purchases drove up the price. Similarly, if he was to be a big seller, she would sell first and profit by closing out her short position at the lower price levels that his sales would establish. After the two get married, wags in the pit snickered that the trader had made her rich, then married her for her money.

Prodigal or not, these guys are all traders like he is, Serfling knows. While he deplores much of what some of them do, he cannot hate these brash young men who lean on his counsel so often.

There is a woman in Scott's life. "I really want to spend the rest of my life with [her]. I want to get out of this, to get my head back together," he will tell a visitor later that year. "But I just never seem to be able to see her enough. I go home from here exhausted everyday by the constant noise, the pressure, standing all day long. I don't want to go out at night after days like that and it's just not fair to her."

Peter W. Casey, thirty-eight, a partner in Serfling & Associates, sums it up succinctly: "He doesn't drink, doesn't smoke, doesn't fool around—what kind of a social life could he have?"

The bell is still nearly an hour and a half off, but this session is over for Serfling. With bid and asked prices continuing to be at least 100 basis points apart—ten times the normal spread—there is no way he will venture into the market again today.

The brash young traders are not so cocky now. The rally they had all bought into had disintegrated despite Solly's and other big index arbs' continued buying—continued buying until about an hour ago, that is. There's been no reversal, none of the usual clear signs. Just a sudden withering in buying demand from Solly and the other big houses. Unlike Scott, who had sold his five contracts at the first sign of slack, many of the others had waited and hoped. Their hopes were dashed now, and the locals were trapped in their morning positions.

"Every price the local named to trade on the buy side was wrong" today, Scott will note later. And the kids bleeding down there now are family to Serfling. "There was so much emotion and pain your body just felt stiff—like you were watching everything in slow motion," he will recall. "Breaths of air were few and far between. You knew many of these guys would never be seen here again after this day."

It has been a terribly close call for Serfling. Normally, when buying looks as right as it did this morning, he keeps at it until he is finally vindicated. It is a strategy that he estimates would have cost him $500,000 to $1 million today. Even if he'd done nothing but hold on to the five contracts he bought this morning, he would be facing a $57,500 loss right now. Scott bows his head and thanks God for the urge that made him cut and run when he did.

OCTOBER 19, 1987. ■ Over the Atlantic, east of the Carolinas, 3:30 P.M., EDT: Two and a half hours into the flight from Caracas, and an hour and a half out of Kennedy, E. Gerald Corrigan could be in a trance as he mentally reexamines the structure of the financial system for the umpteenth time.

He reviews the stress points, the places where leaks may develop, where pipes may burst. After meeting with the Venezuelan president, he had phoned his office in New York and learned that the Dow was down 200. "I knew we'd have a busy night no matter what happened from there," he would tell a visitor months later.

Thank God for the homework, Corrigan tells himself. The market collapse isn't entirely unexpected by Jerry and his Fed colleagues. Increasingly, Corrigan had been worrying about strains in the system caused by an explosion in worldwide financial assets trading over the years. Fortunately, during his nearly three years at the New York Fed, he's had the bank's economics staff worrying increasingly about them, too.

Indeed, early this year his staff had dared to conjure up a vision of a Black Monday situation to study its impact on the nation's financial system. The analytical work in the cluster of studies focused heavily on equity markets and on the "derivative equity markets," as the Fed economists called them—the stock index futures and options markets.

"It wasn't necessarily that we thought something like October nineteenth was likely," Corrigan will explain later, "but we did feel that the changing characteristics of the markets was such and the prices so high that it was conceivable, that we ought to be alert."

Among all the effects of the financial assets trading explosion in the eighties, none makes Corrigan more nervous than the uneven strains this activity sometimes imposes on the banking and markets clearinghouse networks forming the nation's payments system. Partly that nervousness is because no one on earth has a better view of those strains, day in and day out, than Jerry Corrigan. Each day he is supplied with the summary of all the financial transactions occurring in the New York Federal Reserve District. This daily report includes all the checks cashed, stocks, bonds, options, currencies traded, etc., in the district.

"Would anyone care to guess what the total of those transactions is on a typical day?" Corrigan had asked a group of *Wall Street Journal* editors over lunch in the fall of 1985. Some guessed $100 billion, others, $150 billion, and some guessed as high as $300 billion.

"Too low. Too low," Corrigan told the *Journal* editors. The correct answer was a cool $1 trillion. That amount is equal to a quarter of the value of all goods and services produced in the entire nation during an entire year. And this is a routine daily occurrence in the New York Federal Reserve District alone. Now, just two years later, the typical daily total has grown to $1.4 trillion, and Corrigan knows that the securities trading explosion is an important contributor to that growth.

And even as they worried about how to service such growth, many big banks were aggressively contributing to it. They were increasingly relying on currencies and securities trading profits to replace their shriveling earnings from corporate loans. Once the cornerstone of their wealth and power, the corporate-loan business had been lost to the big money-center banks in the eighties. Rather than borrow from the big banks, more and more of their major corporate customers had been opting to raise money by issuing commercial paper—stocks and bonds.

The problem isn't that hyperactive trading vastly increases the total volume of payments. Today's $41 billion of stock and futures trading is barely noticeable in a $1.4 trillion-a-day universe.* What worries Corrigan and his Fed colleagues the most is rather the sudden changes in payment directions and timing that volume surges produce.

Their edginess at the Fed has been growing with stock prices and volume through the year. One of the first things Corrigan and new Fed Chairman Alan Greenspan had discussed back in early September was the vulnerability of the stock market.

Corrigan had seen what Phelan before him had seen: "the technical changes—the linkages between the cash, the futures, and the options markets. These things [futures and options] really did create an illusion of liquidity," Corrigan says.

While investors themselves are skipping back and forth between the stock market and "synthetic" markets with reckless abandon, their money isn't so nimble, Corrigan realizes. He's noticed an intriguing difference in money flows between the stock market on the one hand and the futures and options markets on the other. Stocks are paid for on the fifth business day after the trade, while futures and options margins must be posted prior to the start of trading the very next business day.

For instance, the index arbs won't actually get any of the proceeds of their massive stock sales today in time to pay the margin due on their massive purchases of futures in the S&P 500 pit.

To Corrigan, the import is obvious. "In any crises [involving both cities' markets] the difference in the settlement schedules between New York and Chicago would almost certainly be where the pressure

---

*Indeed, neither today's nor tomorrow's huge trading will produce a remarkable surge in the volume of payments, a Fed spokesman will confirm later.

would be greatest." So, thanks to his own wits and his staff's early 1987 work, Jerry Corrigan, financial master plumber, already knows just where to look for the leaks.

OCTOBER 19, 1987. ■ New York Stock Exchange trading floor, Post 8, 3:45 P.M.: Donny leans heavily on the countertop at his post. His feet ache. So does his lower back. Fifteen more minutes. The Dow is at 1820, after falling at the rate of almost 3 points a minute since three o'clock. It will plunge 6 points a minute in the final bloody quarter hour.

Stone isn't sure which planet he is on right now, and it will be over an hour before he totals up Lasker Stone's more than $5 million trading loss. He and most of the other 480 specialist traders on the floor have been leaning for an hour against a selling hurricane they aren't capitalized to withstand.

The DOT terminal at his post keeps spewing out the Johnson & Johnson sell orders in an endless, ragged procession of blocks: 2,000 shares, 5,000, 10,000, 3,000, 2,000, nearly all are for execution at the market—that is, at whatever the current middle ground is between prospective buyers' bids and sellers' asking prices. Until or unless the specialist has the capital to hold the price up with his own bids, or can find other buyers who will, the cascade must continue. The market is plunging so fast that neither the exchange's computers nor Quotron's monitors can tell exactly what its real level is at this moment.

The Dow will be 90 points lower fifteen minutes from now, as the procession of market orders continues. This isn't arbitrage or portfolio insurance selling anymore. It is panic. According to a view held by some so-called chartists, market analysts who focus on past price behavior, in a panic, the only thing that stands between the Dow's current level and the one from which the bull market began five years ago—767—is the closing bell.

Donny is numb. "You're a little like a trained boxer who gets into a bout where he's overmatched, but just keeps fighting without thinking about it," he explains. "You just keep going."

The NYSE's hoary rules governing specialists' capital needs basically require only that they have $100,000, or enough capital to buy 5,000 shares of each stock in which they are making a market, whichever is greater.

The Federal Reserve and the Big Board won't allow specialists to finance any more than 75% of their trading inventories with borrowed money. If their net capital ever does equal as little as 25% of their inventories, the Big Board considers the specialists to be out of buying power. In other words, they have no free capital available to help make markets in their stocks. The Fed and Big Board rules for specialists are prods to keep them trading the stocks they're assigned. Absent these rules, specialists, like all other investors, would shy away from selling stocks where a loss would result and the markets they make would be less liquid.

While most specialists actually have far more capital than required (Lasker Stone's more than $20 million is a comfortable multiple), a rule requiring only enough to buy 5,000 shares hardly inspires confidence in the liquidity of the markets they make. "The specialists don't really provide much liquidity in size," says Robert E. Rubin, the top trading official at Goldman Sachs. "If you want to sell or buy 1,000 shares, that's fine with them. But try 100,000 and then you have to go upstairs to do it. Guys like Bob Mnuchin [Goldman's equity trading boss] provide the liquidity in this market in cases like that."*

Rubin is right, even assuming all the specialists are going by the book and are going at their jobs hammer and tongs. However, both the SEC and the Brady Commission will uncover many examples of specialists failing to help smooth the price transitions today, and they'll even find that some apparently panicky specialists made matters worse by selling their own stock in the surges, the trading equivalent of pouring gasoline on a bonfire.

The SEC will report, for example, that from two to four o'clock today, the specialist in Exxon stock is buying only 27,000 shares for his own account, but selling 257,000 shares, and that for the day as a whole, he is selling 239,000 more shares than he buys. The SEC will also report that from three o'clock to the close, the IBM specialist is a net seller of 38,000 shares and a net seller of 24,300 for the full day.

---

*Exchange regulations require firms to present the prearranged trades to the appropriate specialist's post on the NYSE floor for actual execution. The requirement is enforced to permit public investors to step in with competing bids so that an unfair two-tier market doesn't develop in stocks traded "upstairs."

Notwithstanding the spotty performance among the specialists, the facts of today's trading will bear out Donny's assertion that "any house in the street can close their desk, or open their bid and asked spreads until nobody will trade with them, but we have to stay." Fourteen large NYSE member trading firms that will be questioned by the SEC (including the leaders in stock index arbitrage) are buying a total of 33.3 million shares, but are selling 27.6 million. That's an average net purchase of just 400,000 shares per firm. They are buying heavily for their clients, all right.* But these big securities firms are selling a net 14 million shares from their own accounts even as the fifty-five specialist firms' net buying totals 21.2 million shares, the SEC will report.

At 3:45 P.M. in the Oval Office of the White House, Chief of Staff Howard Baker and his top assistant, Ken Duberstein, are five minutes into a discussion of the day's plunge with President Reagan. Just past 3:30, virtually as they left their offices for the president's, they'd learned the Dow was down 350 points. Now, as the three men continue to puzzle over the massacre, a presidential aide will pop in to tell them the 350-point decline they are troubling over now is a 508-point decline.

Donny Stone won't stop buying Johnson & Johnson shares until the close. But Donny has an ace up his sleeve, says one well-placed securities firm executive. "I'm told Donny was hedged," Goldman's Mr. Rubin will tell a visitor months hence, "and that he made a lot of money in the crash."

It turns out, Mr. Rubin suggests, that Donny hadn't just weathered the storm at Islamorada and helplessly bitten his fingernails over the market. He had done something about it. Last week Donny had been dealing, for Lasker Stone's account, in a large number of stock index put options—no one will say just how many or which index.

These are the kinds of options whose value increases when the underlying index (therefore, the stock market) falls, the sort of options that the once-proud Mr. Yee of Chinatown has had the misfortune to have sold.

*These clients include bargain-hunting institutional investors and so-called hedge funds, highly sophisticated private pools of capital engaging in exotic trading strategies. The "hedgies," as they are called on Wall Street, were said to be most active during the crash as short sellers (sellers of borrowed stock). Moreover, "short-covering," the short sellers' subsequent purchases to pay back share borrowings, was believed to be a significant source of buying during the crash.

By contrast, Donny had been a buyer, and, although it will be learned that Donny didn't buy enough put options to fully offset Lasker Stone's more than $5 million of trading losses today, the options are mostly hedged.

Dealings in the scorned stock index options or futures markets are regarded by some more conservative specialists as vaguely traitorous, and so Donny will not own up to the hedge. Soon, street-smart Donny Stone will circulate among his badly wounded specialist colleagues, quietly offering to lend them money. He will deny this, later. Yet Stone's actions represent a perfect crisis plan for his friend and boss John Phelan: First ensure that you survive. Then see what you can do to help.

CHAPTER
8

OCTOBER 19, 1987. ■ The Phillips home, Ann Arbor, Mich., 4:20 P.M.: For what must be the thirtieth time today, Douglas C. Phillips dials the Vanguard Group in Valley Forge, Pa., as he watches the market numbers stream silently by on the band at the bottom of the screen on the Financial News Network cablecast.

Now the figures are the summary numbers for today, Black Monday. The Dow, with the specialists finally having been pummeled into submission, plunged an incredible 220 points between three and four o'clock to close at 1738.74. The miracle was that they had been able to find buyers at any price. The decline for the day is 508 points, or 22.6%. On the worst day of the 1929 market crash—Black Tuesday, October 29—the Dow fell only 12.8%. While the S&P 500 index's drop is a slightly milder 20.5%, the December S&P 500 futures in Chicago have settled at 201.50, down nearly 29%. By the trader's rule of thumb that equates a point on the S&P to 7 Dow points, the futures price is saying that the Dow should have fallen to just above 1400.

Total volume is an inconceivable 604.3 million shares, nearly double the prior record 338.5 million, set just last Friday. Only fifty-two stocks, mainly doomsday investment plays like gold and silver mining issues, gained in price. Almost 2,000 declined.

Like perhaps most of those investors around the country who now know about the crash—some won't hear of it until the evening news on TV—Doug Phillips is more frustrated than damaged. He'd watched FNN throughout the day as he tried in vain to reach Vanguard, the big mutual fund management group. Phillips owns a modest stake in the Vanguard World International Fund, which holds a lot of foreign stocks. Over the weekend, Doug had correctly surmised that overseas stock markets, which start trading hours ahead of U.S. markets, would drop badly in sympathy with the U.S.'s Friday decline.* So he'd decided to shed his World International Fund shares early today.

"I've been trying to reach you all day," he tells a harried Vanguard staffer. Doug Phillips wants to sell his mutual fund shares. Actually, there's no public market for such shares, and so you redeem them instead of selling them. The difference could have helped Doug a lot. For, when he redeems his shares, he will be exercising the right that mutual fund holders have to require the fund manager to convert their shares to cash at the net asset value per share on demand.

Net asset value per share is the value of all the stocks held by the mutual fund at their most recent closing prices, divided by the total number of fund shares outstanding. If Doug had been able to reach Vanguard early this morning—before the end of Monday's overseas trading—his redemption price would have been based on Friday's closing prices. But all through the day, the Vanguard number has been busy. Until now. But now his redemption price will be based on Monday's closing foreign stock prices, not Friday's. The difference will cost the twenty-nine-year-old self-described "full-time investor" $1,500.

Others are having even more maddening experiences trying to reach their brokers. On the Street, there are rumors by the ton, all denied of course, that many brokers have taken their telephones off the hook, especially dealers in the smaller stocks traded in the over-the-counter (OTC) market rather than on a stock exchange. One investor will call *The Wall Street Journal* to sputter with rage that when he called his New York brokerage firm and asked for the OTC department, "The operator said she was sorry, but they're not taking any calls today." The firm's telephone operators will refer any questions on that practice to the OTC department, where an official will answer that the department took all calls on Black Monday and never instructed the switchboard to do otherwise.

Hundreds of other investors, complaining about being unable to get their brokers, will besiege an 800 number, a crash hotline to be established three weeks from today by the North American Securities Administrators Association (NASAA), an organization of state securities

---

*The Tokyo market fell 2.35% overnight, and European markets generally fell more than 10%. They were hit by early-bird U.S. institutional sellers at their openings and again, near their closes, by the then just beginning chaos in New York.

regulators. Investor Claude Holloway of Annandale, Va., will call the hotline to complain that he lost over $30,000 today because, instead of his broker, he kept getting a recording telling him the number wasn't in service.

On a day dominated by institutional trading, it often wasn't enough to reach your broker. The SEC would report that of the more than 14,430 telephone complaints and the nearly 1,300 letters that it and the stock exchanges received between mid-October and the end of November, three quarters would involve problems with brokers. Nearly half of the complaints will allege that sell orders either weren't executed or were executed hours and sometimes even days after customers had placed the orders and at far lower prices than those prevailing when the orders were entered.

Many others (10.4%) will complain to the SEC about not being able to get their trades confirmed for hours or days, and still others (10.1%) will be upset because their accounts are liquidated to satisfy calls for bigger margin deposits as the stock prices plummet.

There will also be complaints of broker misconduct, as there always are when the market turns sharply lower. People who had begun to think of brokers as beneficent advisers now suddenly remember that the main thing distinguishing them from used-car salesmen is product.

One midwesterner calls the NASAA hotline to complain that he was put into a margin account by a Minneapolis broker even though he earns only $7,000 a year. He lost a lot of money in the crash because for months the broker had been rebuffing his pleas to sell. The investor is a Catholic priest whose $25,000 nest egg seven years ago grew into $200,000 ("about thirty-five years' pay," the priest says) by the spring of 1987.

Soon his nest egg will be reduced to $25,000 by the sale, to satisfy margin calls, of nearly all his shares of Possis Corporation, a small high-technology stock making up 75% of his portfolio. "I told Phil [the broker] all summer: 'Phil, you gotta get me out of the Possis stock. It's too much all in one place.' But he kept saying: 'Let's wait. An L. F. Rothschild analyst's going to recommend the stock.'"

Still, he takes it philosophically. "I guess I agree with Woody Allen," the Midwestern priest sighs. "A stockbroker is somebody you give your money to and he invests it until it's all gone. Please, now, don't use my name," pleads the woebegone clergyman. "It would give scandal. I'm on the bishop's finance committee."

Some victims will be creative about trying to recoup their losses. On February 15, 1988, a Pittsburgh investor, who received a follow-up letter seeking details of his brief complaint to the NASAA hotline, will write back:

"Please be advised that I do not intend to release anything about my great loss of over a million dollars on Black Monday, unless I am assured of a substantial compensation from your book."

Still, the biggest toll Black Monday will exact on investors—both individual and institutional—is psychological, frightening many investors to the sidelines. "The market has now proved that anything that can go wrong will go wrong," Doug Phillips, the Michigan investor, will say.

The bitterness against brokers won't surprise old hands on Wall Street. New York professional investor Yves F. M. Hentic claims to have "practically built a career" retelling a story he heard long ago from an official in Merrill Lynch's legal compliance department, which checks that the firm's brokers are obeying the law.

Beginning a routine inspection visit to a Merrill branch office in the Pacific Northwest, the compliance man stopped in at the glass-walled office of the branch manager, a grizzled veteran nearing retirement. According to the story, the branch manager, upon hearing his visitor's mission, walked over to the glass wall, smiled, and waved. Each of the young brokers outside responded immediately and energetically. "See them smiling and waving?" the manager asked the compliance man. "They think of me as their lifeguard. But I know half of them are peeing in the pool."

OCTOBER 19, 1987. ■ New York Stock Exchange board room, 4:15 P.M.: "Was this the market meltdown you predicted in 1986?" asks a reporter at the edge of the crowd far to John Phelan's right.

He is one of perhaps fifty reporters jammed in among the equipment of four network television camera crews and a gaggle of newspaper and magazine photographers assembled here in this largest conference room at the exchange. Rich Torrenzano, exchange President Bob Birnbaum, and Executive Vice-Chairman Dick Shinn share the raised platform with John Phelan, who is doing most of the talking into the mass of microphones taped together in front of him.

Phelan has never been better. "Was this the meltdown?" he repeats. "Well, it was certainly as hot as I ever want to see it get. . . . I wouldn't want to be around for one worse than this."

"Is program trading the cause of this?" asks another reporter.

Oh, a lot of things are behind it, Phelan says, including "five years of a bull market without a correction, a rise in expectations of inflation, the [federal budget] deficit, the Iran problem. . . . One thing has led to another . . . a confluence of things . . . ," and, yes, "a piece of that is the new [stock index futures and options] products," he adds, seemingly as an afterthought.

No reason to pick a fight with Solly, Goldy, Morgan, Kidder, and the rest of the program traders at a time like this. This is a time for statesmanship, for class. And Phelan is at the top of his game. His voice is steady, and his delivery clearer and less hurried than the New Yorkese he speaks offstage. Far from seeming frightened or even nervous, he projects an offhandedness that no one would take for studied. The worst disaster in stock market history and Phelan is practically laconic about it. The image is perfect.

John Dorfman, the *Journal* reporter on the scene, will recall that "there was talk among the reporters about how assured and in command Phelan seemed to be. He just dominated that press conference."

"Was closing the market considered at any time today?" asks the reporter from *USA Today*. Phelan rambles easily into the subject:

"We've been in constant contact with the SEC and other people in Washington today. One of the things that we've talked about over the past several months was if in fact we got a kind of break in the market like this is, whether trading should be halted and if in fact it does [get halted], what good does it do?

"And I think the consensus today was that it was better to let the market try and work out of this on its own, rather than stopping trading and getting a pent-up selling demand with no liquidity at all. And of course one of the other problems is world markets as well," he continues, as if discussing some academic subject. United States authorities could shut the U.S. markets, but they "can't shut down around the world, so there's no guarantee that these stocks are not going to trade around the world as well. So I think the thought was that we would continue trading.

"The president has the power to stop trading and the exchanges themselves individually do," he adds. "I think there is no doubt that if the SEC requested that we do so, we would certainly do so," he says, in effect tossing a lateral to Washington. If the market has to be shut tomorrow, count on White House Chief of Staff Howard Baker or David Ruder at the SEC taking responsibility for it, he insinuates.

"Stocks fell 12% [on the worst day of the 1929 crash] and they're off a lot more than that today. Would you call this a correction? Is it a panic?" asks the *Barron's* reporter. Now Phelan is really rolling. "I don't think the word 'panic' is correct," he says. "I think it is a significant fall that we are all very concerned about."

"How confident are you . . . or are you confident that no member firms are in trouble?" Bingo. Practically before the reporter's question has cleared his mouth, Phelan strikes squarely at the rumors abroad on the floor and in Chicago during the afternoon's trading:

"I'm confident that no member firm is in trouble. . . . Now, member firms are complicated mechanisms today. They're into many different businesses. But at this point in time we know of no significant firm that has a significant problem. And we know of nobody in the dealer [specialist] system that has a significant problem. Now that can change momentarily," he adds, "but right now, to the best of our knowledge, the system is in reasonably good shape."

Momentarily? Good shape?

E. F. Hutton & Company is doomed, and L. F. Rothschild, Unterberg, Towbin, Inc., is on the ropes. Hutton itself and a substantial portion of L. F. Rothschild's assets will be sold in fire sales within weeks. Some of their problems, however, won't be known for a few days.

But by nearly any conservative financial test, given today's volume and the likelihood of a similarly huge trading day tomorrow, nearly half the NYSE's specialists are on the ropes. Even by the exchange's own guidelines, specialists need at least 25% of their net capital available at all times, instead of invested in stock. Yet by that test, as the SEC will curtly observe in its massive study of the crash: "By the end of trading on Oct. 19, thirteen [specialist] units had no buying power," and eight of them, as well one other unit, would have no buying power by the end of tomorrow, either.

In addition, measured by the same yardstick, twenty-three specialist firms, or 42% of the total, had less than $5 million of buying power at today's close, and that in a market where $21 billion worth of stock was traded today. A. B. Tompane & Company will arrange overnight to be acquired by Merrill Lynch, but tomorrow morning the NYSE will disclose to SEC staffers that the exchange "had placed 12 of its 55 specialist units on 'closer than normal' surveillance because of its concern about those units' financial conditions." This was despite "assurance from the specialist units whose buying power was exhausted at the close of business on Oct. 19 that they had received capital infusions or additional financing," the Brady Commission will report.

Months from now, Phelan will pooh-pooh any suggestion that he misleadingly downplayed or concealed the financial peril at press conferences today and tomorrow, particularly with regard to the exchange's market makers.

On Tuesday morning "we only had five" specialist firms that were "having severe difficulty," Phelan will say. "They were significantly below our twenty-five percent guideline and if the market went down another 300 to 400 points they wouldn't have enough to make it," he will admit.

"On Tuesday there wasn't any [specialist] firm that told us they couldn't open, otherwise we would have reallocated their stocks [to other specialists]," he will add. How closely were the specialists questioned on their financial health? "At times like this we just want to know whether you're in or not," Phelan will answer. "We're not interested in the details."

Rich Torrenzano has been busy behind the scenes, trying to shadow Phelan wherever he goes "so I had a sense of what was happening," he will say, and then rushing out periodically to brief the press armies that are converging here. "If you panic, the nation will panic," Rich's father has told him. So he will keep the more alarming details to himself.

He'll divulge some of these ten days from now, when he is questioned by reporters at a news briefing about discount brokerage Charles Schwab & Company's revelation that it faces a $22 million fourth-quarter loss. Part of the exchange will go like this:

Q: "Did you know about the Schwab loss before it was announced?"

A: "Yes."

Q: "How much before?"

A: "I won't say."

Q: "What else do you know?"

A: "What is important is that I always tell you the truth. It is not necessary that I tell you everything that we know."

Early in February a caller will tell Rich SEC and Brady Commission studies showed that the exchange was in a whole lot more trouble during the crash than anyone thought. "It must have been murder figuring out what to say to prevent a panic," a caller observed. "We had to do things you wouldn't ordinarily do," Torrenzano will reply, "but decisions had to be made."

Today, Torrenzano's idea of putting cool and collected John Phelan on national display is a big winner. Phelan's calm will be universally noted in the press and on TV. At the barrage of hearings on Capitol Hill in the coming months, Phelan will be greeted as the hero who kept the public calm during the crash.

If tomorrow doesn't end better than today, however, John Phelan's name will live in infamy as that of the villain whose facile assurances helped anesthetize an investing public on the eve of the greatest financial slaughter in history.

And he seems to sense this.

"What do you say to those people who lost their shirts, the little people who own 2,000 shares?" he is asked. "Well, I'd just say that all of us are with them," he answers, "all of us who have our savings plans and our retirement funds and everything else tied up in this that we are as uncomfortable as they are . . .

"We don't know where this market will end up, but I think we are extremely fortunate today that the country is in a very strong position. We're not going through hyperinflation or the tail end of hyperinflation or the other kinds of things that happened in previous periods."

OCTOBER 19, 1987. ■ Paul Steiger's office at the *Journal*, 4:20 P.M.: Steiger has convened National News editor Marty Schenker, Glynn Mapes, and Lewis D'Vorkin from Page One, and Markets editor John

Prestbo. They have both news and packaging problems and damned little time in which to solve them.

All writing and editing in New York must be complete by seven P.M. so the presses in the *Journal*'s seventeen plants around the country can start running the two-star first edition, which goes to nearly half the paper's subscribers. Generally, subscribers in the farthest-out, hardest-to-reach areas get the two-star, which is produced against tight postal and freight schedules.*

He could certainly give over all three major story slots on the front page to the market plunge.† Yet the editorial meeting with Caspar Weinberger that broke an hour ago has reinforced his conviction that the Iran story belongs on Page One, too.

No matter, there is room to maneuver. Norm will back a two-column headline up front if Paul thinks it's justified and so will Peter Kann, Paul has learned. And with the market down 508 points, such a move is pretty clearly justified. "I think we should go with a two-column head on the market leader," says Steiger, looking around the room. He sees nods and hears murmurs of assent.

The decision isn't as routine as it may seem. There hasn't been a multicolumn front-page headline in the *Journal* since January 14, 1952, when Warren Phillips was running the paper and put a two-column head on an interview with Dwight Eisenhower from Paris.‡ (Later, one

---

*The *Journal*'s seventeen printing plants together run off approximately 800,000 copies of the two-star edition, making it alone the nation's eighth largest newspaper. The bulk of the two-stars are trucked to post offices near the printing plants for distribution in the next morning's mail throughout the geographical area served by each plant. Approximately one half of the 1.2 million three-stars go to private delivery services clustered in the suburbs around major metropolitan areas, with about one quarter going to big-city newsstands and the rest into the mail. Overall, 85% of the *Journal*'s slightly more than 2 million copies per day go to home or office subscribers, with the remaining 15% sold on newsstands.

†These slots are: column one (the left-hand column); the column-four space for the "A-head" (so named because it resembles a capital A) and column six, the right-hand column. Columns two and three are given over entirely to the What's News feature, a summary of what editors deem the paper's most important stories of the day and of major world news events that may or may not also be the subject of stories in the paper. Column five has a different feature each day of the week. Tomorrow's (Tuesday's) will be the Labor Letter, a compendium of short items on union developments and trends in the workplace.

‡The *Journal* had a bit of an inferiority complex back then. Headlined EISENHOWER IS HOPING HE WON'T BE NOMINATED, the story was a cloying follow-up on a public statement Ike had made the week before about not being interested in seeking the presidency. "PARIS—Dwight Eisenhower wasn't fooling—he's really reluctant," the story began, and warned that ". . . there's disappointment ahead for those who have chosen to interpret General Eisenhower's statement last week as a subtle, shrewd opening shot in a campaign for the Presidency." What the story and two-column headline were really saying, of course, was, "Look, everybody. *The Wall Street Journal* is an important paper now. Great men talk to us, too." But apparently not much. The

staffer or editor—Pearlstine will claim to disremember just who—will question the decision by noting that the *Journal* hadn't run a two-column head on its Black Tuesday story back in 1929.)

Steiger realizes that in addition to conveying the significance of the market drop, a two-column head will create a "shoulder" on Page One. He could then tuck the day's chart of the Dow and another story underneath that shoulder to make a powerful stock market package. But that would mean using column five, which on Tuesday is given over to the Labor Letter. No, there's no objection to holding back the Labor Letter to make room for another market story. But what will that story be?

The Washington staff isn't getting far on the government action story, Steiger had learned after the Weinberger session. They're still being told there probably won't be any major government action. Congress is upset, but isn't it always when there's a chance to grab some publicity? Certainly not Page One material, that. Meanwhile, Alan Murray and Rose Gutfeld of the Washington bureau's economics reporting group had been filing memos on SEC and Treasury reaction directly to editor Henry Myers at the Page One desk. Much of that material will probably wind up inserted in the main market story that Bea Garcia, the Abreast of the Markets columnist, is deeply involved in putting together up in the Markets Group, Steiger thinks.

Just like editors at any other fully computerized news operation, Steiger and the other *Journal* editors can look over reporters' shoulders fairly constantly without interrupting them, even without the reporters' knowing it. Once a reporter finishes a page and hits the SEND button on his terminal, the page goes right into the system, where a copy of it can be instantaneously retrieved by anyone else linked to the system. Steiger has been using his terminal to stay abreast of the many stories now in progress. All he needs to do is call up the proper electronic desk and scan the list of pages there for the relevant identifying labels, or "slugs," on the pages he wants to read. The first page of the main market story, sent into the Page One desk eleven minutes ago, is easy to spot. It's slugged CRASH. Page Two of the story will be slugged CRASH2, and so on.

---

story contains just one direct quote from Ike, who was known for demanding that interviewers not directly quote him.

But the electronic shuffle has been disappointing so far.

The roundup story on foreign market drops won't do. Foreign investors were reacting mainly to Friday's plunge in New York, not today's. Besides, another whole day of trading in the foreign markets will have passed by the time *Journal* readers get their papers in the morning.

There is a good clean piece on money managers' reactions. But predictable. They're confused. Not a candidate for Page One. There's also a nice little piece on some winners, including Donald Trump, who took his $175 million of profits from the market rise by getting out of stocks during the past month. Too narrow for Page One—and who wants to be responsible if they lynch him.

Also in the Markets Group, there are other pieces on how the mutual funds are coping with the surge in redemptions, on frightened investors' flight to Treasury bills and money market funds. Dick Rustin's Money Group has stories on the ominous explosion in margin calls and on the merger juggernaut stalling in the face of rising interest rates and a recently proposed adverse tax measure. All are strong, clear-cut pieces. But their subject matter is too narrow, too specialized for Page One. Larry Rout is taking them for a Second Front package.

Scott McMurray and Bob Rose, who spent their day at the Chicago markets, have a dandy story on how the futures led the slide in the stock market. But two market reports side by side up front? No way.

Steiger's about at the end of his rope. There really needs to be something along with CRASH. When the stock market falls 508 points, you have to spell out the enormity of that. The numbers, the volume, the huge imbalances, the sickening rides through the day, must be included Steiger realizes. But he also knows that by the time the story does that, it will have run to the bottom of the column and will have to be continued on some page way back in the first section.

"Ideas?" Steiger asks.

"I'll tell you the question I'd want answered most as a reader tomorrow," says D'Vorkin. " 'Does this mean we're going to get another Great Depression?' "

"That's my question, too," Schenker adds.

Who can do it fast enough? Washington Features editor Kenneth Bacon, that's who. Bacon will interview Brookings Institution economist Barry Bosworth, then weave his notes together with Rose Gutfeld's memo on her interview this afternoon with Nobel Prize-winning economist George Stigler and background from a pair of old *Journal* articles into a 1,500-word story reporting on and interpreting experts' predictions that another Great Depression is probably in the cards. (Bacon will begin at 4:45, when he first learns of the assignment, and be finished with the bulk of the story ahead of the seven P.M. two-star deadline. Page One staffer David Sanford will edit Bacon's story and write its six-line, one-column-wide headline ahead of that deadline, too, even though he won't receive any of the seven-page story until after six o'clock.)

Last decision: "Do we go with Iran in column one?" Steiger asks, looking at Mapes. He always has a backlog of Page One material. That spot often goes to the kind of time-insensitive story that would be as appropriate tomorrow or next week as it is today—it's what editors call an "evergreen." "I thought it would look dumb to have an evergreen" on Page One, given the cataclysmic market plunge, Mapes will recall, "but I didn't want to bury the reader with all stock stories on Page One, either. Under those circumstances, the Iran story filled the bill perfectly."

The conferees quickly scatter. Steiger goes over the preparations in his mind once more:

The printing plants have been advised that the news department will need twenty extra columns for this coverage. That'll add three and one third pages to tonight's paper. With the other extra space taken earlier for a blizzard of third-quarter earnings results that must be run, the paper's size will be pushed up to a hefty seventy-eight pages—six more than the usual maximum.

With the NYSE transactions ticker tape, normally right up with trading, over two hours late at the bell, the Associated Press is in trouble. It usually supplies the *Journal* and most other newspapers with individual stock quotes before 5:30 each day. Today, it'll only be able to supply midafternoon quotes ahead of the *Journal*'s two-star deadline. And while Steiger doesn't yet know it, the AP's closing quotes won't be supplied for some five hours. Price movements have been so great today that, over and over again, they will trigger numerical stops in the AP's computer program designed to screen out obviously erroneous quotes. Finally the AP will give up and deactivate the screen so that it can get the list run.

Earlier, Nikki Frost, who supervises the chart artists in Graphics, had encountered a big problem with the usually routine charts of the Dow industrials, transportation, and utilities averages that run beside the start of the New York Stock Exchange quotes. The size of the market plunge would require a redesign of the charts. They could be rescaled, to show the extent of the day's plunge without taking up any more space. Alternatively, they could be made much deeper to show the plunge on the existing scale. Paul opted for the latter course.

From now through the evening, Steiger basically will float from Page One to Second Front, to National News, checking and rechecking emerging stories, headlines, graphics. He will devote special care to the front-page package, especially to the wording of the main market story and its headline.

The story had come down from Markets with a longish, perhaps overdramatic lead:

"NEW YORK—What began as a routine stock market correction two months ago and last week developed into a terrifying rout, yesterday became the stock market crash of 1987—the worst in history and maybe not over yet."

Henry Myers had risen to the occasion, rewriting it as:

"NEW YORK—The stock market crashed yesterday."

That's punchy as hell, but Steiger is prompted to ask himself three questions: "Does the word 'crash' mean what we're talking about here? Are we going overboard calling it a crash?"—perhaps exaggerating the facts—and "Will it tend to panic our readers?"

He will pull out the dictionary to find that the word "crash" "means a sudden drop—collapse. So the answer to my first question was yes," he'll say. Exaggerating the facts? "No, we aren't," Steiger will tell himself. "Today's drop was far more severe than 1929's."

Finally, was the *Journal* being irresponsible by using the word "crash"? "I decided that if a word is precisely appropriate, then you are disturbing your compact with the reader unless you use it. Tell it straight."

Of course, Steiger will add that this decision was made easier by the knowledge that "we would be giving readers a balanced and appropriate perception of what was going on" in Ken Bacon's piece "that pointed out the safeguards in the banking systems and basic health of the economy that likely would prevent a cascading [economic] collapse."

All in a story that would begin directly beside the main market story and just a little bit lower on the page.

The *Journal*'s dubbing today's collapse a "crash" will be a rarity in the press. And employees at some large securities firms, including Merrill Lynch, will be asked not to use the word. Ironically, it was Merrill Lynch, in a bumbling attempt to calm investors through a statement issued just after today's market close, that evoked the Great Depression. The statement noted that: "As Franklin Delano Roosevelt once said, 'We have nothing to fear but fear itself.' "*

OCTOBER 19, 1987. ■ Offices of Lasker, Stone & Stern, 20 Broad Street, 5:00 P.M.: Until this time, Donny Stone has only been exhausted. Now he is frightened—more frightened than he can remember since a day, more than forty years ago, when he was a young soldier, alone and stalked by a squad of Germans in a village the Germans held on the Rhine.

The mine-detection duty, the construction jobs under fire, none of those had frightened him the way he was frightened that day. It was late in the war, General Patton's armor had blown across the Rhine, right past pockets of enemy troops at the river and on into Germany. Donny's squad had been assigned to protect a bridge across the river into a medieval town near Cologne. They had probed the little town's twisting cobblestone streets with a patrol.

Suddenly, Donny had realized there were no members of his squad in his sight or hearing. He'd decided to hurry back to the bridgehead and his comrades. But all of a sudden, as he ran down the cobblestones, he heard many other boots running down them, too. He stopped dead in his tracks. Silence. Then he ran again. More boots on the cobblestones, closer now. He froze. Again, silence.

They had to be well within rifle range if he could hear their footsteps so clearly. He knew it would be foolish to turn his back and run for the bridge. Instead, for what seemed like hours, he inched his way, backward, along the walls of the houses to the bridge, and then bolted across

*FDR actually said, on March 4, 1933, "The only thing we have to fear is fear itself."

to his squad and safety. He would long be haunted by the memory of those boots running on the cobblestones and his agonizingly slow withdrawal, all the while wondering if each backward step might be his last.

The memory had come and gone in a flash.

It wasn't worry about his own or Lasker Stone's financial security that brought on the brief fright. Donny doesn't yet know that today's trading losses at Lasker Stern reached $5.2 million. But the price of stock index put options he'd ordered last week had soared, and so today's trading loss won't be catastrophic.

No, the terror comes from his suspicion that he no longer understands the market. It had happened when he sat down at his desk here in the office building next door to the stock exchange. Nearly blind with exhaustion, he'd initially stared at the Quotron screen without really seeing it. Then, line by line, quote by quote, the enormity of it began to hammer its way into his brain: the Dow minus 508? IBM down 31¾? Digital Equipment, 42¼? Disney, down 19⅛, and Eastman Kodak, 26?

If there was anything that Donny had learned in thirty years as a specialist, it was that the market simply does not work that way. Those losses were impossible, and yet there they were. Suddenly it came to him. Either this was some monstrous aberration—the trading equivalent of a nuclear accident—or it meant the end. If this did not turn soon, the question was not whether Lasker Stone and Donny Stone would be here at the end of the week, or month, or year. It was whether here would be here. How can a stock market exist that behaves like this? Who would risk capital to invest in such a market?

From now until midnight, when the firm's twenty staffers complete all the paperwork the blitz has generated, Donny will turn the frustration of today over and over again in his mind. "The one trick I've learned about specializing is to be willing and able to take losses," he will recall later. "But there was no way you could take a loss as big as there was out there [on Black Monday]. I sold into every rally, but it didn't help. All I did was wind up replacing what I'd sold with more stock."

The fifty-five specialist firms' inventories swelled to $1.3 billion today from about $900 million on Friday. Many of the smaller specialists, who deal in the less heavily traded stocks, saw few buyers at their posts and have their backs against the wall, Donny knows. A second day not nearly as bad as today will finish them and probably a lot of others.

OCTOBER 19, 1987. ■ Federal Reserve Bank of New York, 5:30 P.M.: Jerry Corrigan, behind the massive desk at one end of his cavernous tenth-floor office, picks up the phone and dials John Phelan. The secretaries are still here, but it isn't Corrigan's style to use them for placing phone calls.

Fading sunlight seeps into the room from the double window behind him, but light never more than half conquers this place. Its dark, mahogany-paneled walls, the baroque mantelpiece at the opposite end of the room, and the heavy furnishings seem to absorb light like a sponge absorbs water.

"John? Jerry Corrigan returning your call. . . . Yes, about an hour ago. . . . Well, I've read some things. The driver met me at Kennedy with a briefcase full of paperwork and the market summaries were on top of the pile. Pretty grim."

The two barely have met one another, but oddly they settle into an easy conversation. Corrigan has caught Phelan with his guard down, spent from the day's tension and from the press conference that ended only about forty-five minutes ago. Phelan is letting his hair down.

Corrigan will refuse to share the details of this or any other conversation he has in line with his Fed duties. "It's just not conducive to the trust a Fed official must have," he will explain. "How can you be effective if people have to worry about some day reading what they've told you?"

"I wanted to make sure we were plugged into the Fed," Phelan will say. "I told him: 'We got through today but another one like it tomorrow and the whole system is gonna have a problem.' "

Phelan may or may not be telling Corrigan what he, as a specialist, knows only too well: Unless the specialists can shed some inventory tomorrow, it may be curtains for the market. He may or may not be pointing out that the specialists can start the ball rolling tomorrow, but they can't control the market, so anything that would stimulate buying would help.

Perhaps, too, he is telling Jerry that, yes, some of the specialists are getting flak from their bankers, although it's not yet clear how serious or widespread the problems are. Corrigan could probably find out about those problems ahead of anyone at the exchange. Apparently, the bankers are scared skinny that the roof is going to fall—in Chicago, tomorrow, and here, next Monday, when today's trades settle.

Yes, there was a lot of talk on the floor and in Chicago about big member firms being in trouble. No, Phelan's staff doesn't see it yet and the firms say they're OK. Yes, they're checking. Every hour.

Liquidity? That was a killer. Phelan wished the member firm moguls hadn't punctured the specialist superfund trial balloon before it ever got off the ground this morning. Maybe an extra billion dollars would have made a difference. Maybe not. It would have been nice to see. This morning, chances of the member firms chipping in to form a $1 billion specialists' fund to support stock prices were slim. After today's disaster, there is no chance at all, Phelan knows. The market needs Corrigan's and the Fed's help for sure. It was one of the things the member firm executives had asked Terry to bring up with the authorities. And Corrigan had been down the crisis path enough times now to know that easily available money is crucial now. Sure, Greenspan recognizes that. Tight money and an interest rates spiral right now would be the last straw. Then you might not find enough buyers at any price.

After a time, the two men will agree to stay in close touch. And they will. But even though their offices are but three blocks apart, they won't see each other face to face during the entire two weeks that they stay in close contact.

Corrigan will shortly be in touch with Alan Greenspan, who's in Texas for a speech to a bankers' convention. Greenspan will want Jerry to work with Fed officials in Washington on wording and coordinating a statement on liquidity. Corrigan will leave his office at 9:30 for home in suburban Westchester County. But the project will absorb him at home late into the night and again early in the morning.

"Timing was crucial," Corrigan will recall. "We wanted the maximum impact [on the securities markets]." Accordingly, the Fed officials will decide to release the statement well ahead of the stock market opening, and at the time when Wall Street's big government bond trading desks are preparing to swing into action for the U.S. trading day. A Tuesday morning release also will give Greenspan, Corrigan, and others at the Fed in Washington time for one more review of the statement in light of the overnight trading in foreign securities markets.

Corrigan will recall that "we got up, took a look, and went ahead and pulled the trigger" on the statement, attributed to Chairman Greenspan, at 8:30 A.M. Its entire text reads:

"The Federal Reserve, consistent with its responsibilities as the nation's central bank, affirmed today its readiness to serve as a source of liquidity to support the economic and financial system."

Phelan will head off to be interviewed for national TV news shows, and will finally drag himself home shortly before nine P.M. He and his wife, Joyce, will go to a little restaurant nearby for a hamburger, then stroll in the neighborhood for a quiet chat. "If there is any event you'd want to pick not to happen on your watch, this is it," he will tell her.

By eleven o'clock, exhausted, he will fall into bed. There will be no breathless phone calls. "You don't run the place like that," Phelan will admonish later. "It doesn't do any good to get a call in the middle of the night."

As he drifts off to sleep, there will be reason to hope that Corrigan and Fed can play an ace in the morning. And there are maybe a couple of cards that he and the specialists can play. If that isn't enough . . . well . . . think about that in the morning.

OCTOBER 19, 1987. ■ The Japan Society, 333 East 47th Street, New York, 8:10 P.M.: A young Japanese man rushes a paper napkin with Japanese characters written on it to Setsuya Tabuchi, chairman of Nomura Securities Company, Ltd., whose more than $70 billion of assets dwarf those of any other securities firm in the world.

Tabuchi is the honored guest at tonight's dinner meeting of the society, a group of American and Japanese business leaders with a special interest in Japan. The message he has been handed concerns the early Tuesday trading on the Tokyo Stock Exchange, which earlier in the year surpassed even the NYSE in the total value of shares listed.

Tabuchi gapes at the note and jerks back in his chair as if he has been shoved. Instantly, he rises and in Japanese (simultaneously translated for the Americans present) he announces, "I've been informed that in the first thirty-five minutes of [Tuesday, October 20] trading on the Tokyo exchange, there have been only six trades." The announcement is greeted with "a long silence," recalls Robert L. Dilenschneider, president of Hill & Knowlton, Inc., the big public-relations firm, a reaction "just shy of a gasp."

Operating in a manner similar to U.S. stock exchanges, the Tokyo market assigns stocks it trades to special exchange members called *saitori*, who operate somewhat like NYSE specialists—with a couple of important exceptions. The saitori aren't allowed to trade for their own accounts, and hence are not responsible to supply liquidity to ensure fair and orderly markets in their stocks.

Accordingly, while about 700 stocks, or close to a third of those listed on the NYSE, had delayed openings this morning due to order imbalances, 95% of the Tokyo stocks are delayed, the SEC will report.

In a stunning demonstration of the developing linkage of international markets during the past decade, the Nikkei Dow Jones Industrial Index of 225 leading Tokyo stocks will dive 7.5% in the Tuesday morning session and end the day down 14.7%.

Tabuchi's Nomura, along with three other immense securities houses—Daiwa, Nikko, and Yamaichi—together account for 60% to 75% of the trading on the Tokyo exchange. And during the final two hours of the trading session now getting under way, entering the market as buyers, the four firms will be the main reason why the Tokyo market decline is less than two thirds the Black Monday drop in New York. Less than six months from now, with Japanese institutions shying away from the U.S. and European stock markets and plowing their immense resources into home markets instead, the Nikkei Dow Jones will be back into record territory.

The jolt in Europe is being absorbed over two trading days, since the U.S. stock market mayhem had already been under way for a half hour to one and a half hours before the European markets closed today. Stock prices in Tuesday's London trading, which would begin before dawn in New York, will plummet 11.6% following Monday's 10.1% drop.

Other European markets won't fare as badly. In Frankfurt, prices will fall another 5.08% after Monday's 7.1% drop; In Zurich, prices that were down 3.05% on Monday will fall another 11.3% in the session to begin overnight. Other European markets, with their respective Monday and Tuesday drops, include: Paris, 4.65% and 5.8%; Milan, 4.45% and 6.26%; Amsterdam, 7.81% and 8.40%; Stockholm,

6.4% and 7.01%, and Brussels, 10.5% and 0.48%. The Brady Commission and SEC investigators will find that early-bird U.S. institutional sellers, unloading U.S. stocks that are also listed on major European exchanges, are aggravating their declines.

The bloodbath is worse in Asia. Stock prices in Sydney are taking a 24.9% drubbing, and are plunging 20.9% in the Singapore exchange's Tuesday session.

Meanwhile, the Hong Kong Stock Exchange has already thrown in the towel for the time being. Officials announced the closing of the exchange for the remainder of the week following Monday's record 11.3% drop in the Hang Seng index—a reaction to Friday's 108-point drop in the Dow. Meanwhile, by the end of Monday's session at Hong Kong's highly speculative futures market, many traders face margin calls of up to four times the value of the stock index futures contracts they had bought only hours before. Hong Kong authorities reportedly fear that a deluge of stock sales to meet these huge futures margin calls would collapse the market. And over the weekend, the Hong Kong government will inject $2 billion Hong Kong dollars ($256 million U.S.) to keep the Futures Guarantee Corporation (a sort of clearinghouse) solvent.

The Hong Kong authorities will only delay a crushing reaction to Black Monday, not evade it. And indeed, some market participants will blame the closing for aggravating selling sentiment through this week. On the Hong Kong exchange's next trading day, Monday, October 26, the Hang Seng index will plunge a sickening 33%—half again worse than today's crash in New York. And by Wednesday, October 26, the Hong Kong government will have to inject yet another $256 million into the Futures Guarantee Corporation to stave off a collapse.

John Phelan and others at the New York exchange will point to Hong Kong as proof positive that they were right to tough it out and keep trading.

OCTOBER 19, 1987. ■ Chicago Mercantile Exchange trading floor, 9:30 P.M.: Not long after today's close, Scott Serfling got a cup of soup at the cafeteria and he's been wandering among the tight knots of frightened young men here ever since.

Occasionally, he would think of another relative to call and return to his trading desk and its phones. "I called to let them know that I was all right; that I hadn't lost everything and committed suicide," he will recall.

Scott will stay here until three A.M., wandering and talking, then wandering some more. There will still be about 100 people here when he leaves.

Now, chatting with a small group of colleagues in the aisle near the pit, he feels a tug on his shoulder. It's a young man we'll call Ned and he wants to talk privately. Scott moves back toward his trading desk. "I'll give you first chance at this, Scott," Ned says. "See this Rolex watch? It cost $10,000—new last year. I'll give it to you for $1,000."

"With the check made out to your clearing broker?" Scott asks. Ned bows his head. "I've gotta have $1,000 tonight, Scott," he says, barely above a whisper, "or my clearing broker's going to sell my membership."

"Ned, I'm sorry. But don't worry, it won't take long to get rid of a Rolex at that price."

Ned is not the first to approach Serfling to offer a bargain for cash tonight and he won't be the last. Scott had waited too long to sell this afternoon. But many of these locals still haven't sold the contracts they bought in this morning's ersatz rally. And some face awesome margin calls.

After the S&P 500 contract's price plunged in the early trading, the CME clearinghouse sent out a special intraday margin call, giving clearing brokers an hour to post extra security on all their open S&P 500 futures positions. Later, as the price resumed a steep plunge that accelerated through the afternoon, the clearinghouse had sent out three more intraday calls. They have totaled $1.2 billion.*

The emergency calls go to the mostly large firms that are members of the CME's clearinghouse—an organization that essentially exists to

---

*Intraday margin calls are clearly emergency measures. Margin in the futures market amounts to a security bond—a deposit players have to put up to ensure that if the market goes against them nobody will cut and run without paying. There are two main varieties of margin: initial margin, charged anyone opening a futures position, and variation margin. Under the latter, futures exchanges adjust the margin accounts in the clearinghouse each day (and broker members of the clearinghouse, in turn, adjust their customers' accounts) to reflect price changes in the prior day's trading. But given the unbelievable size of today's decline, the CME clearinghouse, operating under percentage-change guidelines, has put out what amounts to four emergency calls for more margin from those investors with open "long" or buying positions in the S&P 500 contract.

hold and properly allot the margin. It is from the margin on deposit at the clearinghouse that winning futures investors are paid when they close their positions. Therefore, the clearinghouse must be avid about keeping enough margin on deposit to pay off all the winners in case they all close out their positions at once.

This daily adjustment then, amounts to billing those accounts for more margin whose positions were hurt by the prior day's price moves—the buyers, or "longs," on Black Monday—and credits it to the accounts of the winners—today, the sellers, those with what's called "short" positions. Margin applies only to existing positions, called "open," of course.

Most locals at the CME don't have clearing memberships, which are too costly and require far more capital than most locals can muster. In general, established futures brokerages are the clearing members here. The locals pay fees to the clearing brokers to, in effect, use their access to the clearinghouse.

So, when the clearing brokers get margin calls, they meet them by taking money out of the accounts of those clients whose positions are generating the margin calls. In short, the clearinghouse squeezes the clearing brokers for margin, then they squeeze the clients.

Scott Serfling, whose purchase and sale of his five contracts both occurred during the same trading session, has finished the day without any position. So Serfling is unaffected by all the margin calls. However, many of his colleagues are against the wall. The earlier margin calls wiped out the balances in their accounts at the clearing brokers, and now the brokers, faced with demands by the clearinghouse, are turning the screws on the locals, sometimes for ludicrously small amounts.

For example, tonight $100 will buy a Bears season ticket. A few hundred will get you the title to a flashy powerboat. Condos are going for a fraction of their cost. "There were a lot of phone calls to relatives and rich girlfriends looking for money," Scott will recall.

There is a surreal tinge to all this. The young men parting with their possessions do not seem crestfallen. "If you were one of the survivors— one of the fifteen percent who learned how to trade here—then money was not a big thing," Scott recalls a few months later. "For a lot of these guys, if they needed some money, they just walked into the pit and got some. If they got tired of the pit, they went on vacation. On Black Monday, a lot of them didn't seem to care all that much what they got for their things, as long as they could pay the clearing brokers," Scott will say.

"It hadn't dawned on them yet that maybe things were changed here now. Maybe you couldn't just walk into the pit and get some money whenever you needed it. Maybe those days were over."

Soon, Scott will turn down the chance to buy a month-old $62,000 Mercedes for $50,000. The desperate owner will finally sell it for $38,000. The check will go to his clearing broker.

OCTOBER 19, 1987. ■ TWA terminal, JFK Airport, midnight: Paul Steiger sees the flight from Los Angeles taxiing toward the terminal. It carries his wife, Heidi, who'd called him at the office earlier tonight. The crash made her mission on the Coast impossible, she realized. She was aborting her plans, and would be on the TWA flight at midnight. And he had canceled the San Francisco trip, too, he told her.

The evening had been messy, difficult, maybe the worst he'd ever been through at the *Journal.* The two-star press run had begun an hour and ten minutes late, at 8:20, causing the plants to miss the postal deadline for 45,000 copies.

Graphics changes and editing updates seemed continuous, and the presses had to run on a stop-and-go basis. The Associated Press's closing stock quotes hadn't even begun to arrive until after ten P.M., so the three-star deadline was missed by more than an hour, and almost 14,000 three-star editions missed their mail deadlines.

At times, Steiger had felt like a Chinese fire marshal. Fully 150 of the *Journal*'s 500 news staffers had been directly involved in today's coverage. The figure would rise to 300 tomorrow and remain nearly that high for nearly two weeks.

Steiger cannot know it while he waits for Heidi's jet to unload, but he and the returning Pearlstine will be put under enormous pressure in the weeks ahead from both outside the *Journal* and within.

The New York Times has already hit the street with a two-line banner headline the entire width of its front page. There are powerful photos of awestruck traders on the Big Board floor, staring up at the Quotron screens, presumably at that terrifying discount of the S&P 500 futures. Even in the early editions sent to the northern suburbs, the

Times had given the story three quarters of its front page, all its business section front page and three other full pages—five pages of stories to the *Journal*'s three.

There is a scattershot flavor to the *Times*'s coverage, but it is immensely dramatic and will galvanize critics of Steiger and of the Markets Group. The *Journal*'s coverage, these critics will allege, is dull and undramatic, overstocked with numbers and unclear. And while it won't be articulated, there will be a persistent suggestion that the Markets Group's stock market coverage has been soft and uncritical. The suggestion that if the Markets Group had been tougher and more vigilant, the excesses that led to this debacle might have been checked. Maybe if the Markets Group had taken a needle and let the air out of program trading instead of explaining it . . .

It was Steiger's fault, some critics believed. Prestbo was the Markets editor, yes. But he was Steiger's man, selfless and totally loyal, and Steiger called the shots. Yes, the Markets Group had failed the *Journal*. Steiger had failed.

Now, at the airport people are streaming by Steiger. Ah, there's Heidi now. "Welcome home, honey," he says and gives her a kiss.

She is not in a good mood. "This is a terrific story for you to write about. I get to live with it."

Later, back at their apartment, there is a message from Roger, a college friend of Paul's, who also knows Heidi very well:

"Paul, you must have had an incredible day, but I need to know right away about what this means for the price of real estate in East Hampton," where Roger's summer house is for sale.

"He's so solicitous about you and your incredible day," says an annoyed Heidi. "But what about me? I've got 150 clients ready to eat me alive."

CHAPTER 9

OCTOBER 20, 1987. ■ New York Stock Exchange, chairman's dining room, 8:30 A.M.: "This market is gonna go up," John Phelan tells the six men sharing breakfast with him. "It's got to bounce back after falling so far yesterday."

The men agree. Absolutely. Must go up.

Four of Phelan's guests are the NYSE's floor directors, in charge of enforcing the exchange's rules and representing the exchange leadership in operating the trading floor. Three of the floor directors are specialists—Donny Stone, John Lyden, the managing partner of Nick, Lyden & Company, and James Jacobson, a partner at Benjamin Jacobson & Sons. The fourth, David Shields, the managing director at Shields & Company, is a floor trader.

The remaining two men in the room are the quietly proficient exchange president, Bob Birnbaum, and Dick Grasso, the executive vice-president, who will succeed Birnbaum in mid-1988. No one needs to be told how important a market recovery today would be. They discuss how Black Monday had put huge strains on the exchange's trading facilities and left several specialists in a deep financial hole. Dozens more will join them if the market collapses today, all seven men know. Banks have been howling since yesterday afternoon about the sharp decline in the value of the securities they hold as collateral on their loans to the specialists and other Wall Street firms.

Yes, there must be buyers today; real buyers, the kind who deserted the market entirely yesterday afternoon as the Dow plunged 220 points in the final hour of trading. The kind that will have to be convinced that the bottom of this market was yesterday. And the NYSE officials know that nothing short of a thumping good rally today will convince them.

But how likely is that after yesterday's numbing disaster?

Well, there are plenty of buy orders for some stocks already streaming into the DOT system from bargain-hunting institutional investors. At this point, the odds of that don't seem great, a chart in the Brady Commission report will show. DOT, the automated order system, started accepting trades at eight o'clock. Now, after a half hour, there are about $25 million of sell orders and $15 million buy orders entered in the system that will handle more than two thirds of today's record trading volume. About a half hour from now, around the time this meeting breaks, it will be a lot worse—about $140 million of sell orders, nearly double approximately $75 million of buy orders. The ratio will improve by the 9:30 opening of the market ($335 million of sell orders against about $315 million of buy orders), but today's trading will get under way with an imbalance of sell orders in the DOT system.

The buy orders will be highly concentrated. For instance, the amount of money to be paid in this morning's opening trades for just four big stocks—IBM, GM, Exxon, and Atlantic Richfield—will total $276 million.*

Altogether, this is not the kind of climate one usually associates with thunderous rallies. It's clear that the rally so desperately needed now won't come about unless something is done to encourage buying and discourage selling, too. Both are within the power of the men in this room.

Program traders relied on the DOT system to dump billions of dollars' worth of stocks onto the market yesterday. After the George Anders piece in Monday morning's *Journal* that explained how program trading would act to fuel a market meltdown, this morning the press is full of accusations that program trading caused the crash. Phelan knows he can ask all member firms to refrain voluntarily from using the DOT system for program trading today, and no one will dare refuse. And that is precisely what he will do ahead of today's opening.

Meanwhile, the floor directors can help stimulate the needed buy-

---

*Arrived at by multiplying the opening price of each stock by the share volume of the opening trade, then totaling these four results.

ing—just by doing their jobs and conveying the consensus of this morning's meeting to all the specialist traders on the floor well ahead of the opening. The specialists will take it from there. After all, one of their principal tasks is to determine stock prices at each morning's opening.

Supply and demand and market forces and all those technical factors may ultimately determine stock prices, the men in this room know. But it is the specialist who decides where they start trading each day, and today they will start higher. Much higher. "We had two goals Tuesday morning," Phelan will recall, "One, get rid of [the specialists'] inventory; two, but don't go too high [with the price] or you won't get rid of it."

Of course, that is far easier to say than do. Phelan knows that it won't just be a matter of the specialists' setting high opening prices, selling their excess inventories into the openings, and living happily ever after, not in this stunned and wobbly market. Today the wrong opening price could be disastrous, and a price too temptingly high could easily attract more sellers than buyers.

The higher opening prices Phelan and the others have in mind are a double boon. They'll allow the specialists who are selling into the opening to both trim their losses on their inventory sales and raise more capital to help cope with the still-powerful army of sellers that Phelan and his colleagues know is lurking out there.

Thanks in part to yesterday's chaos, specialists will have greater than usual latitude at today's opening. Many investors yesterday who made their orders contingent on specific prices—the usual practice among institutional traders—saw prices fall so fast that they were obsolete in the market before the orders could be executed. Chastened, they will enter today with orders to be executed "at the market"—essentially, at whatever price the specialist determines the market to be. The Brady Commission will find that "the vast majority of orders to buy at the market's open were 'market orders,' enabling the NYSE specialists to open stocks significantly higher than Monday's close."

The Brady Commission's report will cite order imbalances in the delayed openings of 92 stocks (compared with 187 on Monday). Again, specialists will operate under crisis procedures that allow them to hold back any indications of the bid and asking price spreads on the delayed stocks for a half hour after the trading day begins. Yet even the relaxed rule will be widely ignored as some specialists delay their indications for hours, and as "many specialists" begin trading at prices far above yesterday's closes without putting out any preopening indications at all.

One explanation could be the "Bambi" theory—if you can't say something nice, don't say anything at all. It's clear that "something nice" this morning would be an indication that suggests an opening price sharply higher than yesterday's close. But alas more than a few specialists will be staring at imbalances of sell orders, not buy orders. Howard Kramer, the SEC staffer who will analyze specialist trading in a sample of sixty-seven blue-chip stocks, will find that twenty-six of them have had delayed openings today. Among that group "most of the imbalances—certainly the biggest ones—are on the buy side." But, in a look at the data six months from now, he will see many sell-side imbalances in the group, too. "Looking at the data here in front of me, I estimate about sixty percent have buy-side imbalances and forty percent sell imbalances," he will say.

Many of the indications that are posted on the ninety-two stocks where trading is delayed at the opening will be of limited value. The SEC's report will note that many of the preopening indications have such wide price spreads that they will offer no real guidance to potential buyers or sellers. For example, General Electric, which closed at 41⅞ yesterday, will have an initial opening indication of 45 bid, 65 asked, at 9:52 A.M. and another of 40-55 at 10:30 before it opens at 46½ just before eleven o'clock. The GE specialist will be telling the world that more than twenty minutes after the day's session has begun, would-be buyers and sellers are still as much as $20 apart, and that an hour into the trading day they'll still be at least $15 apart in one of the most heavily traded stocks on earth. To a professional trader, such indications amount to a KEEP OUT sign.

Other specialists will open their stocks sharply higher in spite of seemingly small buy-order imbalances. For example, Atlantic Richfield, one of the thirty Dow Jones industrials, will open at 75, up 10 on opening volume of 267,000 shares, and a buy-order surplus of just 13,000 shares.

Shortly before ten o'clock, as the SEC will report, a Lasker, Stone & Stern specialist will open Coca-Cola stock, another thirty Dow industrial, up 10, or 33%, Donny Stone's Johnson & Johnson stock, not one of the thirty industrials, but an important S&P 500 component included in nearly every program trader's market basket, also will open late and up 10 points.

The trader specialist for Spear, Leeds & Kellogg will list indications of 35-45, then of 40-50 on shares of J. P. Morgan & Company, the bank holding company, which closed yesterday at 27¾. Trading will begin shortly after ten o'clock—at 47, up 69%. J. P. Morgan will be one of seven NYSE stocks to be reallocated to other specialists over the next six months because of improper or inadequate specialist performance during the crash.

Close observers will see the disciplinary moves as ironic in light of the clear pattern of openings that will follow Phelan's breakfast meeting with the floor directors this morning. The punishments will seem perfunctory and in response to pressure from the SEC, whose report will cite "several instances of specialist performance in opening their stocks that raise questions about the specialist's maintenance of a fair and orderly market."*

Phelan, the floor directors, and other officials realize that to achieve today's goals, the exchange must keep the program traders on the sidelines; which is now being arranged. At the opening, the NYSE will announce that it has asked members to refrain from using the DOT system to execute program trades today.†

The Dow will soar 127 points in this morning's first thirty minutes of trading and 196 points in the first hour. The specialists will be "very heavy sellers on the opening transactions and during the first 30 minutes of trading," the SEC will report, "as many used the opportunity to liquidate their large positions from the previous day."

---

*The SEC report discloses that the NYSE had begun "several investigations of specialist performance during the week of October 19" and that specialists in two issues (to early February) had agreed to withdraw them and allow their reassignment. Spear Leeds will be one of the two. Yet the loss of Morgan stock is hardly a disaster. Even after it loses Morgan, Spear Leeds, the exchange's largest specialist firm, will still be making markets in 153 Big Board stocks.
†The exchange will allow program orders loaded into DOT ahead of the opening to be executed. The SEC will find that a few members apparently ignored the request and that still others completed program trades manually, by carrying orders around to the specialists' posts. However, overall, program selling of all types totaled only 24.4 million shares, or 4% of volume on Tuesday, October 20, down from 89 million shares, or just under 15% of the trading on Black Monday. At tomorrow's opening the NYSE will announce an indefinite extension of the ban, but will partly lift it on November 3 to allow use of DOT for programs loaded into the system ahead of the opening. All restrictions on the use of the system for program trades will be dropped on November 9. Then, early in 1988, the exchange will adopt a measure prohibiting the use of DOT for program trading at any time during a trading day after the Dow Jones Industrial Average has moved more than 50 points from the prior day's close.

"You can make a case that what they did was entirely fair and reasonable," Brandon Becker, the SEC official in charge of dealing with self-regulatory agencies, will say six months hence. "You can't really make a judgment one way or the other without examining a whole lot of individual openings." Yet the massive report he and his colleagues at the SEC's Division of Market Regulation produce will be less charitable: "As with October 19, the Division believes the openings on October 20 deserve scrutiny by both the Commission and the NYSE."

Even as Phelan and the floor directors complete plans to avert another disaster on the stock exchange floor today, the electronic media have arrived to watch and wait for one. Cable News Network, which beams newscasts via satellite to fifty-eight European and Asian nations, was the only TV network camped here yesterday. Now trucks and cables from NBC, CBS, and ABC have joined CNN's outside the exchange building. Throughout the day camera crews will peer down on the trading-floor chaos from the press gallery catwalk up near the ceiling, waiting for the story—the market—to break: "Live from New York, the collapse of the stock market!"

Instead, beginning an hour from now, the media will unknowingly witness what may someday be judged an even worse calamity. In a desperate attempt to make their individual markets orderly, many NYSE specialists will open stocks at prices that make them unfair.

OCTOBER 20, 1987. ■ The Federal Reserve Bank of New York, 8:45 A.M.: Back to work. Jerry Corrigan, who's already been at his desk for more than an hour, picks up the telephone. Minutes ago, the Fed staff in Washington released Chairman Alan Greenspan's statement pledging to supply liquidity during the crisis. Corrigan will make sure everyone here believes that and pitches in.

Within the hour, in Dallas Greenspan had approved the text of the one-sentence statement after an insubstantial wording change. Corrigan had signed off on it from here and Vice-Chairman Manuel Johnson had done so in Washington. Fed governors had been consulted by phone at their homes around the country, too.

Greenspan has canceled his speech to the bankers in Dallas. Instead, he'll shortly check out of his hotel room and fly back to Washington to monitor the crisis from there. Over the days ahead, he'll be in daily touch with the Fed district bank presidents and with other Fed governors, as well as with Treasury and other administration economic officials.

Greenspan will arrive in Washington at one P.M., and go straight into a crisis meeting at the Treasury. James Baker will arrive at two P.M., having flown back from Europe with Wall Street investment banker and former New Jersey Senator Nicholas Brady.

Yesterday White House Chief of Staff Howard Baker had reached Brady, the chairman of Dillon, Read & Company, in London. Baker told Brady that the market was falling apart and that most of the people who could help him figure out what to do about it were out of reach. Greenspan was en route to Dallas at that time, and James Baker was in Sweden since shortly after leaving German government finance officials at the Frankfurt airport on Friday. Brady then phoned the Treasury secretary in Sweden and arranged to fly to Washington with him today.

Notwithstanding Alan Greenspan's inopportune travel schedule, the Fed is on a far more solid footing today than anyone would have dared hope even two months ago. And that is thanks to the homework by Corrigan and his staff and to the attention he and Greenspan had given a few weeks ago to examining possible responses to a stock market emergency.

Last night, in addition to working with Greenspan, Fed Vice-Chairman Manuel Johnson, and other Washington-based staffers on the language and timing of the chairman's statement to be released within a half hour, Corrigan had also discussed with them the implications of the crisis. These and wider discussions involving the other Federal Reserve Board governors led to a plan aimed at keeping money flowing in sufficient quantity to accommodate the added loan demand just ahead.

Rather than making low-cost loans to banks or securities firms in danger of failing, the Fed will radically increase the lending power of the nation's banks. It will then be up to the banks to sort out who gets the new loans. Almost anybody would rather borrow than go under, and as long as the Fed makes sure the banks have plenty of lending power, that is exactly what will happen.

During the next two weeks, the plan will completely reverse the

Fed's policy of slightly restraining bank lending that has been in force since just before Labor Day this year. Through traders working for Peter Sternlight, the executive vice-president of the New York Fed for open-market operations, the central bank will tremendously stimulate loans to securities firms by creating a mountain of new reserves for banks to lend.

First, working at the open-market operations trading desk two floors below Corrigan's office, the traders will make massive purchases of government securities. The money the Fed pays for those securities will be deposited in bank accounts.* Deposits are bank reserves and, under Fed regulations, the amount of its reserves determine how much a bank can lend.

A bank doesn't have to sell some of its government securities to the Fed to get access to the reserves the central bank injects. Once the reserves are created, they can be loaned from bank to bank. Banks with more reserves (hence, lending power) than they are using typically lend unneeded reserves in an arena called the "Federal funds market." Conversely, banks whose reserves aren't large enough to allow them to service all their loan demands can borrow the additional reserves they need from the Federal funds market.

The interest rate in the Fed funds market floats in line with the bidding among prospective borrowers and lenders of reserves who use it. And, as in any other open market, the rate is sensitive to supply and demand. The more plentiful the reserves are, the lower the Fed funds rate (that is, the price) of those reserves will be. The more scarce the reserves are, the higher the Fed funds rate will be.

---

*When the Fed buys government securities, it deals only with an approved group of primary dealers. There were forty dealers in this exclusive group in October 1987 (in contrast to forty-two in mid-1988). The primary dealers buy new bonds, notes, and T-bills directly from the Treasury as they are issued and then resell them to investment institutions. At other times, the primary dealers trade in an average of more than $100 billion of already issued government securities a day. The group of dealers includes most of New York City's largest banks, as well as Harris Trust and Continental Illinois in Chicago and the West Coast giants, Security Pacific and Bank of America. Wall Street's largest securities firms—among them Salomon Brothers, Merrill Lynch, Goldman Sachs, First Boston, Morgan Stanley, Bear Stearns, Prudential-Bache, PaineWebber, and Dean Witter—are primary dealers, too. No matter which type of primary dealer the Fed buys bonds from, its payment will be in the form of an instant addition to bank reserves. Of course, all the banks themselves have their own accounts at the Federal Reserve, which are credited with the Fed's payment for any bonds they sell to the Fed. Voilà, instant reserves! Similarly, any made by the payments Fed to the securities firms among the primary dealers will become reserves, too, since these payments will be credited to these firms' bank accounts. Customer deposits also qualify as reserves.

Injecting reserves has a powerful multiplying effect on lending. The Fed's regulations require member banks to have just 12 cents of reserves for every dollar they lend. So for every dollar the Fed injects, banks can make $8.33 of new loans, according to a Fed staffer. The Fed's government securities purchases this week and next will inject a whopping total of $11.85 billion of new reserves.* So U.S. banks will be authorized to respond to new loan demands of up to a staggering $98.7 billion, if necessary.

Of course, "it never works out anything like that," says a Fed spokesman in Washington. And the Fed's objective isn't to stimulate anything near that much new lending, anyway. Rather, the intent is to flood the Fed funds market with reserves, to show that no bank needs to worry about finding the money it needs to fund new loans now.

Today alone, the central bank will inject enough reserves to drive down the Fed funds rate to 6¾% from 7½%. In response to the stimulus, loans at the ten biggest New York City banks to finance the purchase of or carrying costs of securities will soar. By tomorrow night, the total will be $12.04 billion—$5.5 billion more than last Wednesday. Nationwide, the increase will be $7 billion.

Corrigan's and the Fed's plan is the essence of simplicity, John Phelan will tell the *Journal*'s Daniel Hertzberg a few weeks from now: "The banks would be kept liquid; the banks would make sure everyone else in the system would stay liquid." The Fed's massive reserves injection amounts to a pledge to drown this crisis in liquidity if need be.†

Until early next month, when the Fed stops injecting reserves, Greenspan will rely on Jerry Corrigan to be the central bank's point man on Wall Street. Corrigan has already begun touching base with the top New York City bank officials today. He is speaking for Alan Greenspan and the Fed, assuring them of the Fed's commitment to keep funds plentiful throughout the crisis, and encouraging them to keep those funds flowing into the securities industries as needed, consistent with prudent lending standards.

---

*This figure represents the net total increase in daily average reserves affected by Fed open-market operations in the weeks ending October 21 and October 28, as cited in Federal Reserve H.4.1 reports, which will be made public on October 22 and October 29, respectively.
†The Fed injected additional reserves into the banking system for seventeen consecutive business days, from October 8 through November 2, 1987.

Corrigan knows it is vital that banks keep open the lending spigots for their Wall Street customers during the payments crunch this week for the futures and options investors and next week for stock market investors.* He deals with some of the most powerful banks in the world, including Citibank, Chase Manhattan, J. P. Morgan, Bankers Trust, Chemical Bank, and Manufacturers Hanover.

But Corrigan also knows the banks must not get the impression that the Fed's prudent lending standards are being relaxed somehow to accommodate this crisis. For one thing, this is no Fed bailout of Wall Street or Wall Street's bankers. The New York Fed president makes sure everyone he or his staff talks to understands that. Any expanded lending to alleviate the crisis must be undertaken "within prudential standards," he will stress.

Notwithstanding all the liquidity the Fed is creating and the rationality of Corrigan's pitch to the banks, Jerry will face an uphill struggle to convince some of the banks to keep Wall Street afloat. It's clear the circumstances are grave. Phelan, who reached his office at 6:30 this morning, has been informed that of the thirteen specialist firms ending yesterday at or under the NYSE's warning level for capital, five were so far below it that they might not survive another market plunge today. Yet rather than easing and speeding their lending procedures in the crisis, some major banks are slowing and tightening them.

Journal reporters Hertzberg and James B. Stewart will find that specialist firm A. B. Tompane & Company hadn't been able to get Bankers Trust to commit on a loan of desperately needed additional capital, and as a result had agreed to sell out to Merrill Lynch in the middle of the night. Bankers Trust also had denied a commitment on a $30 million loan to Henderson Brothers, Inc., one of the NYSE's best-capitalized specialist firms, despite five phone calls extending past midnight, the *Journal* reporters would learn. Other specialists were telling Phelan that this morning their banks are edgy about collateral. There were rumors, too, that Salomon Brothers and Goldman Sachs could have big-ticket margin payments to make in Chicago that may become a problem.

Corrigan won't get involved in any of these individual tugging

---

*The different schedules reflect next-day margin requirements in the futures and options markets and regular settlement after five trading days in the stock market.

matches—it would be an unthinkable abuse of the central bank's power. However, the horror stories that he and his staff are hearing help them gauge the strains bankers and customers are facing today and for the next ten days, as actual payment is made for the 2 billion shares being traded on the NYSE this week. These stories show that the dominant emotion among Wall Street's bankers this morning is fear.

Some foreign banks, including an unnamed Japanese bank, are freezing their lending levels, even to their biggest and strongest Wall Street customers. Other banks are raising their interest rates to discourage borrowing and to test whether their customers have other sources of credit, the SEC will report.

The SEC will also find that one European bank, which will raise its lending rate ¼ of 1% today, will nonetheless see its securities industry customers borrow up to their usual daily limits. So tomorrow the bank will bump up the rate another ¼ of 1%.

Cynical as it may seem, some banks will also use "selective intraday margin calls" on their stock loans "as a means of 'testing' particular borrowers." If the targeted borrower meets the margin call, the banks' credit fears will be allayed. If he does not, the bank is forewarned to reduce, or at least not expand, lending to the troubled borrower. Meanwhile, the targeted borrower must divert time and energy from his life-or-death trading struggle to round up the cash for an "exploratory" margin call. Risk arbitrageurs, the takeover stock players who have been on the ropes since last week's threatening tax news, are being targeted in particular, the SEC will learn.

A major New York City bank, fearing it won't get paid, will raise the SEC staff's hackles by blatantly violating foreign-currency-market settlement practice. The *Journal*'s Stewart and Hertzberg will report that even though this bank will refuse to deliver $70 million of German marks it sells to a big Wall Street firm until tomorrow, it will demand payment in U.S. dollars today. Other banks will have to step in and bridge the gap with overnight loans. The SEC staff, which won't specify this transaction or name the bank, will sputter that such an action could have "frozen the foreign exchange market and precipitated a widespread credit constriction that would have worsened the difficulties experienced by the financial community during the break."

The banks' skittishness is understandable. They are faced by clamorous demands from customers for new loans at a time when the value of the collateral posted on existing loans is plummeting right along with the stock market. And even where there isn't a substantial fear that borrowers will default, there are huge paperwork logjams forming as part of the regular credit-checking routines of the banks.

"Sure, the banks were going slow," Chicago Mercantile Exchange Executive Committee Chairman Leo Melamed will recall six months from now. "They were getting asked for $100 million by people who normally ask for $10 million."

OCTOBER 20, 1987. ∎ Chicago Mercantile Exchange trading floor, 9:45 A.M., EDT: "Trading?" Scott Serfling asks a young local a few feet below his trading desk.

"Just watching," the young man says with an exasperated sigh.

"Your clearing broker?" Scott asks the fellow. He gets back a dejected nod.

Along with a hundred or more other thinly capitalized young traders at the S&P 500 pit, Scott's acquaintance has been reined to the sidelines by his clearing broker. Few of the locals have either the capital or the inclination to become members of the CME's clearinghouse. So a number of large futures brokers who do maintain their own clearing memberships earn fees by using them to clear and settle the locals' trades.

However, today they have been eschewing that business. Given the risk of more losses like yesterday's, which certainly would exceed many of the young clearing customers' financial worth, the last thing the clearing brokers want to see is their local clients opening new positions today. Doing that would generate heavy new margin requirements— something the locals might not be able to meet if the S&P 500 futures market swings as savagely today as it did yesterday.*

No, that is a risk the already strapped clearing brokers do not need now. Not with stories circulating about traders pulling bales of cash out of Chicago banks and rumors that defaults by any of several large securities firms could bring down the Chicago clearinghouses with

---

*The risk to the clearing members is that their clearinghouse memberships make them responsible for their customers' margin requirements. If the locals can't come up with the margin money, the firms they clear their trades through will have to come up with it.

defaults in the billions. So the big clearing brokers have in effect refused to clear any trades for their less capitalized local clients. The locals have been walled off from the market because they have no way to settle any trade they may make.

It was a weird opening. There'd been talk of buy-order imbalances in New York. Then, practically at the bell, the Big Board pulled its rabbit out of the hat: no program trades on DOT today. Anybody wanting to do them would have to have their traders walk orders around to various specialist posts on the New York Stock Exchange floor. There'd been some frantic headscratching among the locals to divine the impact of that move here in the pit.

The way Serfling analyzes it, the Big Board was trying to sever the link that lets the pit influence prices in New York, then push back the selling pressure into Chicago. Denial of DOT should pretty much shut down index arbitrage trading here, Serfling figures, since trying to execute the trades at the New York end by hand will be a horror show that the index arbs almost certainly will choose to avoid. So he figured some buying would be missing here this morning.

New York's kicking the portfolio insurers' programs out of DOT will probably shunt most of their selling today to the pit here, Scott figures. But maybe it won't be too bad. Because the December futures price sank to such a tremendous discount to the index yesterday, portfolio insurance sellers using the pit got far less money for the futures they sold here than they could have realized by selling the underlying stocks on the NYSE. So, if the index arbs' not buying here today does lead to another big discount, the portfolio insurers just might make them fairly reluctant to use this market as heavily as they did yesterday, Scott guesses. (He will be wrong. Portfolio insurers will sell more than 28,000 contracts in the pit today, or 2,000 more than yesterday.)

Serfling had seen in the past ten minutes that the big Wall Street firms apparently figured today's scenario differently. The first trade in the pit was 221. That's not far off the 225 close of the index last night, but a discount on the opening. Then the Wall Street buying hit. The next trade was all the way up at 225, then 229, 229, 229; then 230, 232, 233—233 again. Then there was another gap up to 237, 238, 238, 239, and 239. Oh, heavy, heavy trading. Maybe 3,000 cars in the first minute.

The big houses' alternate brokers have been selling while their usual brokers were buying. Serfling can see that the big houses are buying aggressively from their customers, the portfolio insurers. It has to be that way, he figures. With orders that size, portfolio insurers wouldn't be dealing through any but the big firms.

He also realizes that with DOT sealed off, the big houses' buying isn't simply related to arbitrage as it was yesterday morning. Yes, it must be real, honest-to-God speculative buying! There can be only one rational explanation for Solly's and Goldy's and Morgan's and Kidder's buying—the simplest explanation of all. The big boys are buying so avidly because they are convinced the market is going up and will stay up at least long enough so they can get out with a trading profit.

Now, fifteen minutes into the session, they've moved the price to a premium of a dozen points. Scott knows it's a phony premium, what with all those S&P stocks delayed and being counted in the index at yesterday's closing prices. And he sees that as time passes and more stocks open in New York, the index is taking off. In ten minutes it will catch up to the December futures price here—and keep right on going. Prices seem stuck now, with the bidding bunching around 240. This is too rich a game for most of the locals, yet some are opening long positions, too, along with Solly and other big houses. Trying desperately to get back what they lost yesterday, Serfling reckons.

Despite the aggressive buying by the majors, Scott senses there's something wrong with this bullish scenario this morning. But what is it exactly? There's no time to really think; so many calls coming in from clients, trying to figure out if yesterday was a fluke and a killing can be made if they dive into this rally early today.

Ten minutes from now, Serfling will speak on the telephone to a West German money manager client as he puzzles over the action in the pit. The German has a $20 million wad to bet here, if Scott says go. Now 242, but, oops, back to 240, 240, and 240 again; now 241, 242. Oops! 239, 239, and 239 again. Now 240, 241 . . . Nobody's even bothering with basis points, they're bidding on the whole numbers. The rally already acts like it's topping out, but why?

Then Serfling will understand. Barely a minute ago, with the locals buying avidly, a floor official of one increasingly nervous clearing broker had stopped by the rim of the pit and, shouting like a lifeguard, had pulled the plug on all the firm's local trader clients. "All locals out!" he had yelled.

Of course. That's it. The locals are so decimated that the Wall Street trading houses are pretty much alone on the buy side against their portfolio insurance clients on the sell side today. Missing perhaps 300 or more of their local pilot fish to follow them and magnify their trading power, the Wall Street houses will eventually be ground down by even moderate portfolio insurance selling, Serfling realizes.* And given yesterday's 20% drop to hedge against, the portfolio insurers might be very aggressive sellers today—unless the rally on the floor in New York can continue strong and frighten them away. Yes, that will be the key today. Wait, and watch New York.

"No, Otto, I don't think you need to hurry," he tells the West German. "I think you'll be able to buy 'em below 200 today."

OCTOBER 20, 1987. ■ Dow Jones Tower, World Financial Center, 10:30 A.M.: Odd place for a story conference, the elevator.

". . . Not the professional investment types, but a broad range of prominent people. Interesting people," says the tall moustached man in the dark suit. "People everyone would recognize. What are they doing? What do they think people should do? It might be very readable and useful, too."

Paul Steiger listens thoughtfully and nods. "I like it. We'll take a good look at that."

Yes, the suggestion is intriguing. It could indeed be readable. It could be nicely illustrated, too, from the *Journal*'s now extensive files of sketched portraits. And it comes from none other than Warren H. Phillips, the man in the dark suit who is chairman and chief executive of Dow Jones. No worry about executive complaints on this unconventional story.

Phillips's story suggestion, and Steiger's response, reflect a yet undefined uneasiness they and others at Dow Jones will increasingly feel about the *Journal*'s coverage of the crash—especially when matched up against the thunderous and broadly varied *New York Times* approach.

Both men examined the *Times* coverage carefully this morning, and both were impressed. Any way you want to measure it, the *Times* has

*Indeed, the Brady Commission will report that the locals' activity on October 20 declined sharply. And while they sold $2 billion less in contracts than they did on Black Monday, they bought $3 billion less.

given the story far more space today (33 columns) than the *Journal* (18.5 columns). True, today's *Times* is much thicker—120 pages to the *Journal*'s 78—but the New York daily has committed 34% of its news and business section space (other than ads and lists) to the crash story, while the *Journal* has devoted about 25% of its available space.

The *Times*'s coverage also has a sledgehammer visual impact. The front page is a nuclear explosion of banner headlines, a four-column-wide chart of the five-year bull-market rally, with an inset showing yesterday's swan dive; three multicolumn front-page stories on the crisis and a prominent three-column-wide summary of the related stories inside.

And the pictures! A dramatic three-panel sequence of thunderstruck Spear Leeds specialist trader Terrence J. McManus on the Big Board floor. First, he is shown looking up in fright at the Quotron screen above his post, then covering his eyes with his hand, and finally leaning forward, holding his head in his hand.

Just as it will all through the week, everything about the *Times*'s coverage screams "Wow!" And historic or not, the *Journal*'s two-column front-page treatment today seems colorless, and perfunctory by comparison.

Some magazines and newsletters in the weeks ahead will carry unfavorable comparisons of the *Journal*'s coverage with that of the *Times*. In his newsletter, financial press critic (and former *Journal* reporter) Dean Rotbart will sing praises for the *Times*'s coverage and contend that the *Journal*'s main Black Monday story is narrowly technical and too densely packed with numbers. Yet today it's the *Journal*, not the *Times*, that is calling what happened yesterday a "crash" (instead of a "plunge") and is labeling yesterday's trading "panic-driven" (rather than just "frenzied"). And the *Times*'s main report on the Black Monday market activity is half again more crowded with numbers than the *Journal*'s. (Numbers account for 4.5% of the word count in the *Times*'s main front-page story contrasted with 3% of the *Journal*'s.)

No, the *Times*'s undeniably greater impact is primarily visual—stemming from its lavish use of space, big bold headlines, graphics, and powerful photos. It is an awesome broadside at the crash story by a newspaper whose editors seem to be competing with network television.

And the *Times* will rock and roll again tomorrow, giving the main market story a three-line front-page headline two thirds of a page wide. Four big stories will eat up two thirds of the front page, led by a report of today's market action under a three-line, four-column-wide headline. G.O.P. (PRESIDENTIAL) FIELD FEARS CAMPAIGN DAMAGE, and an explainer—THE MARKET: WHY DOES IT MATTER?—are tying together the market, the economy, and average Americans' lives, and there's a visceral look at the threat to residential real estate, too: AMID TURMOIL, HOME BUYERS ARE PUTTING DREAMS ON HOLD.

Three quarters of the front page of the Business Day section and eight full inside pages are given over to a smorgasbord of pictures, graphics, news stories, and features ranging in tone from utility (CAUTION IS URGED BY ADVISERS) to amusement (OLD JOKES STRIKE RESONANT CHORD).

In CAUTION IN THE PRESS: WAS IT REALLY A CRASH?, media reporter Alex S. Jones will deftly needle his own paper, noting that judgments in other papers on just what to call Black Monday "varied widely. For instance, *The Washington Post* and *The New York Times* decided not to refer to the market action as a 'crash.' " Jones will go on to quote a *Post* executive arguing to justify his decision, but there won't be a single word of defense from anyone at the *Times*. Jones will note the *Journal's* straightforward label and quote a certain deputy managing editor, "Paul Stiger [sic]," as saying that "if '29 was a crash, this was also."

Richard J. Meislin will stake out one of the more fascinating, emotionally charged aspects of the crash: the yuppie impact. In a deliciously tongue-in-cheek story headlined YUPPIES' LAST RITES READIED: SOME SEE END TO EXCESSES, he will note that "psychologists and marketers said the market reversal, if it endured, was likely to force a shift in values among people who had seemed to find it difficult to distinguish self worth and net worth."

One of Meislin's sources will be the widely quoted Faith Popcorn, chairman of Brain Reserve, Inc., a New York consulting company:

"It's like almost drowning—you become a very, careful swimmer. Yuppies are compulsive. They're compulsive spenders, and I think we're going to find out they're compulsive non-spenders."

She said people had suffered from a "yuppie glut—too much, too soon, too disgusting." And she predicted there would be a lot of young professionals who, after taking a beating this week, would trim back on the items they consider to be necessities. "One house, one car, one raincoat—that's what it's going to be," Ms. Popcorn said.

The *Times*'s coverage represents modern metropolitan daily journalism at its best, Steiger will assert. "They gave it the same kind of treatment that the *L.A. Times, The Washington Post,* and other good metro dailies gave it—only more so," he says. "At a metro daily, the editor in chief and the other editors would huddle. They'd give the financial editor all the space and all of the reinforcements from the general news staff he asks for and then hit it with everything they've got. That's the way they mobilize for a truly huge story—a *Challenger* disaster, assassination of the president, or whatever."

That approach, however, isn't appropriate at the *Journal,* Paul Steiger will argue. Steiger and Pearlstine (who'll arrive from Europe in midafternoon and take the helm tomorrow) see the *Journal*'s role as vastly different. "A story like this isn't something we cover in addition to the other things we do," Paul will contend. "It is a story for everyone here that affects everything we do."

So, months after this week's barrage of special story packages, the crash and its implications will infuse the *Journal*'s coverage of the U.S. and international stock, bond, currency, and commodities markets, as well as industry and other corporate news, management, the media, politics, and the economy—nearly everything the paper covers. Most of the scores of crash-aftermath stories produced by *Journal* reporters will focus precisely on the subject matter of their regular assignments. John Prestbo, the *Journal*'s Markets editor, is blunt: "Of course, the reporters' focus is tight. They know their pay and career prospects depend on how well they cover their beats."

The group Steiger convenes in the ninth-floor conference room this morning isn't an *ad hoc* crisis team of generalist reporters and editors. It's the people who cover the markets and the financial services industries. Present are Prestbo and more than a dozen of the Markets Group staffers, Dick Rustin and a half dozen of his chargers from the Money Group, and some other editors.

Tomorrow, the *Journal* will lead on Page One with a precisely aimed story from senior economics writer Alan Murray in Washington on how the crash has put new Fed Chairman Alan Greenspan on the spot.

The left-hand leader will be a "roundup" (produced from the memos of many reporters around the country) on consumers who are suddenly reassessing their spending plans. There'll be two other roundups in tomorrow's package, and fifteen of the sixteen remaining stories will explore the crash's impact on the various industries or activities regularly covered by their authors.

Steiger's between-floors conference with Phillips will spawn a note to domestic *Journal* bureaus minutes hence and an offbeat story that might do *People* magazine proud. The latter is a roundup, illustrated by line drawings of, among others, the irrepressible Donald Trump. (He'll confide that he reinvested in the stock market today. But for less well-heeled mortals, "It's better just to have a good time and watch," he'll advise.) Pop psychologist Joyce Brothers will urge people to nest, "Just as in a storm, birds nest." Hollywood producer Burt Sugarman will advise against borrowing money (but a few months hence will be ready to borrow a bundle for his proposed $1.57 billion takeover of Media General, Inc.). There'll even be advice for Wall Street out of Cleveland—from advertising executive and corporate etiquette expert Lois Wyse, who will remind *Journal* readers that "you need to assure everybody in your life that you still love them, even if they're now part of the newly poor."

In another roundup story (forced into the Who's News section and thus buried on page 42), a frantic Pittsburgh-based stockbroker will tell a client: "Don't say, 'Oh no!' Shut up and listen to me!" Pittsburgh bureau staffer Clare Ansberry will report: "By noon, he is answering the phone, 'John-End-of-the-World-Posteraro. He bluntly tells the caller: 'You're in bad shape. I told you guys to get out, but you don't listen. What should you do now? Pray a lot!' "

At the regular 4:30 meeting this afternoon, Steiger and the other senior editors will decide headline sizes and placement of the dozen or so stories they consider the most important. Murray's piece on Greenspan and the Fed will lead Page One. The offbeat advice roundup suggested by Phillips will lead Larry Rout's Second Front.

Arguably the hottest story of the day, today's market drama, which will get a four-column headline on the *Times*'s front page tomorrow, won't run on Page One in tomorrow's *Journal.* Instead, in line with a practice peculiar to the *Journal,* the story will be summarized in a blurb at the top of the daily What's News column on the front page, where it also tells readers that the story is on Page Three.*

The *Times*'s more freewheeling coverage, lavish use of space, and strong graphics emphasis will powerfully convey the fear, the rage, the frustration associated with the crash. The *Journal* will carefully, precisely tell its readers what has happened and what may happen as a result of the crash in each of many specific industries and business areas. The difference will be between a honeycomb at the *Journal* and free-flowing honey at the *Times*.

As time passes, Paul Steiger's uneasiness will grow. He will begin to feel that the *Journal* coverage is missing something. And even after the dozens of tightly focused stories commissioned in the days ahead, he will be dissatisfied. Two weeks hence, Steiger will recall, "Somehow I felt that I still hadn't read anything that sorted it all out. I yearned for a story that would tell me: 'Here's what really happened to the stock market on Black Monday, why it happened, and what it really means.'"

No one capable of the task in Prestbo's highly specialized and segmented Markets Group will be disposed to try to satisfy this hunger for an elementally broad story. They will be busy thinking, reporting and writing about what the crash means in the tightly focused coverage areas for which they are held responsible. Therefore, in the first days of November, Steiger will turn to Dick Rustin and ask if the Money Group's formidable reporting team of James B. Stewart and Daniel Hertzberg can tackle the task. For a year, both Stewart and Hertzberg have been covering the continuing government crackdown on insider trading almost exclusively. Now, with the insider probe temporarily sidetracked by the market crash, they are itching to get involved in the crash coverage. "The Markets Group people already were so involved in the day-to-day developments and also I thought we could really do

---

*This practice reflects a traditionally slower work pace and a higher level of rewrite and tinkering with stories by the Page One staff that for decades has made it ill-suited to handle stories that develop late in the day, especially market stories, which can't even be written until after four P.M. While feats such as the Page One staff's efforts on Black Monday are no longer rare, they are not commonplace, either. So the day's hottest story usually goes to Marty Schenker's National News desk, where editing speed is at a greater premium, and space and deadline requirements are more flexible than on Page One. Yet, for all the editors' painstaking efforts, many readers aren't aware that the stories they encounter toward the front of the paper are displayed according to an extensive hierarchical ranking system.

something with the combination of Dan's and Jim's skills and a fresh eye on the situation," Steiger will remember.

Even as Stewart and Hertzberg plunge into their task, tension is escalating among the *Journal* staffers, *Journal* staffers who have never seen the *Times* stake out what is quintessentially a *Journal* story and hit it like this. Many are awestruck. While the *Journal* is the nation's biggest newspaper, many of the staff, and especially the native New Yorkers, believe in their hearts that the *Times* is the best paper in the country—able to do almost anything it chooses. And now it was choosing to upstage *The Wall Street Journal* on its own turf.

Slowly, the fear will begin to spread like a cancer among some *Journal* staffers; the fear that maybe, just maybe, the unthinkable will happen. Maybe *The New York Times* will win a Pulitzer Prize covering the stock market crash.

OCTOBER 20, 1987. ■ Chicago Mercantile Exchange trading floor, 10:40 A.M., EDT: The pit is eerily quiet, but Serfling's trading desk is a madhouse. "No, this is Jay Poole, Scott's clerk. I'm sorry, he's on another line. There are two other calls holding. Okay, but it may be a few minutes."

Serfling has his hands full dealing with questions from fifteen clients. He doesn't need this. "Yes, all right. I'll talk to him a few minutes if he can talk right now," Scott says. "I've got calls backing up."

Serfling stares gaping into the pit as he waits for his friend from Shearson's trading desk in New York to put his boss on the line. "Scott Serfling . . . hi. Yeah, I know . . . insane. Just insane. . . . No, just about everybody's a seller now . . . the houses, most of the locals. No, there's hardly any trading going on now . . .

"No buyers, except I see a few guys who sold an hour ago. Yeah, they're covering . . . Oh yeah, they've got everybody right where they want 'em now. They can just about name any price they'd like to pay now. . . . Oh, I don't believe it . . . twenty cars at 220! The last trade was 225. Can you believe it?" Serfling asks. "I think somewhere below 200 is the next stop in this train. I'll take another look then. . . . Here's a little flurry now. Oh, God, 250 cars at 215 now! Fifty more at 214; nine cars at 213; one hundred at 213; fifty more at 212!"

Scott will also be asked what he thinks is happening and what he expects by three callers he's put on hold. One's a client, another's a friend's boss from PaineWebber in New York, and the third is a money manager he doesn't know, also in New York. Must be that word of Scott's strategic location here at the pit has gotten around New York, he will tell himself. Scott will be tempted to ask the money manager why he's calling, but won't. The guy has to be a client of Solly's or Goldy's or Morgan's—maybe of all three. Why isn't he talking to them? Serfling will conclude that he probably is talking to them and can't believe his ears.

Scott hasn't seen trading at such a dribble since the first few weeks the pit operated back in 1982. The market is literally drying up before his eyes. Nor has he or anyone else ever seen such a price descent, like a bowling ball in a vacuum.

For more than an hour now, many of the floor brokers in the pit have refused to accept any orders except those that let them buy or sell "at the market," according to a General Accounting Office study of the crash. Conditional orders, where the customer specifies the price—so-called limit orders—are the norm in the pit. But there are no norms today, with prices moving so fast that many "limit orders" are unfillable even before they reach the broker in the pit.

Scott can see the shorts are just killing everybody. The Brady Commission will report one representative example during this period. One large investor sold a total of 500 contracts at an average price of 229 this morning. (That puts the sales at about fifteen to twenty or twenty-five minutes ago.) The investor will buy back contracts to cover the position at an average price of 201, according to the commission. His profit on the trade will be $7 million. That represents a 12.2% return on the total value of all those contracts (or a 17.5% return, based on the 7% initial margin requirement for that size trade), all "within 40 minutes."

Many of the locals left in the pit have changed course 180 degrees and are chasing the shorts. Which means they have even bigger monkeys on their backs than when the day began, Serfling realizes. A lot of them gave up a half hour ago and dumped the contracts they had bought during the burst of euphoria around the opening, just breaking even at best. Now the gaps down are being led by these locals trying to open short positions, growing ever more desperate to sell. In the past fifteen minutes, Serfling's seen trades of seven cars, forty, fifty, seventeen, twenty—local-sized trades for sure. Caught long in today's abrupt reversal, some locals are now trying to recoup not only yesterday's losses in the pit, but additional ones incurred this morning.

Every time he sees another trade, Serfling thanks God he took his losses early yesterday and has stayed out of any positions today. Somewhere in here it will be time to buy, he senses, but certainly not until after this free fall ends. The collapse tempts him to think about opening a short position, but he doesn't have anywhere near the capital it would take to risk any trades in this kind of volatility. After all, he'd seen prices gap up 3 and 4 full points early today, and now they've been gapping down as much as 5 full points. No thank you. He'll need to be a lot more confident about the price direction before he thinks about getting into today's game.

So far, the December contract price has fallen 30 points from its high of this morning and it has another 30 points to fall to its low an hour and twenty minutes hence. The collapse will total an astonishing 27% in two hours, or twice as steep a nosedive as anything else in a comparable time period on Black Monday. Today's nadir for the December contract price will be 181, or the equivalent of the Dow below 1400.

OCTOBER 20, 1987. ■ New York Stock Exchange, chairman's office, 11:15 A.M.: *The New York Times* has put a full court press on the crash story, and at the moment, its veteran business reporter Bob Cole's question has Phelan cornered behind his big desk.

"About as well as you could expect," says Phelan. He tells Cole that senior officers and the floor directors of the exchange had discussed over breakfast what they'd all heard overnight in three areas. They were market surveillance (the NYSE monitors trading for signs of illegal or unfair practices), capital requirements, and the logistical implications of the huge trading volume, he tells the deceptively mild-looking *New York Times* reporter. "Our conclusion was that everything was about as well as can be expected."

In his late fifties, Cole is among the most persistent and effective business reporters on the *Times*. And assertive. He's arranged this interview with Phelan amid today's chaos on little notice. Bespectacled, balding, and slightly round-faced, Cole looks like everybody's favorite uncle. And he acts that way, too—as long as he gets exactly what he asks for, when he asks for it, without sugar-coating or public-relations gimmicks.

Cole makes it crystal clear that neither the *Times* nor he are to be trifled with. He has a supreme disregard for and mistrust of public-relations people, which he frequently demonstrates by using them as verbal punching bags. Thus, when New York corporate professionals have nightmares, Bob Cole is usually in them. He is a Runyonesque newspaperman, the old-fashioned kind who's as good at his trade as anybody and a lot better than most. He's admired and respected inside the business press and feared and respected outside it.

Cole's face is a welcome sight to Phelan and to Sharon Gamsin, Rich Torrenzano's media director, who is also sitting in on the interview. Both she and the press-savvy Big Board chairman realized that Cole's call late yesterday would present a major opportunity in the exchange's high-profile campaign to try to help calm the nation. An effective story in *The New York Times* was worth more than almost anything else in this regard, except perhaps for an effective national TV appearance.

No one from *The Wall Street Journal* has yet sought to interview Phelan. No one from the *Journal* will do so until a month from now when Rustin dispatches Daniel Hertzberg to rendezvous with Phelan at the Connaught Hotel in London for a vital interview for "Terrible Tuesday," Dan's and Jim Stewart's retrospective story on the crash.* "Rich and I were puzzled for a while. Then we decided that the *Journal* was attacking the story very specifically, piece by piece, mainly with features that looked at this or that facet of it. The *Times* just treated it as a big news story," Gamsin will recall.

The major problem in accommodating Cole had been finding a block of time in which Phelan and he could talk uninterrupted, and Sharon hadn't succeeded.

A buzzer interrupts the interview. It is Phelan's secretary, Mary Tater, with a return of one of his phone calls. "Yes, Mary, I'll take it." Perhaps a minute goes by, interrupted only a few times by brief, even

---

*"We really wanted to run the story on Friday the twentieth of November, exactly a month after the day the story was about," Hertzberg's boss, Dick Rustin, remembers. "Phelan was in London. So, early that week, I sent Dan to catch up with him. He got some great stuff for the story."

monosyllabic replies or questions from Phelan, as Cole studies the canned biographical summary on the NYSE chairman that Gamsin has given him.

"What do you mean 'as well as can be expected'?" Cole apparently asks Phelan after the call. Cole's notebook will show that he gets a less-qualified answer, which tracks perfectly with Phelan's PR objective now. Months hence, Bob will read in his notes on the interview: "No firms are in trouble. No problems as of now."

Another buzz. Another phone interruption. Phelan handles it the same way. He hangs up. Cole goes over parts of the biographical summary with him. Another call.

And another. This one ends the interview—at least for now. The caller is Donny Stone, Phelan recalls. The Big Board chairman does not say so, but there is trouble below. Cole jots down in his notebook that Phelan has interrupted the interview to "go to a quick conference on the floor."

CHAPTER

10

OCTOBER 20, 1987. ■ New York Stock Exchange trading floor, 11:20 A.M.: "Look, let's get these stocks up and trading and get on with it. We've got to trade out of this," a grim-faced John Phelan tells his colleagues.

But no amount of cheerleading or whip-cracking is going to solve the problem that Phelan has had to come down to the floor to deal with, and he knows it. He must know the options now are down to a very few.

Phelan, Stone, and Donny's fellow specialists and floor directors, John Lyden and Jim Jacobson, huddle behind a canvas flap separating the trading floor from a 12,000-square-foot area under construction at its southwest corner that soon will be added to the trading space. Phelan has the power to close the exchange. So does the president of the United States. No one else can take such an action, but Phelan and the three floor directors all have the power to halt trading in individual stocks.

The cries of specialists to close the exchange are ringing in the floor directors' ears now, and they urgently report the rising hysteria to Phelan.

Since around 10:30, it's been clear that the opening strategy has failed. Later the NYSE chairman will recall the eerie feeling as the trading pace decelerated during the past hour like a car whose engine has overheated to the point of melting. "The scary part about Tuesday morning was this vacuum developing. The volume slowed way down and you had the idea of it just going into a 500-point free fall with absolutely no bids."

Phelan's nightmare is exactly that: "What if we have another 500-

point day?" an exchange official will quote him as asking this morning. Now, following the collapse of the carefully orchestrated opening rally, that looks like a real possibility.

Donny and the other specialists are being steadily driven to their knees. Trading data compiled from the NYSE's transactions tape by New York–based Francis Emory Fitch, Inc., an exchange member firm that sells this information, will show that between 10:30 and 11:00, Donny handled blocks of 11,000, 13,200, 35,000, and 10,700 shares all at the same price as during the prior trade. However, that is getting tougher and tougher to do as Stone's trading capital is used up. Now the blocks are starting to crack the price. A few minutes ago, Donny handled a 11,000-share block at 66½, down a modest ⅛ from the last trade. In a few more minutes, he'll be hit by another block, this time, 15,500 shares, and this time the price will fall ¼, to 65½, as the Fitch figures will indicate.

The SEC report will show that today's first large program sales by the portfolio insurers are being rammed home on the floor this half hour. At 11:10 the floor brokers dumped sell orders on 2.1 million shares into Donny's and other blue-chip stock specialists' hoppers in a $75 million sell program. The stock won't trade again until after one o'clock, the Fitch-supplied data show.

As Phelan, Stone, and the others huddle behind the canvas flap, demoralized Big Board specialists face what some will view as the final blow—another huge portfolio insurance sell program. This time it will be 4.2 million shares, or $150 million worth of stock. The more than 7.4 million shares being sold by program traders (without the aid of the DOT system) between 11:00 and 11:30 will be greater than twice their selling total in any other half-hour period today, the SEC report will note.

If the crushing selling assault is to be met by a coordinated response, it will have to be ordered here and now. "Tuesday, we didn't let specialists close stocks at will," an exchange official will say.

"All right. If there's pressure, let 'em close," Phelan will recall saying.

So what was just a dribble of trading halts allowed in major stocks near the start of this hour will grow into a wave. Dozens of major blue-chip stocks included in the S&P 500 index will be among the eighty-three stocks that will be halted between eleven o'clock and noon. In particular, a wave of super-elite blue chips is about to break, as specialists making markets in some of the largest, most heavily traded stocks in America close down trading, citing order imbalances. The timing of the halts of the stocks involved reveal the coordination. The following table shows some examples:

STOCK	TIME OF HALT
Eastman Kodak	11:28 A.M.
IBM	11:30 A.M.
Minnesota Mining	11:31 A.M.
Goodyear	11:31 A.M.
Philip Morris	11:30 A.M.
Primerica	11:26 A.M.
Sears	11:21 A.M.
Union Carbide	11:18 A.M.
Westinghouse	11:26 A.M.
Woolworth	11:29 A.M.

Source of data: Francis Emory Fitch, Inc., member of the NYSE

All ten stocks above are components of the Dow Jones Industrial Average. Other Dow stocks include Merck, which hasn't traded since 9:54, and DuPont, which hasn't even opened yet. The ten Dow stocks that were halted between 11:00 and 11:31 account for over 36% of the index's value. Merck and DuPont account for almost 19% more. All told, for more than an hour beginning about 11:30, there will be no market here for the stocks that comprise more than half the value of the Dow Jones Industrial Average.* These stocks, and dozens of other components of the S&P 500 index, also have a major influence on that market measure.

Close students of John Phelan's public utterances will read a familiar rationale behind the massive halts just ahead. Early in 1987 Phelan had told an Investment Dealers' Digest reporter that the exchange was working on a defensive plan in case the market meltdown he feared occurred:

*In addition, DuPont, IBM, Philip Morris, Sears, Merck, Minnesota Mining & Manufacturing, and Dow Chemical (which will halt trading at 11:43) account for well over half the weight of the twenty-stock Major Market Index. The American Stock Exchange trades an options contract and the Chicago Board of Trade, a futures contract on the MMI.

To head off a meltdown, Phelan says he is preparing a still unan-
nounced plan to build a safety net which would prevent program
trading from greatly magnifying a bear market, turning it into a
free-fall. Trading would be halted on as many as 100 stocks at once
if program trading drove the market down more than about 25%,
he says.

The trading halt would "give the market time to breathe,"
Phelan explains. "Rather than just let it sell right down, we halt
trading and put out indications that let the world know that the
last sale of stock X was 56 and it's quoted at 40 [bid]. Rather than
let it somersault down, we try to establish a new equilibrium by
reaching out to all the buyers and sellers.

The halts will have another effect. Each few seconds, when Quotron
and other market monitors automatically recalculate and display the
S&P and the Dow averages, the prices of halted stocks won't be moving
steadily lower. Instead, they will be counted in the averages as unchanged. And, in this desperate hour, that will have the blessed effect
of understating the disintegration now under way on the Big Board
floor.

The NYSE's Market News Center will not be informed immediately
of the halts. "When they halt a stock we get a call from the floor and
then we call Dow Jones and Reuters immediately and inform them,"
Market News Center manager Rosa Johnson will explain. "But during
the crash—the second day—they didn't," she says. So there will be no
immediate calls to the Dow Jones ticker and the Reuters financial
report to inform the financial community of the halts.

Therefore, many professional traders who might otherwise discount
the seeming improvement will take it at face value. Indeed, less than
an hour from now, despite Rich Torrenzano's conviction that it is
important that the press always be told the truth, the halts will actually
be denied.

The effect will be to give the world the impression that the selling
pressure in the stock market is diminishing more than it really is. The
Dow will soon seem to be leveling off.

At least two ghosts here at the exchange must be stirring now.
Outside, on the Georgia marble exterior of the exchange building, a
little-noted bronze plaque commemorates two men and the trade paper

they first published at 15 Wall Street in 1889, before this building was erected on the site. The paper was *The Wall Street Journal.* The men were Clarence H. Dow and Edward D. Jones.

OCTOBER 20, 1987. ■ American Express Tower, World Financial Center, 11:30 A.M.: "There's 36 points [of potential profit on index arbitrage] and we can't capture any of it," Shearson Lehman Brothers' Executive Vice-President William Breck complains to the *Journal*'s George Anders.

That isn't because of the DOT system ban. Shearson Lehman is big enough to send an army of traders around to the specialists' posts on the Big Board floor to hand-deliver program trade orders. No, partly it reflects the extreme public pressure against program trading now, and—although Breck doesn't tell Anders this—a temporary trading capital pinch is being imposed on him from above. Since midday yesterday, a good portion of Shearson's capital reserves have been committed elsewhere. Today, the firm finds itself caught in a futures margin payments gridlock in Chicago. All told, Shearson's trading capital is therefore badly encumbered and Breck has been ordered to the sidelines.

Much of these reserves were spoken for quickly yesterday by another highly regarded Shearson executive—Peter DaPuzzo, the senior executive vice-president who heads retail equity trading.

Yesterday DaPuzzo was determined to continue buying over-the-counter (OTC) stocks (those often-smaller issues that are not traded on exchanges) from many Shearson clients who wanted to sell them. Operating through a network of thirty-six traders in its headquarters office at the World Financial Center and twenty-nine others in its offices elsewhere, Shearson makes markets in a whopping 2,750 OTC stocks, more than any other firm. DaPuzzo had built Shearson's OTC trading business into Wall Street's largest by making markets under any or all conditions, and nothing, including Black Monday, would stop him from continuing to make markets.

Normally, DaPuzzo's department gets $50 million of the firm's money to buy OTC stocks. Some are acquired as inventory to back the Shearson brokers' selling efforts; others become ammunition in the continual wars among Wall Street's huge trading desks. If he thinks it's necessary, Peter can commit up to $80 million of Shearson's money to his trading sector without getting higher approval. Yesterday he'd committed $80 million by ten o'clock, just a half hour into the trading day.

So "I called [Shearson Vice-Chairman] Herb Freiman and asked for permission to bump it to $100 million," DaPuzzo will recall. An hour later, he was back, recommending that "we either double up, or stand back and stop trying to make markets." The capital was bumped to $200 million. By noon, Peter was again proposing the same either/or scenario, with the same outcome. Now $400 million of Shearson's money was behind DaPuzzo and his OTC desk.

Through the afternoon, DaPuzzo, and some of the young trading tigers and tigresses who'd drunk a champagne toast with him on Friday to the end of the stock market correction, struggled against an insurmountable mountain of selling. DaPuzzo walked among them and, he will tell *The New York Times*, saw their ashen faces and teary eyes.

Today the OTC market is in shambles. Some institutional and aggressive individual investors who spent yesterday dumping blue-chip NYSE stocks from their portfolios have gotten around now to their holdings of smaller stocks. And they are at least as eager, maybe even more so, to sell OTC stocks today as they were to sell blue chips yesterday.

Moreover, sellers are being enormously frustrated by many smaller brokers', and even some big Shearson competitors' refusing to acquire stock from them. Unlike a Big Board specialist, an OTC market maker has no affirmative obligation to step in and trade to keep the market going. In any case, after the horrendous losses they took on Black Monday, many OTC market makers are effectively out of the picture. The SEC will report that some securities firms' OTC trading desks are even refusing to take calls today. The agency will also cite a suspiciously high occurrence of improper price entries into a computerized OTC trading system that is making it impossible to trade the affected stocks.

In this environment, DaPuzzo won't make significant headway in shedding Shearson's excess inventory of OTC stocks. And, in the over-the-counter market as a whole, today will be the worst day of the crash. Following its record 11.35% plunge yesterday, the National

Association of Securities Dealers' (NASD) NASDAQ composite index of OTC stocks is plummeting another 9% on record volume of 284.1 million shares, 61 million more than the day before.

The averages will understate the calamity. This drop represents for holders of the smallest, least liquid OTC stocks, some of which seemingly cannot be sold at any price now. This afternoon, John Pinto, senior vice-president at the NASD—the OTC market's equivalent of the NYSE—will tell the *Journal*'s OTC reporter, Priscilla Ann Smith, that "we're scared. Of course we're scared. We're looking at conditions in the marketplace that are indescribable; gigantic losses, it's staggering."

Peter DaPuzzo for the most part will have traded his way out of his risky oversupply of stock by the end of this week. Many of the companies that issued the stocks will be asked to acquire some. With the implicit alternative being that Shearson will eventually be forced to dump its inventory onto the market, many firms will respond and buy it from Shearson.

It will be a hard blow to DaPuzzo, who has come in with monthly losses only three times in his twenty years in the business, none ever amounting to more than a couple of hundred thousand dollars. This month he'll lose $10 million of the firm's money, and will be pleased to end the year in the black.

Why would Shearson give DaPuzzo so much capital to put behind OTC stocks that other parts of its trading business would be temporarily starved of capital? DaPuzzo's answer is devastatingly simple. "A good many of the stocks we trade have only 1,000 or so shareholders," he will tell a visitor after the crash. "And maybe 700 of them work here."

OCTOBER 20, 1987. ■ Chicago Mercantile Exchange trading floor, 11:40 A.M., EDT: Serfling scratches his head as he watches the bidding escalate below. "They have either lost their minds or this is their stand, right here, right now," he tells himself.

It was "New York all the way," Scott will recall months from now. "Seemed like most of the big New York firms were in on it, with Solly in the lead." Suddenly, beginning about ten minutes ago, they have driven up the December contract price 11 points. Way over 1,000 cars so far and what a ride.

They began in a tight bunch, with the price down around 189. "Fifty for fifty—189.50 for fifty cars!" Then it was 190, 190.50; 191 for a couple of trades, then it was 191.50; 191.50 again, and, boom, they broke out. "One ninety-three for 100," then "194.50 for 100," then "195, 195 for 120," then, just a 5-point gap up to 200, and instantly another trade at 200. The gap up clearly showed "they were trying to get the price up, they didn't care how many they were buying," Serfling will say.

Kalo A. Hineman, the acting chairman of the Commodity Futures Trading Commission, will tell the Senate Banking Committee in early February that he had talked to Leo Melamed, chairman of the CME's executive committee, about the market situation on Monday. Leo had told him then that the CME and the NYSE were "in frequent communication and had agreed to cooperate in addressing the unprecedented volatility in the market." Later, Phelan will recollect having had "three or four" conversations with Melamed on Black Monday.

Could this be part of their cooperation to deal with the frightening discount? Phelan closes down the key S&P stocks in New York, slowing the nominal decline of the S&P 500 index. Meanwhile, here in Chicago, the CME looks the other way while the December contract price is rammed skyward. Good-bye, ugly discount!

Six months hence, Hineman will say he can't recall the details of his Black Monday discussion with Leo Melamed. However, the NYSE's many halts of S&P 500 component stocks would fit nicely in a coordinated strategy to reduce the terrifying discount of the S&P futures contract price to the index itself. A determined upward drive in the price of the S&P contract here would be aided if it appeared that the stock market decline was decelerating. Neither Melamed nor Phelan will acknowledge any such plan. Salomon Brothers' John Gutfreund will refer queries on trading matters to Stanley Shopkorn, the firm's top equity trader, who will say he wasn't aware of any such strategy in Chicago. However, "in an effort to keep the New York market open on Tuesday, we repeatedly told specialists we'd bid to break sell order imbalances," Shopkorn will say.

Whether planned or a happy accident, whether Leo Melamed is looking on or not, something wonderful is happening in the pit now.

It is an awesome display of nerve. God, how the arbs at Harry's would love it! "Go, big Solly, go! C'mon, Big Solly, you can do it! One more time!" At its zenith a few minutes hence, with the S&P 500 index itself still falling, the rally will cut the discount of the December contract price to the index about half, to around 20 points.

Scott and the other locals don't realize it, but the New York firms' buying rampage is a bluff—another desperate tactic on this most desperate of days. The SEC will learn that much of the money they are plowing into the pit right now isn't the firms' own. Rather, in many of their buys, they are acting as agents for big banks and insurance companies that positively use Wall Street firms as trading brokers here in the pit. Some stocks being sold in New York are being replaced in their owners' portfolios with futures contracts. It is index substitution, a tactic considered to be part of the portfolio insurance family of trading strategies. Thanks to the huge discount, it's a lot cheaper now to buy stocks in their synthetic form here than to buy the real thing in New York. The SEC will find that these portfolio insurers acquired 1,337 S&P 500 contracts during this half hour in Chicago.

The diminished corps of locals in the pit are mostly scratching their heads over the New York buying binge, just as Scott is. Many of them are flat now—that is, without any position in the market. And while they do not realize it, everything in this latest gambit depends on their deciding to buy contracts, to go long.

The pit traders for the New York firms will continue to push up the price—to 200.50, then 202, 202 again, 203, 204, and 204 again. This time there is no eager school of young local pilot fish to follow their lead. Only the veterans, the richest and savviest locals, are left in the pit today; and for the most part, they stand aside, watching the screens through narrowed eyes.

The climax, minutes from now, will bring the worst of all possible outcomes for the New Yorkers. Far from jumping on the bandwagon the Wall Street firms are now laboring to keep rolling, the suspicious and hungry locals will smell blood. Instead of opening long positions, the locals will open short positions. Instead of buying, as the New York firms so urgently want them to do, the locals will sell.

So the strategy that at this moment offers hope to alleviate the problems of the big securities firms and the specialists will soon actually worsen them.

When the locals start selling to the New Yorkers, the latter will break and run. The market will literally reverse its direction. The SEC will find that in the end the portfolio insurers' sales during this half hour will wind up exceeding their purchases by 724 contracts.

Just past 11:45, the rally will start to fizzle, and then the December contract price will immediately begin to fall. It will go quickly: 204, 204, 203, 203, 202, 201, 198, 196, then a sickening whoosh downward to 190 on the next trade.

First there had been the irrational buying flurry on the opening. Then, an hour ago, came the second rally attempt. Soon the morning's third, and last, embryonic rally will sink out of sight. If this were a swimming pool, the New York firms would be drowning here this morning.

Soon they'll have "a whole bunch more contracts . . . [whose prices will be] falling like a stone," Scott recalls. "There was a feeling they had to do something. But no one could think what."

OCTOBER 20, 1987. ■ Federal Reserve Bank of New York, president's office, 11:55 A.M.: A worn-out Jerry Corrigan nonetheless already has plenty of reason to be pleased. Both this morning's telephone blitz, which showed the Fed's colors in the banking community, and the aggressive reserves injection program which Peter Sternlight is running, are going very well indeed.

Corrigan and Sternlight have worked a month this morning—and bankers are now confident that the Fed will indeed supply enough liquidity to handle their extraordinary demands. None of the banks would have any problem going along with Corrigan's request to lend bountifully to Wall Street, within prudential standards.

Well, at least Corrigan could take satisfaction that the single biggest contribution the Fed could make to calming the markets, the liquidity program, had been handled correctly, and was already an unqualified success. He'd done his part throughout the morning by assuring the big banks that the Fed would supply all the liquidity they'd need to meet Wall Street's huge requirements for short-term loans. Since there's no substitute for actually seeing the Fed supply that liquidity, Peter Sternlight's crew in the eighth-floor trading room furiously shovels more reserves into the system so the bankers can see the results for themselves.

The window they look through to do that is the Fed funds market—the banks' marketplace for borrowing and lending the reserves the Fed requires banks to maintain in a prescribed ratio to their total loans.* The Fed funds rate is directly influenced by the government securities trading activities—the so-called open-market operations—of Sternlight's crew. When it buys government securities, the Fed credits payment to accounts the sellers' banks maintain at Federal Reserve banks around the country, thus creating reserves. When Sternlight's people sell securities, the buyers' payments are deducted from the accounts, thus draining reserves from the banks involved.

When a bank finds that its reserves exceed the Fed's requirements, it doesn't have to stuff them under the mattress until it can persuade its customers to borrow more money. It can make some money on the excess reserves by lending them to other banks that have lined up more loans than they have reserves to support. The banks don't deal with one another directly, but rather through a small network of specialized brokers who are largely unknown outside credit-market circles.

The market for these itinerant reserves, or Fed funds, isn't conducted in an imposing neoclassic building like the New York Stock Exchange, with a big sign reading FEDERAL FUNDS MARKET. Rather, it resembles the over-the-counter stock market in that the Fed funds brokers, sitting in offices, communicate with prospective borrowers and lenders of Fed funds, and with each other, via telephone and other telecommunications systems.

As in the OTC stock market, there isn't one single specialist appointed to keep the book on all the bids and offers for Fed funds. Each Fed funds broker firm posts its own bid and ask prices, which change as banker clients' needs to borrow or to lend reserves change. There is a major difference from the OTC stock market. Fed funds market

*The original idea behind the Fed's reserves requirement was to make sure that banks were sound—that they had enough money on hand to meet their depositors' needs. If a bank lent out every penny of its depositors' money, there'd be no funds left from which they could withdraw when necessary. So, the Fed makes its member banks (the vast majority of U.S. banks operating under federal rather than state charters) hold back some of their deposits, generally 12%, as reserves for possible withdrawals. That way, federally chartered banks can lend up to about $8 for every $1 of reserves on hand. Subsequently, the reserves requirement has served as the fulcrum by which the Fed carries out its monetary policy by adding to those reserves or draining them through its "open-market operations."

participants are lending and borrowing the reserves, not buying and selling them, so the bid and ask "prices" in this market are expressed in annual interest rates, rather than in dollar amounts. The bid price is the interest rate the would-be borrower of Fed funds offers to pay, and the ask price is the rate the would-be lender wants to be paid on his excess reserves.

Historically, many of the big and tremendously aggressive money-center banks in New York, Chicago, and California have skated on the edge of the Fed's reserves requirement. In fact, according to a New York Fed spokesman, these banks have often run with slight reserves deficiencies on days between the biweekly reports of their reserves position they must make to the central bank. Conversely, many smaller banks around the country usually have more reserves than they need.

Therefore, money-center banks traditionally borrow Fed funds, especially around report times, and the smaller banks around the country traditionally lend to them. The big banks are careful not to lend too much in excess of their reserve limits because they don't want to get caught needing to borrow too much just ahead of reserves report deadlines. For if the country-mice banks sense that their own excess reserves are desperately needed by their big-city cousins, they will gladly rush forward with the necessary amounts—at rapacious interest rates.* As it happens, the very banks that are suddenly facing the greatest demand for added loans as a result of the stock market crash—the big money-center banks—are precisely the ones with the thinnest reserves positions to accommodate those loan requests.

That's one reason why Sternlight's reserves injection effort is so critical, and why if Sternlight is to err now, it should be on the side of excess. An insufficient injection of reserves would mean that when the big banks rush to borrow the added funds needed to service their surging loan demands, the Fed funds rate will spurt even higher. And because that rate is the single most closely watched indicator of the direction of interest rates by stock and bond market players alike, it could worsen the current crisis unimaginably.

It would work like this: A surging Fed funds rate would make both banks and investors regard Fed Chairman Greenspan's statement on

---

*Banking may therefore be the only field where usury can be a professional courtesy.

liquidity this morning as insincere, a meaningless gesture dropped in the hopper to help psych the markets on the opening. That, in turn, would suggest that the Fed basically won't change its monetary policy—to continue the slight tightening under way since Labor Day. The prospect of still higher interest rates would make bond prices fall and their yields go up. Holders of bonds, then, would be under pressure to sell now, before bond prices drop further. Their sales will in fact hasten that drop, and lift yields still higher.* The higher yields on bonds (not to mention the lower investment risk associated with, government bonds in particular) will make them an even more appealing alternative to stocks, creating still more selling pressure in a market that is already literally at the breaking point.

Conversely, falling interest rates would be as helpful now as rising interest rates would be damaging. If interest rates fall, the rates being paid on existing bonds become increasingly attractive and their prices rise. Lower rates also mean lower borrowing costs; therefore, higher profits for corporations, higher dividends for shareholders, and higher stock prices. People in both the stock and bond markets would be given reason at least to stay put or even increase their holdings.

If there are two things that the stock market and the nation need desperately right now, Phelan has repeatedly been telling Corrigan, they are added liquidity and lower interest rates. Of course, Corrigan knows even better than Phelan that Sternlight's aggressive reserves injection program is providing both, in spades.

The measure of this program's success is reflected in the cost of Fed funds, which is plummeting as the Fed floods the market with reserves. This afternoon broker Fulton Prebon (U.S.A.), Inc., will tell *Wall Street Journal* Credit Markets columnists Matthew Winkler and Tom Herman that today's average cost of Fed funds sank to just 7.16% from

---

*The yield of a bond is a function of its price and the coupon interest rate. Under the right circumstances, a previously issued 8% Treasury bond can yield its buyer 10%. Here's how: The Treasury will pay $80 per year per $1,000 bond to holders of 8% bonds until those bonds reach their maturity date, at which time the holders will reserve a final payment of the $1,000 face amount. However, in the meantime, if prevailing long-term interest rates rise above 8% to 10%, then anybody wanting to sell the 8% bonds (instead of holding them to maturity) won't be able to find buyers, unless he cuts the price. Specifically, the price will have to be cut enough to make the $80-per-year interest payments on each bond equal to a 10% return on the buyer's money. In other words, the price will have to be cut from $1,000 to $800 per bond, giving the 8% bond a "yield" of 10%. Conversely, if prevailing bond rates fall to 6%, their holders will demand that potential buyers pay more than the $1,000 face amount (specifically, $1,333) to reflect that fact, thus making the 8% bond yield 6 percent.

7.61% yesterday. And Fed funds will be quoted at just 6¾% bid at day's end.

Yet for all the success of the Fed's prime thrusts, several of the big banks, especially the foreign ones, remain leery of substantial new loan commitments to the Wall Street houses, and some are quietly tightening the conditions on existing loans.

Corrigan's pitch to the banks couldn't have been more straightforward: The Fed is making sure there is enough liquidity, so would the banks please use that liquidity to see their securities industry clients through any payments-induced cash crunch by advancing them additional loans, made within prudential standards, of course.

"Within prudential standards." During this morning's big stock market rally, that term seemed to be a harmless qualifier, a bit of legalese to let Corrigan cover for the Fed in case anyone in or outside of the banking community should assert later that the Fed was running a loan-guarantee bailout effort.

Yet, with the market falling back more than 200 points in less than two hours, and with wave on wave of rumors sweeping the Street about Goldman, Shearson Lehman, and other firms being in margin trouble, in Chicago, trouble that was threatening the Chicago options and futures clearinghouses. Under these conditions, "within prudential standards" looks like a major hurdle to many bankers.

And that kind of thinking will only spread further now. At this moment, a report is coming out over Knight Ridder's Commodity News Service wire, printing out in major futures pits everywhere, and soon will be talked about all over Wall Street, too: "NY commercial banks restrict forex dealings with U.S. invest firms. Fear insolvency." Clearly, a loan to a firm you won't trade with in the foreign currency exchange (Forex) market because you fear it may be insolvent would not fall "within prudential standards."

Corrigan knows what is behind the fears of insolvency. It is precisely the problem he'd identified long before as the biggest potential threat a market crash would present to the financial system. It was the difference in settlement schedules. You could trade simultaneously in New York and Chicago all you wanted. But you would have to pay, or be paid, on vastly different schedules in the two markets. The continuing huge volume in the stock market today means continuing payment and settlement dangers, too, Corrigan knows. And the price collapse that has Phelan's and the exchange specialists' backs to the wall sharply increases the peril.

OCTOBER 20, 1987. ■ New York Stock Exchange, chairman's office, noon: Bob Cole continues cooling his heels outside Phelan's office, an unaccustomed situation. Public-relations concerns will have to wait until the Big Board chairman can determine if there will be anything left here to promote after today.

"Well, we don't want to (close)," Phelan tells the three executives on a conference call from Chicago, but it's an option the Big Board leadership has to consider, he tells the futures exchange executives.

Phelan and Melamed will differ on the exact wording of the statement and its meaning. The NYSE chairman will insist he never meant to convey that a New York closing was imminent. This is how the Chicago Merc officials will explain what has occurred over the past few minutes:

"I was in executive session with the executive committee," Melamed will say. "Me, Chairman Jack Sandner, and President Bill Brodsky. We'd been advised that the CBOE had closed its OEX option market [at 11:54, New York time] and so did the American Stock Exchange" stop trading earlier in its options contract on the Major Market Index. "That frightened us a lot," Melamed recalls.

"We said to Phelan that we're hearing rumors they're closing. He said: 'It's getting very close to that, we're going into that meeting in a few minutes. There are no buyers.' We just assumed that meant their closing was virtually certain and we were already being clobbered by the selling from the closed options pits," the CME executive committee chairman will say.

The CME executives tell Phelan they plan to immediately consult the CME's ten-member executive committee, which has been in session almost continuously since yesterday morning, and end their call. Phelan will say he didn't know "or care much at that point" whether Melamed closed his S&P pit or not.

Yesterday very few people on the floor had talked about wanting to close the exchange. But by this time today "it seemed like everybody wanted to close," Phelan will recall. Nor is all the pressure coming from the floor here. Exactly a month from today, the *Journal* story by Jim Stewart and Dan Hertzberg will quote Phelan as saying that "several big securities firms 'called the SEC and asked them to tell us to close.' Mr. Phelan won't name the firms, but market sources say Salomon Brothers, Inc., and Goldman Sachs & Co., major firms with huge inventories of securities that were being rapidly devalued, were among those pushing to shut the exchange." (The *Journal* reporters will add that a Goldman official allowed that the firm did discuss a temporary halt with SEC Chairman David Ruder, but denied that Goldman recommended one, and that a Salomon spokesman didn't return their call for comment.)

Being an ex-marine doesn't make Phelan a masochist. No one here would like to avoid the agony of watching the market continue its plunge for the next twenty minutes any more than Phelan. And he knows that it may very well come to that unless the market is turned soon. In an interview seven months from now, he will refer to an unspecified "fallback plan," after which the only alternative would be for the market to be closed.

If the exchange were forced to close, it would be proclaiming defeat, like a fighter who cries "No more!" and quits in the ring. It would raise serious concerns about the financial soundness of the exchange and its members that surely would exacerbate pent-up selling pressure during any halt.

Phelan will talk in vague terms about another call during this period. "Tuesday a guy from one of the member firms—no, let's not say member firms—called me and said: 'We gotta close the exchange. We're doing five times the volume we normally do. We can't handle it. Gotta close.' I told him you're just gonna have to find some reason to stay open. If you can't find any other reason, do it for God and country. He said: 'OK. I thought I'd make the pitch.'"

The caller's rationale was powerful, Phelan concedes. "If the market was going down another 500, why not just close and open it there in the morning, rather than wasting any more capital trying to stop it."

Now it's lunch hour and six floors below Phelan's window the streets are more clogged than ever. The TV trucks, the news bulletins on the market have brought hundreds of the curious and an odd festive atmosphere. In his *Times* story tomorrow, Bob Cole will note the crowds, the TV crews interviewing traders as they emerge to take cigarette breaks, and a Bible-toting preacher holding forth at his accustomed spot across the street from the exchange.

Through lunch hour scores of people will stare over at the exchange building as they stand on the wide steps in front of Federal Hall where the statue of Washington stands, and where still larger throngs had stood vigil at the crash of 1929. Across Broad Street, NYSE public-relations official Sharon Gamsin will recall, black humorists hold a banner reading: JUMP! JUMP!

The Big Board chairman rises from his chair and walks out to Bob Cole, who's seated on one of the gray couches just outside his office. "I'm not going to be able to talk to you anymore. I've got some things to do," Cole will recall Phelan telling him. Cole writes in his notebook: "At noon, the market was going back down, flat—a bit off. After [waiting] 30 minutes [Phelan]—couldn't see me—that was 12:05."

He also writes names of people for Phelan's secretary to reach for him now: "Baker, Ruder, Corrigan . . ."

CHAPTER
11

No one yet has told the full story of how the disaster that began on Black Monday was finally brought under control. Maybe no one ever will. This chapter sets out some startling facts about stock and futures markets trading on October 20, 1987. To me, those facts strongly suggest that only a broadly coordinated manipulation of stock and futures markets information and prices averted a stock market plunge on October 20 that could have rivaled, or even exceeded, that of the day before. Bluntly stated, the question these facts forcefully raises is whether some leaders and market makers at the New York Stock Exchange and the Chicago Merchantile Exchange collaborated to save the stock market by rigging stock information and prices.

OCTOBER 20, 1987. ■ Chicago Mercantile Exchange trading floor, 12:10 P.M., EDT: "Are they crazy?" Scott Serfling wonders aloud.

The New York firms' last buying flurry ended in disaster less than a half hour ago and the situation looked even more hopeless at 12:05 when they started this one. From about ten minutes to twelve until five minutes ago, the December contract price was practically in free fall, amid a building swirl of rumors that New York might close—which of course would force a closing here. Why would they dare buy more in a climate like this?

But buy more they had. Scott noticed the traders for the big Wall Street houses heaving up again on contracts, albeit more conservatively now, 100 to 200 at a crack. There have been a dozen or so trades, maybe 2,000 cars, Serfling estimates. And they've been obviously anxious buyers, "bidding 183 when the last price was 182, and 184 when the last was 183," Scott recalls.

"Eighty-five for 100! Eighty-five!" comes a shout from the pit. Was that Hutton? "Eighty-five for 100!" Shearson? Scott and the other locals are puzzled.

Just minutes ago, the consensus around the pit was that the price would keep falling and test 180, and if it broke below that level, the betting was it wouldn't stop until 150 to 160. Scott had his West German money manager clients on hold. They'd been itching to buy contracts earlier. They couldn't believe how cheap they'd become.

Scott had been watching the December contract's roller-coaster ride, beginning from above 240 more than two hours ago. After the opening rush into the low 240s, the price had dipped to the high 220s, traded flat to slightly higher for a bit over a half hour, then headed into a sickening dive below 200. From there, it recovered to 215, whooshed down again to below 190, bounced back above 205 and, less than ten minutes ago, back down to 181.

The pattern couldn't be more clear-cut to traders who pay particularly close attention to price charts—and that includes Scott and most other futures market professionals. An unbroken succession of lower peaks, followed by deeper valleys, suggests a continuing, cascading decline. And those locals who have been selling—going short—into the last two buying flurries are licking their chops at the prospect.

The New Yorkers' latest buying spurt has been more sporadic and febrile than the others. Unlike during their previous short-lived buying binge, the New Yorkers hadn't seemed intent on turning back the selling momentum in the pit. "No. Not at all," Scott will say later. "They weren't buying enough for that." Already the price has sagged back to 182. Like many others in the pit, Scott is braced now for the fresh sell-off that should follow this latest failed rally attempt. After that, Scott thinks, it might be time for Otto, his German money manager client, to spend some of the $20 million burning a hole in his pocket.

Later, Scott and many other locals will remember this latest buying spurt with suspicion. "We all thought that they must have known there was something else coming," he will say, "but they said: 'Oh no. We just bought at the lows of the day.'"

Then, for all their half-anticipation of it, the sound startles them like the first clap of thunder in a storm.

"Clang! Clang! Clang! Clang!" The bell! That jarring, nerve-shredding bell that's rung every time trading ends in one of the pits. They ring it at one o'clock for meats, at 1:05 for lumber; at intervals from 1:14 to 1:24 for the various foreign currencies; at 1:30 for gold futures trading. It is just thirteen minutes after eleven, local time. There's no scheduled close right now, and momentarily all is confusion.

Suddenly a worried-looking Leo Melamed, the volatile little chairman of the CME's executive committee, bursts through the security turnstiles at the main entrance straight ahead of Serfling and moves toward the south rim of the pit. The door opens onto a stairwell that connects the trading floor with the CME executive suite one flight above. Melamed is flanked by a coterie of executives and staffers, including CME Chairman Jack Sandner. Now an exchange staffer moves briskly through the throng of traders, just back from the pit, who are mainly just watching today. He raises a battery-powered bullhorn and reads a brief two- to three-sentence statement closing the pit. (Six months later, a CME spokeswoman will say she is unable to locate the exact text of the announcement.)

It is a strange scene with a number of elements that, later, will not seem consistent or rational. Some traders are already responding irrationally.

"That's it. I'm gone," a young local tells Scott. "After all that stuff in the papers about program trading causing the crash, there's no way the president is ever gonna let this pit reopen." And he is gone in an instant—upstairs to the CME membership office to sell his S&P 500 trading membership. "He told me there was a line there. Can you believe it? A line!" Scott recalls, "and they just moved up and took the bids that were on file."

The CME membership office records for today will show a depressing chain reaction. The first seven of eight S&P 500 pit memberships will be sold at steadily diminishing prices of $125,000, $120,000, $116,000, $115,000, $113,000, $111,000, and $110,000. The eighth will go for $110,000, too.

Melamed will stay on the floor for about a half hour, waiting, as he'll say later, "to see what New York would do."

To see what New York would do? Later he will assert that when he talked with Phelan ten minutes ago, there was no doubt in his mind that the NYSE's closing was imminent. Indeed, it had been the virtual certainty of a Big Board halt that galvanized the executive committee to act here, he says.

The big danger to the CME from a New York closing, Melamed will explain, would be the added selling pressure it would transfer to the

S&P 500 pit at a time when the pit already has additional selling pressure from this morning's recent halts of Amex and CBOE stock index options trading.

Yes, but selling pressure here and selling pressure in the stock market are two entirely different animals. Unlike stock exchange specialists, market makers don't have any responsibility to trade to keep the market going. So selling pressure can continue only as long as there's a supply of willing buyers. With the December contract price down about 25% so far today, buyers are getting more and more scarce, and trading volume is beginning to dry up of its own accord. In the first hour and a quarter of trading, as the price fell a bit more than 10%, volume hit 11,722 contracts in ninety-six trades, but when it dropped another 14% in the next hour and a quarter, trading shriveled to only 4,282 in thirty trades.

Anyway, an exchange-wide trading halt in New York almost certainly would end all the selling pressure here, not exacerbate it. Fully 465 of the S&P 500 stocks are listed on the NYSE. Even this under-states their influence on the index, which is calculated in a way that gives the most weight to the largest companies' stocks.* Therefore, a closing in New York almost certainly would result in a spontaneous closing here.

Six months from now, when asked if any lawsuits were filed against the exchange for closing, Melamed will answer, "Oh no, none at all. We made sure we closed it right." Made sure they closed it right? Was there time in the scant few minutes that elapsed between the phone call to Phelan and the present moment to do legal research on the closing? And, for that matter, was there time to draft the written announcement just read to the traders in the pit?

Some will begin to suspect that this closing might have been planned all along, for reasons other than those proclaimed here—reasons that might best be shielded from public scrutiny. Shortly after this morn-

---

*Indeed, the calculation of an S&P 500 index would be absurd. Unlike the Dow, the S&P 500 isn't a simple average of stock prices, adjusted by a divisor. It is "capitalization-weighted"—that is, it is computed by multiplying each stock price by the number of shares outstanding, summing these dollar "capitalization" figures, and dividing by 500 to get the index value. This gives the largest, most expensive stocks the most weight in determining the index. The thirty Dow industrials, for example, which are also S&P 500 components, account for 25% of the weight of the index, according to Elliott Shurgin, publisher of research/index services for Standard & Poor's Corporation. At the end of 1987, the eighty largest capitalization stocks combined accounted for 57% of the index.

ing's opening, Scott McMurray, who moved here from New York in August 1986 to cover this and the other financial futures markets more closely for *The Wall Street Journal,* and all his press colleagues were barred from the trading floor.

"Apparently there'd been a flap over a local radio personality who was upsetting people by going around the floor with a microphone asking traders if they'd lost everything," McMurray will recall. But the CME has barred all press from the floor this morning. Not just the radio interviewer or all microphones, but *all* press. In mid-1988, McMurray still recalls it as a singular event—the only time he has been barred from the CME floor.

The press may be out of sight here now, but it is not out of mind. "When Melamed came down to close the pit, he asked everyone not to talk to the press about it," Scott Serfling will recall. There are, of course, compelling reasons to close this pit now. The major facts of the markets' current predicament suggest some fairly obvious ones. It's just that they aren't the kinds of reasons that officials of free markets could be expected to admit to.

At bottom, the decision to close the S&P 500 pit today was motivated by price concerns, Melamed will concede in June 1988. The CME leadership decided that "it would be irresponsible to allow a price collapse like [the one they foresaw] in a panic," he will say. Furthermore, intended or not, the closing here will help John Phelan defuse some of the selling pressure he is facing in New York.

While Phelan and his people have almost completely stopped the transfer of selling pressure from the portfolio insurers in this pit to the NYSE floor through index arbitrage, the investment world at large isn't hip to that yet. So, institutional bargain hunters—the major buyers they need in New York—have been looking at this morning's deepening discount of the S&P 500 futures contract price and the plunging Dow as proof that massive program selling is under way or at least imminent, the Brady Commission will report. Therefore, the institutional buyers are staying stubbornly on the sidelines. Wouldn't anyone? Why jump in and buy stocks at the equivalent of 1700 on the Dow when it appears certain you'll soon be able to snap them up at 1500, 1200, maybe even lower? Similarly, short sellers, who have sold borrowed stock in the expectation of price declines and still haven't "covered" by buying the stock they need to repay in the market, have little incentive to buy now, either. Why cover the position now when you'll surely be able to do so later at a much lower cost (and thus a far bigger profit)?

In addition, both the wave of trading halts of big S&P 500 component stocks on the NYSE between eleven o'clock and noon, and the futures rally here a half hour ago, have backfired. New York's retarding the decline of the index with trading halts should have emboldened buyers here during the latest aborted rally. Who knows, maybe it did. But once the rally failed, the retarded decline in the S&P index instantly became a liability. For the rapid collapse of futures prices that has occurred since the short sellers and portfolio insurers broke the rally is down so against a backdrop of an S&P 500 index that is falling at an artificially impeded, far slower rate.

As a result, the discount of the futures price from the index itself has grown more, and more rapidly, than ever before. Moments ago, it reached a record 46 points, a gap so terrifyingly huge that it has all but totally dried up buying both here and in the stock market.

As long as this situation continues and New York stays open, there is no reason for the slide to stop until all of the specialists' capital is gone and the market is literally in free fall. Melamed knows that Phelan's and the others' serious consideration of closing the New York Stock Exchange is anything but premature.

But turning out the lights here would certainly ease the pressure. For one thing, it would instantly transform the sinking S&P 500 futures price discount from the dominant influence on trading in the stock market into a historical curiosity. Now the vast majority of would-be buyers and sellers among the institutions will be focusing solely on the S&P index itself, which (due to all the halts) is making the market's decline seem much shallower and more orderly than it actually is.

In addition, the closing here means there is just one way left for investors to gauge the overall selling pressure across the blue-chip stocks and the futures markets. That is the spread between the futures contracts on the Major Market Index and the index itself, which is based on prices of twenty big blue-chip stocks (including seventeen Dow industrials) and is designed to track the Dow.

At the Chicago Board of Trade, which is continuing to trade futures contracts on the MMI, the contract price is in a headlong dive that has deepened the contract's discount from the level of the MMI index itself to more than 40 points.

Something will be done about that soon.

OCTOBER 20, 1987. ■ New York Stock Exchange, chairman's office, 12:20 P.M.: At last the options are narrowed to two—one of them is closing the New York Stock Exchange.

John Phelan puts down his telephone and swivels around once again to look at the two-foot-square screen of the deluxe market-monitor terminal that sits on the credenza behind him. Rich Torrenzano, Donny Stone, and Sharon Gamsin squint as they read with him. Bob Birnbaum and Dick Grasso have been in and out of Phelan's office. They're out right now.

Writing in next Monday's *Financial Times,* a London newspaper that distributes an edition in the U.S., Roderick Oram will describe this gathering as involving "very tense, thoughtful and deliberate discussions." Indeed, it's all but impossible to overrate the causes for concern at this moment. So far today:

—The planned higher openings backfired, burying the specialists in sell-order imbalances, sometimes after just minutes of trading. Starting from a nearly 200-point gain at the opening, the Dow has fallen more than 15 points below even yesterday's close.

—Rumors are rife among the specialists that further huge selling, stemming from unmet margin calls and mutual fund redemptions, is imminent.

—Specialists trying to aggressively draw down credit lines to stay afloat have encountered foot dragging by their bankers, some of whom have tightened collateral requirements on existing loans. (Phelan, who has been publicly denying financial troubles, will concede at today's press conference after the market close that "three or four" specialist units "needed some help" now.)

—There's talk of trouble between several big Wall Street firms and their bankers, as well as of possible insolvency at the big Chicago futures and options clearinghouses.

—Even though blue-chip trading halts had slowed the descent of the

S&P index and the Dow, the buying flurry in the S&P 500 pit a half hour ago was a miserable flop. Far from disappearing, the S&P contract's discount to the underlying index is now at its deepest, most frightening level of the day and is worsening fast. The S&P contract's price descent will stop with the closing of the pit less than five minutes from now. The collapse of the MMI futures contract price will not stop even then. At noon its price discount from the index itself was a record 29 points, the SEC will report. Now the discount is 59 points.

—The trading-halt situation clearly is threatening to spin out of control. Through Birnbaum, Grasso, and floor directors Stone, Lyden, Jacobson, and Shields, Phelan has been entreating the besieged specialists all morning: "Could you just hold out a little longer" an exchange official will recall. Yet each new hope for a turn has been dashed, and now many of the specialists won't hold out anymore. Most of the eighty-three halts during the hour that ended at noon came in orderly clusters. Now the floodgates will open as 161 issues are halted during the hour that will end at one o'clock.

The closing of the S&P pit will at least remove one important flashing red light to institutional buyers. However, the closing also means that the S&P pit is out of the picture as a potential aid in any turnaround that might be generated. At least for the time being.

But even if the market's decline could be slowed to a standstill, it will not be enough at this point. After this morning's string of defeats, the only thing that will bring the real and substantial institutional buying needed to end the catastrophe will be evidence that the market has turned. It is not enough that it stops going down. It must go up.

At this moment, a thunderous rally is beginning in the MMI pit at the Chicago Board of Trade. However, it is not rational to expect that this turnaround alone would spark a stock market reversal now. For one thing, the stock index arbitrage that would otherwise automatically begin an answering rally here has, for all practical purposes, been banned today. Also, the MMI pit is a much smaller and therefore less credible market than the S&P 500 pit at the CME, which can't mirror (or undercut) the MMI rally because it is closed.

So while the MMI contract price hurtles skyward during the next ten minutes, most investors—even the pros—won't even notice. Nobody really believes that a rally produced by purchases of just over 800 MMI stock index futures contracts in Chicago means the end of the

Stock Market Crash of 1987. Especially after this morning's string of disasters, if there is to be a genuine reversal, it will have to be indicated in a far more credible marketplace.

There is no more credible marketplace in the world than this one. And no more credible market measure, despite its narrow base, than the Dow. The only way investors will be convinced they are not witnessing a fluke in the MMI pit will be for the Dow to run up, too.

How? In a spontaneous burst of public buying? In response to a surge in an obscure futures contract price in Chicago? Under these market conditions? There are two probabilities of any of this happening—slim and none. Surely any professional investor savvy enough to understand the relationship of the MMI futures and the component stocks here will want confirmation elsewhere before jumping into the stock market. So while the record 59-point discount of the MMI futures price from the underlying index is almost halved in the next ten minutes, the Dow will barely budge.

No, there are only a couple of realistic hopes that this market might reverse, and either would surely seem to need the help of the specialists.

Most obviously, specialists could simply buy their own stocks and "buy them sloppy," that is, pay higher and higher prices until institutions perceive the market turn is real and leap on the bandwagon. Also, whoever is behind the buying binge that runs up the MMI price in Chicago could conduct a coordinated buying program in the component stocks of that index here in New York. But imagine how much buying it would take to produce a riproaring rally in the very stocks that are under the heaviest selling pressure in history right now. Unless specialists helped such investors, a market-turning buying program quite probably would take far too long, and cost far too much, to be feasible.

The alternative to a market turn seems certain to be another horrendous collapse today, Phelan is convinced. So for the past fifteen minutes he has been placing what he calls "warning" phone calls. With Donny here and Torrenzano listening in, he has spoken to the people whose names appear in Bob Cole's notebook: Howard Baker at the White House, SEC Chairman David Ruder, and Jerry Corrigan at the Fed.

"I told them: 'There's a fallback plan here, but you ought to be warned that if this goes another 300 or 400 points, we'll have to close,' " Phelan will say in May 1988. And Torrenzano will recall a few weeks from now that Baker told Phelan: "You're at the helm. Do whatever you have to do. You have our full support."

Baker will order the White House counsel to draw up the document needed for President Reagan to declare the stock market closed. "But I told Phelan. 'I hope you will exhaust every other alternative before you consider [asking the president to order a] closing," Baker will recall in mid-1988. Both Ruder and Corrigan will decline the opportunity to discuss these calls from Phelan.

In a few minutes, Donny Stone's fellow floor directors, John Lyden and Jim Jacobson, will come up from the floor and join the group here for a few minutes around 12:30 with the pleas of many specialists to close the exchange still ringing in their ears. ("I told them to check back every half hour or so," Phelan will remember.) Then, all of them will stare transfixed at the big square monitor with the orange figures and hold their breaths.

OCTOBER 20, 1987. ■ Federal Reserve Bank of New York, president's office, 12:15 P.M.: For Jerry Corrigan, lunching in again today as usual, it's one down, one to go.

Twenty years ago, an extraordinary trading spurt like the one that went on this week might have strained the payments system, too, but not in the ways it will be strained this week and next. Mainly that's because twenty years ago, institutional investment strategies were far more tightly focused and specialized. If an institution was a heavy hitter in the futures game, it tended to identify itself as a futures firm and live pretty much within that identity. Ditto for firms with a predominant focus on stocks, bonds, currencies, etc.

But the Wall Street megafirms of today—Salomon, Goldman, Merrill, First Boston, Shearson, Morgan, Bear Stearns—take immense positions almost everywhere, it seems, in stocks, in bonds, in futures and options, and all coincident with one another.

Right now Shearson Lehman Brothers and Goldman Sachs still haven't received hundreds of millions of dollars in futures margin payments due them and their customers an hour ago. And they won't get the money for hours. The payments are caught in a game of financial Ping-Pong involving the Chicago Mercantile Exchange's clearinghouse and a gaggle of Chicago and New York banks. This tangle epitomizes the very financial gridlock that Corrigan knows could soon mushroom, in this day of highly internationalized markets, into a world financial crisis of the kind all those nutty books are written about.

Capital-rich Shearson and Goldman routinely invest tens of billions of dollars in securities and other financial instruments positions for their own and their clients' accounts—and their positions are financed aggressively by borrowings. Both firms have huge "agency" trading businesses as well, acting as brokers to major investment institutions like banks, insurers, pension funds, and the like, and major portfolio insurers.

Meanwhile, the CME clearinghouse administers and holds the security, or margin, deposits required of all investors at the exchange. Both buyers and sellers must put up an "initial" margin deposit when their trade opens a futures position, and they must leave the initial margin on deposit until the position is liquidated. To adjust the size of these deposits to reflect changing prices, the clearinghouse requires the daily assessment of a supplemental deposit called "variation margin." It is a zero-sum exercise, with the clearinghouse requiring increased margin deposits in the accounts of investors whose positions were adversely affected by the prior day's price movement, and then distributing all this variation margin among the accounts of investors with the opposite positions.

Netting out all of Shearson's and Goldman's heavy trading activity in the pit yesterday, both in their own and in their clients' behalf, the two Wall Street giants were heavy sellers and today their open positions are overwhelmingly selling ones. That, of course, was the winning bet yesterday, since S&P 500 futures prices plunged almost 29% then. But because they traded so heavily yesterday, they've also had to pay a substantial initial margin on their own and their customers' new positions.

Both the Brady Commission and the SEC will report that winning accounts at two unidentified clearing members of the CME are due to collect a total of $1.5 billion of variation margin today. Wall Street sources will say that Shearson's winning customers—those who are short—are owed more than $900 million in variation margin and Goldman's are owed almost $600 million. Both firms have plenty of losing accounts, too. For example, after netting out its losing (or long) customer positions, Shearson is owed only $97.5 million net on its customer accounts, and its own house account had to pay $11.5 million of variation margin today, a Shearson official will later disclose.

Neither report will reveal how much Shearson and Goldy contributed to today's $997 million addition to initial margin on deposit at the clearinghouse, which lifted the initial margin total to $3.9 billion.* A senior executive at one of the two companies will say his firm paid $120 million in initial margin to the CME today.

The CME clearinghouse deals with its members through four big Chicago banks.† At each, it maintains a clearinghouse account, with subaccounts for each clearing member. Each member is required to maintain two accounts in one of these four "settlement" banks—one containing the broker's own funds and the other his customers' funds.‡ He must also sign a paper giving the bank permission to credit or debit these accounts on the orders of the clearinghouse.

At five o'clock every weekday morning, having recorded the new positions taken, and having sorted out those traders' accounts to be debited from those to be credited to reflect the prior day's position and price changes, the CME clearinghouse sends out instructions to each settlement bank.

By seven o'clock in the morning, in accordance with a rigid tradition, the settlement banks must confirm that all payments and deductions ordered by the clearinghouse have occurred or will occur. If the banks confirm a transfer that hasn't actually taken place, they advance the money involved under prearranged lines of credit set up for their clearing member customers.

Also, if a deduction ordered by the clearinghouse is larger than the balance in a clearing member's account, plus the line of credit, the bank

---

*Initial margin—which on Black Monday rose to $12,500 from $5,000 per contract for CME members and hedgers, and to $20,000 from $10,000 by CME members' speculator customers—must be posted by both buyer and seller on all positions opened, and it must remain on deposit at the CME clearinghouse until the positions are liquidated.

†The Harris Trust & Savings Bank, Continental Illinois National Bank, The First National Bank of Chicago, and The Northern Trust Company.

‡Securities law requires brokers to keep their money segregated from their customers' money at all times.

decides then and there to make up the difference to the clearing member by allowing a so-called daylight overdraft.* Such occasions aren't rare at all, since a number of the clearing members, including Shearson and Goldy, do most of their banking in New York. And rather than leave a lot of excess margin money sloshing around in their clearinghouse accounts at the Chicago settlement banks, they routinely have those accounts swept and any unneeded balances wired to their New York bank accounts.

This morning there was a grand total of $4.3 billion of margin on deposit at the four settlement banks, or $400 million more than the required initial margin of $3.9 billion. Since there's also the $2.5 billion of variation margin to deal with, all CME clearing members, had to come up with $2.1 billion more than they had on deposit in the settlement banks this morning, or ten times more than there would be on a normal day.

At its usual time of five o'clock this morning, the CME clearinghouse instructed the settlement banks to assess their clearing member customers' accounts the total $2.1 billion. A good many of these account balances weren't sufficient to meet the margin calls, the Brady Commission will find.

No sweat, you may say. Just net out the margin that Shearson and Goldy are owed and credit them with the difference.

Sorry, no cigar. All four settlement banks are now busy beating the bushes trying to collect a record amount of variation margin from the losers and a record amount of initial margin to boot. Shearson's and Goldy's respective settlement banks are due to credit more money to their clearing member customers, as a group, than will be collected from them.

That's a common and foreseen imbalance, and there are routine provisions for resolving it. One of the four banks, Harris Trust & Savings, acts as a "concentration bank." Any of the four banks whose margin collections from their customers under the clearinghouse instructions exceeded their margin payments to those customers are

---

*If the settlement bank decides not to extend an overdraft, it informs the CME, formally placing the clearing member in default. The bank must receive the funds to eliminate all daylight overdrafts within the same business day they are allowed. Also, the Fed closely regulates the total of daylight overdrafts that each bank may grant; and once that ceiling is reached, no money may be credited to the accounts of customers with daylight overdrafts until the overdrafts are covered.

instructed to send the excess over the Fed wire to Harris Trust. The clearinghouse then instructs Harris Trust to send the appropriate amounts via Fed wire to those banks whose margin payments to customers are greater than the monies collected from them. So, if Shearson's and Goldy's settlement banks butted in now and simply netted out their accounts with credits, those banks would be on the hook if there are significant margin defaults elsewhere in the collections loop today. Whatever money Harris Trust doesn't get, the other banks won't get, either.

Around dawn the big question at the settlement banks was, how much did they dare advance to the clearing members with insufficient funds? In many cases, the margin calls would force the banks to exceed intraday lending practice. And if their big customers failed to cover the overdrafts with deposits by the close of business, the banks would find themselves far over their federally imposed overnight lending limits.

The way out would have to be to make regular loans to many of the clearing members. But the Brady Commission will report that the settlement banks "were reluctant to undertake credit risks to the extent required . . . without receiving some comfort from their customers and the New York banks," the main bankers to the biggest clearing members, including Goldy and Shearson. "However, Chicago bankers responsible for credit decisions reportedly experienced serious difficulty locating their counterparts in New York," the report will say.

Moreover, the Brady Commission will continue, the Fed's funds transfer wire was open for only an hour (beginning at six A.M. Chicago time) to move any needed funds from the New York banks to the settlement banks ahead of deadline to confirm the clearinghouse-ordered debits and credits. Nevertheless, three of the settlement banks went ahead and confirmed the CME clearinghouse instructions at the usual seven A.M. deadline and the fourth confirmed by 8:30.

When some Chicago bankers finally reached their New York counterparts this morning, they got a rude shock. The funds they hoped would be there to cover the overdrafts in Chicago had already been credited to some of the Wall Street firms' institutional clients' accounts to reflect yesterday's gains on the futures they sold.

Some competitors will speculate that Goldy is in this pickle, but the firm won't discuss details of its operations.

Shearson isn't in this fix, but some $37 million of special intraday margin calls by the CME have been covered by daylight overdafts and Harris Trust, Shearson's Chicago bank, has reached its overdraft limit and must receive the funds to cover the overdraft from Shearson's New York bankers before it can credit Shearson with the variation margin. So the Chicago banks can't credit their two big customers with CME variation margin until the daylight overdrafts are paid. But the daylight overdrafts can't be paid until the swamped New York banks clear any loans needed to do this and get the funds transferred to Chicago on the busy Fed Wire.

And so, adding to the terror already stalking the stock and futures markets today, is a massive payments gridlock.

OCTOBER 20, 1987. ■ New York Stock Exchange, chairman's office, 12:30 P.M.: "Hey. Look . . .," says John Phelan as he peers at the big square screen of his monitor.

Phelan has been pensive during the past ten minutes. "We are a symbol," he tells Torrenzano and the others, "of not only the strength of free markets, but of the strength of this nation." Torrenzano will recall that "we talked about the psychology of staying open." I asked, if we did decide to close, would we be able to open again. John said: 'We have an absolute responsibility to stay open.' "

Phelan's words had hit the group—Rich, Donny, Sharon Gamsin, John Lyden, and Jim Jacobson—with sledgehammer force, for "we knew how much worse it was than anyone else knew," Torrenzano says. At noon, what seemed certain was that the final phase of the meltdown Phelan has feared and struggled to prevent had begun. The Dow hit its low of the day, 1708, down more than 30 points, at 12:21, the Brady Commission will note.

To be sure, at 12:20, the price of the Major Market Index futures contract at the Chicago Board of Trade had begun to run. And oh, Lord, how it had run! Brady's task force will report that between then and now, the price had already recovered half of its unbelievable 59-point discount to the value of the index itself.

But had it run in vain?

There'd been nothing remotely resembling a confirmation. The Dow had barely budged, up less than 4 points during the same period when its supposed identical twin in Chicago had been soaring 10%.

Ominously, a news item circulated in the financial community fifteen minutes ago that might doom any effort to eliminate the big discount in the MMI pit, and might make institutional investors skeptical of any confirmation that could occur here. The item had been carried by Knight-Ridder Financial News services, including its widely followed Commodity News Service. It said:

CBOE STOPS TRADING IN INDEX OPTIONS, CITES NYSE TRADING HALT

CHICAGO—Oct. 20—KRF—The Chicago Board Options Exchange has halted trading shortly before 11 A.M., CDT [noon in New York], in all index option contracts as well as option contracts on some blue chip stocks. An exchange spokesman said the New York Stock Exchange had halted trading late this morning in some blue chip issues, including IBM.

Since some of those issues are heavily involved in various stock indexes, the spokesman said, the trading values for the underlying indexes were not a true reflection of market values and the exchange moved to halt index options trading. "We'll trade whatever New York is trading," he said.

According to CBOE [records], trading in the OEX [the S&P 100] was halted at 10:54 CDT. Trading in options on IBM stock stopped at 10:39 CDT.

Then, when Knight-Ridder had called the exchange for comment, Martha Cid, who works for Sharon Gamsin, had batted down the CBOE man's contentions. So Knight-Ridder had followed up with this report just a minute ago, at 12:29:

NY STOCKS SPECIAL: ALL DOW STOCKS TRADING EXCEPT UNOPENED DUPONT

NEW YORK—Oct. 20—KRF—All stock components of the Dow Jones industrials continue to trade at midday with the sole exception of DuPont, which has not yet opened due to order imbalances, according to Martha Cid, manager of the exchange's news bureau.

Cid said rumors were untrue that many selected blue chips had halted trading due to severe order imbalances and the great number of margin calls that are known to have been issued by mailgram from brokerage houses last night and early this morning.

By mid-1988, Rich Torrenzano, speaking for Martha Cid, will say she "doesn't know" why she said that. The fact is that the rumors are true. At this moment there are ten Dow stocks not trading: DuPont, Eastman Kodak, Goodyear, IBM, Merck, Philip Morris, Primerica, Sears, Westinghouse, and Woolworth, together accounting for more than half the weight of the Dow average.* Six of these stocks are also MMI stocks, and another one of the twenty MMI issues, Dow Chemical, is halted. The halted issues also account for more than half the weight of the MMI.

". . . Look at this," Phelan says.

"It was the Dow. He was talking about the Dow," Torrenzano recalls almost seven months later. He is very sure about the time. "It was right at twelve thirty, give or take a minute, or two, or three." Indeed, Torrenzano describes the moment as almost a mystical experience: "John Phelan looked at the big orange screen—and the market turned."

These faint stirrings in the Dow observed by a roomful of anguished and breathless exchange officials pose the central mystery of the Stock Market Crash of 1987. Is the market reversal that is beginning now a miracle they had prayed for—or something they have manufactured? "It was no miracle," Phelan will say. "Markets turn."

Or are turned.

The Dow is beginning to bubble a bit, all right. Indeed, a look at F. E. Fitch's October 20 trading breakdown shows the drama beginning to unfold among the Dow industrials about now.

—American Express: which was 22½ at 12:26, is already 23¼ on five quick trades involving a total of just 7,000 shares. Nearly 5 million shares are changing hands today.

---

*A number of these stocks are high-priced issues, and the Dow Jones Industrial Average is actually an index, not an average. It is derived by adding the NYSE price of each component stock and dividing the sum by a less-than-whole-number divisor that is adjusted periodically by Dow Jones to reflect stock splits. Thus, the higher a stock's price, the greater its impact on the Dow.

—Boeing: 20,000 shares traded at 34, at 12:26; 3,700 shares at 34, at 12:27; 1,000 shares at 34, at 12:28. Then, 600 shares traded at 34½, at 12:29, and 200 shares at 35, up another ½ point, at 12:30—a full point gain on 800 shares, one twentieth of 1 percent of today's volume.

—International Paper: five trades, 5,600 shares between 12:22 and 12:29, all at 28½. Then 2,700 shares at 29, also at 12:29; 500 shares at 29½, at 12:30; 1,600 shares at 30, at 12:31. Two minutes, three trades, 4,800 shares, up 1½.

Roderick Oram will note the moment in the *Financial Times* of Monday, October 26: "We looked at each other and said: 'We've got a shot at it," one of the specialists said."

They do indeed have a shot at it. More seeming miracles remain to be performed in Chicago and New York. Ten minutes later now, the MMI futures price will have caught the index itself and will then actually trade at a premium of between 10 and 12 points until 12:50, the SEC will report. But the SEC will note, seemingly with a straight face, that the brief premium "resulted in only one index arbitrage program purchasing 40,000 shares of stock and selling 25 MMI contracts—constituting less than one-tenth of one percent of NYSE volume from 12:30 to 1:00."

Fitch's figures will show that in the Dow stocks, especially some of those that are also components of the MMI, the fun is just beginning.*

Today, between 12:37 and 12:39, American Express will squirt up another 1¾, or 7.2%, to 25 on a total of nine trades involving 20,700 shares in all. International Paper will rise 5 to 35, between 12:33 and 12:43, on turnover of 32,500 shares. General Electric will run up 4 to 44½, between 12:31 and 12:51, on 4.4% of its volume. Philip Morris, halted at 77½ at 11:30, will soon resume trading at 79 and run to 88 in seventeen minutes. See Procter & Gamble run between 12:42 and 12:45: 10,000 shares at 66; 2,000 at 67; 5,000 at 68; 2,500 at 69; 5,000 at 69, again; 6,000 at 69¼, and 3,000 at 70. A 4-point rise in three minutes on 23,500 of nearly 1.7 million P&G shares being traded. By

---

*Major Market Index components that are also Dow industrials are: American Express, American Telephone & Telegraph, Chevron, Coca-Cola, DuPont, Eastman Kodak, Exxon, General Electric, General Motors, IBM, International Paper, Minnesota Mining & Manufacturing, Merck, Philip Morris, Procter & Gamble, Sears, USX Corporation. The remaining three MMI components are Dow Chemical, Johnson & Johnson, and Mobil.

12:49, the stock will be at 72. General Motors, with more than 4.2 million shares trading, will shoot up 7⅞, or more than 15%, between 12:30 and 1:00, including a 2-point burst between 12:37 and 12:39, on seven trades involving less than a total of 21,000 shares.

While all these big Dow stocks are also components of the MMI; a few that aren't in the MMI are turning in amazing gains, too. Bethlehem Steel will rocket up 2, or more than 18%, between 12:35 and 12:58, on just 43,800 shares, less than 3.5% of today's volume. And from 12:30 to 12:44, Union Carbide will reach for the heavens when it vaults 5 to 20¾, a 32% gain on a little over 3½% of volume.

Yet the rally will be somewhat selective until the institutional bargain hunters step into the market in force, beginning about 12:50. For example, Minnesota Mining will surge from 48 now to 56 at one o'clock, but it will have only reached 50 at 12:44 as the MMI rally peaks. And some of the Dow stocks that aren't also MMI components will turn in unremarkable performances during the next fifteen minutes. Allied-Signal and Navistar International will be unchanged at 31½; McDonald's will gain but ¼, to 34¼, and United Technologies, ¾ to 33½.

However, the stocks that are on fire will propel the average from 1712 at 12:30 to 1780 at 12:44, up 68 points. The gain from 12:30 to 1:00 will be more than 115 points, and will break the back of the Stock Market Crash of 1987.

In a few minutes the group will dissolve. Donny Stone will return to the floor and resume making a market in Johnson & Johnson stock. But it will not seem like a chore now. By 12:42, Johnson & Johnson will have scrambled to 57, up 1½ from its price now.

Over the next thirteen minutes, Donny will see it soar like an eagle— up 13 points, to 70. Along the way, there will be forty-nine trades, ten of which, while involving 1,000 shares or less, nonetheless will move the Johnson & Johnson stock price up by at least ½ point. Donny will be no help in understanding the surge. Seven months from now, he will tell a visitor to Post 8, "I remember selling into the rally that started at twelve thirty, but basically I only remember the bad things that happened that day."

In a late May 1988 interview, John Phelan doesn't mince words, either. "I can't explain the trading," he says.

EPILOGUE

OCTOBER 20, 1987. ■ Federal Reserve Bank of New York, president's office, 1:15 P.M.: John Phelan's alarming call an hour ago had decisively strengthened Jerry Corrigan's hand in galvanizing the banks to use aggressively the liquidity the Fed has been so freely providing today.

Phelan's news was so alarmingly bad that there finally was no room for anyone to rationalize continued inaction. Almost 170 Big Board issues were halted, including many of the biggest, supposedly most liquid stocks on earth. Specialists were screaming to close the market. He was down to one fallback plan, the Big Board chairman had told Corrigan, and unless it worked or there was a miracle, the exchange would have to be closed, no matter whether that would fuel the panic; no matter what message that might send the world about the strength of the U.S. free-markets system. The specialists simply could not stand against another 300- or 400-point slide.

Then, the incredible 115-point rush of the Dow between 12:30 and one o'clock had come with all the spine-tingling drama of a cavalry charge. It said that while the situation was past desperate, the day could still be won. The momentum was established and the banks hopped aboard.

The Wall Street Journal's Jim Stewart and Dan Hertzberg will report in their November 20 reconstruction of today's events that by one P.M. the big New York banks "had finally pledged their support after receiving reassurances from the Fed, giving specialists and other firms the financial confidence to execute orders."

That confidence is vital right now, with the S&P 500 pit reopened ten minutes ago, again scaring the daylights out of institutional investors. While the December contract's price had opened 30 points above its level at the closing of the pit less than an hour before, it was still at a horrendous 17-point discount to the S&P index itself. The Dow is midway into a half-hour dive of nearly 80 points, but, with the banks solidly behind them, the specialists and the big trading houses are standing firm. Indeed, in his own reconstruction of this day, the *Financial Times's* Roderick Oram will report that "tension eased further when word spread around Wall Street that some big brokers, notably Salomon Brothers and Goldman Sachs, were willing to buy whatever volume was necessary to reopen closed stocks."

Soon, the army of short sellers—those aggressively cynical investors who have borrowed stock and sold it in the expectation that the collapse will continue—will begin to realize they are wrong. So they will rush to close out their short positions by joining in the institutional buying and help push the Dow up more than 160 points, to nearly 1920, between 2:00 and 3:30. A drop of nearly 80 points during the last half hour of trading won't frighten market pros, who will recognize it for what it is: profit taking by the "day traders"—agile traders who dart in and out of the market all in the same day, avoiding the risk and margin costs of holding stocks overnight.

A decisive turn is nearly at hand in the stalemate over Shearson Lehman's and Goldy's margin calls at the CME clearinghouse. As the Brady Commission reports, and a senior Chicago Merc official will indicate, Goldman's Chicago bank will get a $141 million transfer to the firm's New York bank before three o'clock, and then will credit Goldy's account with the variation margin that reflects the appreciation in value of Goldy's and its clients' short positions on Black Monday.

Similarly, Shearson's New York bank will be completing a $595 million transfer to its Chicago bank, Harris Trust. The latter bank will then post the variation margin due on Shearson's and its clients' futures position as a result of the Black Monday price changes. The menacing gridlock will be broken. Corrigan's and the Fed's answer to the problem is elegantly simple. Rather than temporarily expand the Fed's daylight overdraft limits for the Chicago banks, the Fed Wire will be run into tonight—until all the transfers needed to eliminate the overdrafts are completed.

The banking industry won't be publicly vilified for its conduct during the crash and, indeed, its proponents soon will cite it as justification for a long-sought business objective. The industry's backers will renew calls for banks to be allowed to compete in the securities industry again after a half century's absence.* With prime rates above 20% at the start of the decade, the bankers effectively drove their blue-ribbon corporate customers into seeking needed financing in the securities markets, where the banks have since been trying to get legal approval to pursue them.

Their argument will be that Black Monday showed the banks' huge capital resources are needed in the securities industry. But some observers will see it as a galling attempt by the bankers to capitalize on the very disaster they had helped to produce. Virtually every major study of the crash will conclude that wave after blind wave of selling by portfolio insurers was a principal cause of the calamity. And, of course, executing portfolio insurance strategy is an activity dominated by the institutional money managers at large banks.

The Federal Reserve Board will pursue a cautiously relaxed monetary policy into early 1988, partly out of concern that the crash might trigger a recession or depression. But the three-year downtrend in the dollar will finally have revived U.S. exports, and so the economy will turn in surprisingly strong growth in the fourth quarter of 1987 and even stronger growth in the first quarter of 1988, despite rising caution and reduced purchases by consumers.

Commodities prices, also reflecting a flight of capital from the febrile stock market, will surge and the Fed will respond. The situation will have come full circle to where Jerry Corrigan and Paul Volcker began the decade—with the Federal Reserve worrying about inflation. In the spring of 1988, a concerned Fed will gradually snug the Federal funds rate by about ¾ of a point. Early in that process a half-point prime-rate hike will quickly spread among the banks. This time the brunt of the impact will fall not on the major corporations (many of which stopped using banks for major financing needs years earlier), but on the many tens of thousands of average Americans who have taken out home equity loans with interest rates tied directly to the prime.

Fed Chairman Alan Greenspan will run interference. In mid-May

---

*From which they have been excluded by the federal Glass-Steagall Act since the Great Depression.

he will tell a bank structure conference sponsored by the Chicago Fed that banks must be allowed to raise their rates to compensate for the mediocre quality of corporate borrowers they have been left with as a result of the flight of their blue-ribbon clients to the securities markets. His stance is consistent with a key Fed objective. The central bank, concerned over the seemingly endless round of banking crises, is pushing the nation's banks hard to increase their loss reserves against the loans they make. And the more money they earn, the more can go into reserves.

That the banks will come away from Black Monday relatively unscathed in the eyes of the public will be thanks largely to E. Gerald Corrigan. Both the SEC and Brady Commission studies make it abundantly clear that, left to their own devices, free from Corrigan's constant prodding and reassurance, the banks would almost certainly have made the calamity far worse.

Corrigan's efforts will win high marks from his former mentor. With typical understatement, Paul Volcker will tell *Minneapolis Star Tribune* reporter Mike Meyers: "This is pretty detailed stuff where you have to react very deftly. His job involved more than making assessments and providing money. It required a bit of hand-holding." According to Bankers Trust Chairman Charles Sanford, Jr.: "Our job was to assess the credit of our customers in a crisis and not to worry about whether we were going to run out of dough. He made it clear we didn't have to worry." And Chase Manhattan Bank President Thomas Labrecque will put it succinctly: "It's important for a person in his job to understand what's going on. He did."

But the highest praise will come from a grateful John Phelan. "It's impossible to overstate the importance of Jerry's contribution," Phelan will say. Big Board specialists and member firms "were screaming on Monday about how the banks were treating them." But by the crunch on Tuesday, "when it counted most, they were telling us the bankers finally seemed to understand. The difference was Jerry Corrigan."

Corrigan's charges, the big New York banks, will emerge from the crash stronger and richer. The additional $6 billion of loans they are making to securities industry participants the rest of this week and next will be profitable.

They also are in the forefront of banks earning immense profits and fees by trading in currencies for themselves and their clients now, shrewdly capitalizing on the decline of the dollar, which helped to bring on the crash. They will also reap a bond trading bonanza, as investors plow much of the money they are pulling out of the stock market into bonds.

Early next year, *The Wall Street Journal* will report that the fourth quarter, 1987, foreign exchange profits of the nation's nine largest money-center banks* more than tripled—to $818.6 million. Their bond trading profits in the quarter rose 43% to $232.3 million, the *Journal* will report.

Leading the pack in both categories will be Bankers Trust, whose refusal of a desperate A. B. Tompane & Company's loan request on Black Monday helped to drive the troubled NYSE specialist firm into the arms of Merrill Lynch in the middle of the night. Bankers Trust's foreign exchange gains, negligible in the 1986 fourth quarter, will be $337.7 million in this quarter,† and its $145.5 million of securities trading profits will be about triple the third quarter's record $46.6 million and more than five times those in the final quarter of 1986. Citicorp and J. P. Morgan will finish second and third behind Bankers Trust in the foreign exchange profits derby, and Manny Hanny, Chemical, and Chase Manhattan will all show big securities-trading profit gains, the *Journal* will report.

All their gratitude will not win him a rest. Not yet. Phelan's last business call today, at 5:30, will go to Corrigan, partly to thank him, but also to talk about the next hurdle, clearing—matching Black Monday's buyers and sellers at the National Securities Clearing Corporation, tomorrow and Thursday. The percentage of unmatched trades for Black Monday will rise to 3.4%, a bit more than double the usual percentage, but not a major problem. Then there will be next Monday's settlement date for Black Monday trades, where the anxiety will be over whether everyone will pay. They will.

In November the stock market will settle into what will be its normal post-crash condition; reed-thin, nervous, and uncertain—devoid of investor confidence.

---

*In New York they are: Bankers Trust, Chase Manhattan, Chemical, Citicorp, Manufacturers Hanover, and J. P. Morgan. Elsewhere: First Chicago, BankAmerica, and Security Pacific.
†But in July 1988, Corrigan's New York Fed will rule the bank overvalued its currency options positions and order Bankers Trust to restate the foreign exchange earnings by $80 million.

Jerry Corrigan and John Phelan will be in frequent telephone contact for the next two weeks. They will not see each other face to face. They will not need to. As with all survivors of catastrophes, there will be a bond between them from this time on.

Yet the mystery surrounding Corrigan, the mystery of what he knew and what he did, and its impact on his career at the Fed will remain. Months after the crash, a spokesman for Alan Greenspan will say that the Fed chairman will have no public comment on Corrigan's performance.*

OCTOBER 20, 1987. ■ Washington, The White House, 1:30 P.M.: Call him Howard Baker the investment banker. The president's right arm has put his shoulder to the wheel today along with many Wall Street investment bankers, phoning the heads of some of America's largest corporations, asking them to help in the crisis.

Baker has carefully avoided direct language in his appeals, but his urgent plea for them to buy stock has been unmistakable. And the effort is beginning to pay off. A trickle of major companies began announcing new or accelerated stock purchase programs shortly before one o'clock.

The trickle will grow into a flood this afternoon, and so, partly thanks to the White House Chief of Staff, some of the big blocks of stock being offered for sale on the trading desks of the large securities firms will at last find avid buyers—the companies who issued them.

OCTOBER 20, 1987. ■ Chicago Mercantile Exchange trading floor, 2:30 P.M., EDT: After a big scare, finally it seems to be about time for Otto to buy, Scott Serfling decides.

During the past hour Scott has seen, and the Brady Commission will confirm, that "major investment bank buying activity dominated the futures market and narrowed the discount [of the December S&P 500

*"Of course," New York Fed public-relations Vice-President Peter Bakstansky will be eager to explain, "Fed officials don't congratulate one another in public."

futures price to the index itself] to approximately eight points" from about 30 points.

In the last few minutes, the big New York firms' buying has slackened, Scott sees. But he sees the brokers with smaller, aggressive trading accounts beginning to get busy now. Not many people have noticed that, Scott is sure. They have only noticed the big houses' buying slowing down. That should give them pause, while they assess the situation, he expects, and the price should fall back a few points now before they also see the expanded institutional buying.

Accordingly, Serfling has talked to Otto, his West German money manager client. He was sorry the European investor didn't own contracts at the 181–185 price level in effect just before the trading halt, Scott said, but there was no way he could have honestly recommended a purchase under those conditions. Now that the corner had been turned, however, Scott had told Otto it made sense for him to think about wading in.

Otto had agreed and empowered Scott to place a conditional order. With the price now at 215, he instructed his broker in the pit to buy thirty cars for Otto, if he can get them for no more than 213, and then look up to Scott's desk for instructions on whether to buy twenty more cars. That was the price at which trading resumed at 1:05, and it should be the floor price for the rest of today's session, Scott figures.

Serfling knows it is out of the question for him to risk holding a position open for his own account in this market. But Otto's capital will easily let him post the margin to hold his position open overnight, and it's smart for him to get in about now, as Scott sees it. There may not be much price rise left in today's markets, but news of the recovery will be everywhere tonight and the price might very well run away from people trying to get in on tomorrow's opening. Indeed, the December contract's price will open 26 points above tonight's close of 216.25 and finish tomorrow above 258.

But in the meantime the price will not return to the 213 level, and Otto's cars will never be bought.

OCTOBER 20, 1987. ■ Dow Jones Tower, World Financial Center, 3:00 P.M.: Norm Pearlstine has just arrived at *The Wall Street Journal*'s offices from JFK Airport after coming home from Europe, but Paul Steiger "was up to his ears in plans for that night's paper and so I pretty much steered clear and left him alone," the *Journal* managing editor will recall.

Pearlstine heads one flight up the backstairs on a "show the flag" mission to greet and encourage the Markets Group staffers as they begin actually writing the stories for which they have been gathering information all day.

Steiger divides his time among checks with Washington bureau Features editor Ken Bacon, Page One editor Mapes, National News editor Marty Schenker, and John Prestbo, whose Markets Group staffers are producing most of the crash-related stories for tomorrow morning's *Journal*, and with the Graphics executive, Nikki Frost, on the eight special drawings, tables, and charts being produced for the crash-coverage package.

Steiger's one remaining major decision today is whether to give the choice right-hand column on the front page to the Alan Murray story on Greenspan and the Federal Reserve's being forced by the collapse to reverse the nation's monetary policy, or give it to a report of today's stock price turnaround. The Dow is up 140 points now, but has been extremely volatile today, and the trading—over 530 million shares so far—is immense. There might not be a clear reading until the last few minutes of trading. Meanwhile, the Murray story is already flowing, via Bacon, into the front-page desk. It is crisp and insightful—a story unlikely to be duplicated by other papers tomorrow. And so Steiger will go for the Murray piece.

Newsstands this morning were furnished with an extra 108,000 copies of the *Journal*, about a third more than they normally sell. But they sold out anyway. Tomorrow, they will get 178,250 additional copies. "We never did sell out again," a Dow Jones executive will say, however. "About the best we did after that was to sell seventy-five percent of the additional copies run off." In fact, some 189,000 of the 865,000 additional copies of the *Journal* produced for newsstands during the rest of the month won't be sold and Dow Jones will stop turning out extra copies after the Friday, October 30, issue.

Harder times await the *Journal* in the months ahead. During October, the amount of Wall Street–related advertising—a huge source of profits during the five-year bull market—will be down 25% from a year earlier. For November, the year-to-year decline will be a sickening 57%. This category of advertising will firm a bit in early 1988, but the 28% decline through April will account almost entirely for a 10% overall decline at the paper, financial advertising director Geoffrey E. Meyer will report. The paper's circulation will drop about 5%, to slightly below 2 million, by mid-1988.

OCTOBER 22, 1987. ■ Chicago Mercantile Exchange trading floor, 9:30 A.M., EDT: The price volatility in the pit has seemed to lose its rhythm and any semblance of predictability, with this terrifying exception: The word has spread everywhere at the CME this morning that Shearson Lehman Brothers plans to sell thousands of cars on today's opening.

Scott Serfling almost stayed too long in his upstairs office and he had to run for the elevator to make it to his trading desk on time. But he is here now, and today's opening will burn in his memory:

"Shearson's floor broker offered 6,000 cars on the opening. Nobody would say anything [that is, make a bid]. Finally he got a bid of 198, down 60 points from Wednesday's close. And he took it. Then he sold 8,000 more cars in the first minute of trading. It had to cost them $300 million to do that. And then, in another minute and a half, the price was back up to 230," he will remember.

Serfling's memory will be amazingly accurate, the Brady Commission report confirms. Noting that the contract opened "an unprecedented 60 points lower," the Brady report will explain that:

"Apparently it became known in the pit that there was a large customer order to sell several thousand contracts, and given the uncertainty of the market, many of the locals backed away. However, beginning suddenly at 9:36 A.M., the futures began to rally sharply, reaching the 230 level within three minutes. Approximately two hours later, the S&P futures were back above 250." It was an instant 24% decline followed by a 28% rally in two hours.

Goldman Sachs bought some of the contracts at the opening, Bob Rubin, the firm's top trading official, will confirm.

So did Shearson, acting for its own account, another official will confirm. "I was mad as hell when I found out it was one of our own customers' sale," he will add. The seller was a high-stakes Wall Street investor, George Soros. "You ought to talk to George about that trade, if he'll talk to you," Rubin suggests. But attempts to reach Soros will be unavailing.

The incredible bust will be a miracle that changes the life of one of Serfling's local colleagues, who on Wednesday, yesterday, mistakenly neglected to close out a short position of twenty-five cars. The mistake could have been a disaster if the market had opened sharply higher.

Instead, the price break caused by Shearson's selling will let him buy the twenty-five contracts he needs at less than 200, giving him a profit of "$700,000 to $800,000. I only knew him by badge number and he wouldn't talk about it. He just walked out the pit, sold his seat, and he hasn't been seen back on the floor since that day," Serfling will recall.

DECEMBER 11, 1987. ■ Dow Jones Tower, World Financial Center, 10:00 A.M.: The Stewart and Hertzberg "Terrible Tuesday" story that ran in the November 20 *Wall Street Journal* had turned heads everywhere. Now Steiger had moved to ensure their effort wouldn't be in vain.

The "Terrible Tuesday" story detailed some of the troubles among banks and their Wall Street customers that made the crash a far more grave threat than generally understood, and it broke the explosive news of the mysterious, seemingly manipulated turnaround in the MMI futures pit in Chicago. Both the Brady Commission and the SEC, with more time and vastly greater authority and manpower, will confirm the basic Stewart and Hertzberg account with thousands of supporting facts.

While the story did reduce the fear that *The New York Times* would win a Pulitzer for its crash coverage, it didn't eliminate it. Early in the week, Dick Rustin got wind of *The New York Times*'s plans to begin a series of interpretative stories on the crash in Sunday's paper, two days from now. The effort would very much enhance a *Times* Pulitzer submission. It would be hard for the *Times* to package up page after page after page of stories, photos, and pictures from its crash-week coverage as a Pulitzer Prize submission. But if they made the tightly focused five-part series the centerpiece of their submission, then the *Times* entry could be formidable!

The best defense against that would be a good offense. So today's *Journal* contains the first part of the paper's own four-part front-page series, complete with its own logo, "The Crash of '87." Not even assigned to Stewart and Hertzberg until Tuesday, December 8, it is a Fast and Dirty story to end all Fast and Dirty stories, with its unremarkable central premise spelled out in the headline: SPECULATIVE FEVER RAN HIGH IN THE 10 MONTHS PRIOR TO BLACK MONDAY.

No matter, "The Crash of '87" is a defensive project, not an offensive one. Stewart and Hertzberg's crown-jewel story on the crash ran three weeks ago. The rationale behind today's launch is to undercut the *Times*'s Pulitzer chances by beating its series to the punch. "Rustin says this will keep the *Times* from a Pulitzer," another *Journal* editor notes today.

Nonetheless, the *Times* staff will be confident of victory. Early in 1988, the paper's Business Day staff—the heart of its crash-coverage contingent—will be asked to pose for a group photograph without being told why. Many will assume the picture is intended for promotional use after the expected Pulitzer.

But among the Pulitzer prizes for 1987, to be announced early in April 1988, none will go to the *Times* for its crash coverage. Instead, Jim Stewart and Dan Hertzberg will win one—for explanatory journalism—with an entry containing some of their insider trading probe, but based mainly on their coverage of the crash.

There will be disappointment but little rancor at the *Times*. "I still think our day-to-day coverage of the crash was better than the *Journal*'s," *Times* reporter Richard J. Meislin will say, "but we had nothing to match Stewart's and Hertzberg's story on the day after Black Monday."

DECEMBER 31, 1987. ■ Chicago Mercantile Exchange trading floor, 4:15 P.M., EDT: Scott Serfling records the day's trades, and closes the books on his most profitable year ever. Despite trading at only a bit better than break-even since the crash, his 1987 income from trading is about $700,000, and his profit is around $400,000 after absorbing the losses of his struggling young futures brokerage.

But there will be trading losses rather than profits from the outset in 1988. In the first quarter the losses will total $120,000. With the locals in the S&P 500 pit decimated by the crash, trading will continue to be sporadic and price movements, volatile and unpredictable. Trading volume that had routinely been 70,000 to 80,000 contracts a day before the crash will continue at only about half that rate into mid-1988.

Serfling's anxiety over meeting his firm's $200,000 annual payroll cost is mounting with his trading losses. The S&P 500 pit is Camelot no more, he will glumly concede by the end of the first quarter. So, while he will hold on to his strategically valuable trading desk on the CME floor, he will join the Chicago Board of Trade a few blocks away and arrange to do most of his trading in its giant Treasury bond futures pit.

At the end of the first quarter, Scott will huddle with three of his farmer clients. Once each quarter, the farmers come close to Chicago. This time, the three men, and the wife of one, will all ride in the same car, traveling six hours from central Iowa, to learn about their investments, but also just to meet with him. They will stop at the Marriott Hotel in the suburb of Oak Park, and call Serfling to come out here to join them because they mistrust the city too much to come any nearer.

Scott will tell them of his plans and that he will leave the S&P 500 pit with resignation but without regret, for the pit has yielded him much. And it has let him do what he believes is important.

For the past three years, he has worked the pit to provide his three farmer clients with annual profits of $30,000 to $40,000 each on their $50,000 accounts. The income has been sufficient to let them continue meeting heavy debt payments and thus save their farms.

The farmers will tell Serfling that their businesses are improving, so he needn't worry about their accounts not having grown since the crash the way they did before it.

The farm wife will tell Scott that she is praying for him every day; praying that he will get married, raise children, and find an easier job.

JANUARY 8, 1988. ■ New York Stock Exchange trading floor, 4:00 P.M.: Just as the program traders have struggled on since the crash to produce profits for their firms, so futures prices in the underpopulated S&P 500 pit at the CME have zigzagged and stock prices here have gyrated ominously.

As a result, program trading has been implicated in a pair of terrifying aftershocks: drops in the Dow of 77 points on November 30, 1987, and 57 points three days after Christmas.

Today program trading has again exacerbated a market plunge, and this time the Dow has fallen 140 points. It will also be implicated in a 57-point plunge on January 20.

So this month, responding to a near-hysterical chorus of opposition to program trading from their big institutional investor clients, Shearson Lehman Hutton, Merrill Lynch, and Goldman Sachs will stop program trading for their own accounts. But Salomon, Morgan Stanley, Kidder Peabody, and Bear Stearns, among others, will be determined to struggle on. "We are convinced that we are in a commanding position to capitalize on the opportunities resulting from the growth of derivative instruments markets around the world," Salomon's John Gutfreund writes in the firm's 1987 annual report. "It is clear that this area, even with appropriate market regulatory reform, will continue to evolve."

However, on April 14, the Dow will take a 101-point swan dive, sparking powerful new calls for an end to program trading. On May 2, the NYSE will begin requiring the program traders to extensively report their activities to the exchange each day. This will seem the final straw, and on May 10, Salomon Brothers, Morgan Stanley, Kidder Peabody, PaineWebber, and Bear Stearns will throw up their hands and announce indefinite moratoriums on program trading for their own accounts.

A decline in volume to levels of the early 1980s during the ensuing three weeks will drive home the awful truth—without the program traders, the stock market, seven months after the crash, is relatively deserted. Hyperactive but neutral in-and-out trading by Japanese insurance companies in utility and other stocks paying high dividends will obscure the malaise, inflating NYSE volume by as much as 25% on some days.* But Wall Street pros will see that real stock market trading in mid-May is running at not much more than 110 million shares a day, as low as in the middle of the sleepy summer doldrums of 1986. That's too low a level to pay the overhead costs at the vast majority of Wall Street brokerage firms, and indicates that the more than 12,000 layoffs already implemented by Wall Street firms since the crash might have to be augmented by at least that many more.

Suddenly, on May 31, when trading resumes after the long Memorial Day weekend, the market will seem to awaken. Volume will pick up by some 50%, and will even top 300 million shares one day in early June, as the Dow soars some 145 points during the first half of the month. The pros will examine the trading, including a flurry in the S&P 500 pit, and whisper to one another that program trading is back. Are the firms getting a lot of orders to do program trades for customers, or are they back in the business of using the strategy for their own accounts? Nobody knows, and with the market finally seeming to be taking off, nobody will want to ask.

So as summer approaches, fingers will be crossed here and all along Wall Street that the post-Memorial Day flurry, which program trading at least helped to launch, will blossom into a rally long enough, strong enough, and broad enough to repair the financial damage wrought by Black Monday.

As these lines are being written in the summer of 1988, there is no way to know whether Wall Street's hopes will be rewarded or dashed. Yet, if you believe what Scott Serfling saw in the S&P 500 pit between early 1982 and October 1987, then you also believe that more than all other forces it was program trading that sent the Dow soaring above 2700 in the summer of 1987.

Therefore, if America's highest priority is to return the Dow to 2700 and beyond, then the surest route would seem to be the one originally taken—program trading, complemented by an S&P futures pit brim-

*The Japanese insurers' trading responds to discrimination by the industry's regulators in favor of dividend income, as opposed to gains from trading securities. So they arrange huge block trades of sometimes tens of millions of shares of utility or other high-dividend stocks in order to establish themselves as the shareholders of record for the payment of the next quarterly dividend. Once in line to receive the next dividend, the Japanese insurer immediately resells the shares at a price that is lower by the amount of the pending dividend. The strategy is called "dividend capture."

ming with eager, easily maneuvered locals and a towering overabundance of investment capital.

However, let no one labor under the delusion that a Dow thus driven will accurately reflect the value of America's corporate assets or the strength of her economy, any more than it accurately reflected them between 1984 and October 1987. Black Monday and its resolution signaled the passing of an era on Wall Street and in America. Indeed, the Dow may never again mean what we thought it meant before Black Monday.

JANUARY 20, 1988. ■ Dow Jones Tower, World Financial Center, noon: Paul Steiger sits silently beside Norman Pearlstine as the managing editor begins the noon meeting in a conference room jammed with double the normal number of attendees.

"I used to think only wimps stayed within their budgets," Pearlstine tells the sixty New York *Journal* editors and writers he has summoned to this meeting by memo invitation, "but I have lately been told in the most forceful terms that if I value my job, my thinking had better change."

His message is painfully clear. Dow Jones is tightening the screws on its cost-cutting programs to help offset the *Journal*'s advertising and circulation slippage. Pearlstine tells the staffers that he will be meeting with each of them individually in the coming days to discuss any impact this may have on their assignments. And five days from now, the managing editor will issue another memo, reshuffling or demoting seven top editors.

Paul Steiger will not be named in the memo, yet nonetheless it will confirm him as the heir apparent to Norman Pearlstine. The memo will report that Stew Pinkerton, the only other deputy managing editor, will lose that title and instead be made Finance and Investments editor. He will be abruptly inserted in the chain of command as the new boss of John Prestbo and the Markets Group. Pinkerton will leave his spacious office near Pearlstine's and go down to the tenth floor, displacing Prestbo from his office there. Stew will report to Steiger, and his former office will be turned into a third conference room. Five other *Journal* editors in all will be demoted at about the same time.

A worse fate awaits some lower-ranking staffers. In April five clipping clerks in the *Journal*'s library will be told there is no longer any work for them. Four will be invited to interview for one open position elsewhere in the company. The fifth clerk, a sixty-year-old veteran, who's worked at the paper for nearly thirty years, and who holds a master's degree in library science but is emotionally handicapped by severe depression, will not be interviewed.

The man will be confused and crushed. He is single and his job has been his life. He will not go away. Instead, he will come, day after day, to sit for hours in the library, or on one of the green couches in the tenth-floor reception area, or in the men's room. Reporters and editors alike will be emotionally shattered. On the fourth day, Sanford Jacobs, a veteran former *Journal* columnist who has been reassigned to the Spot News desk, will write a letter appealing to Chairman Warren Phillips to help the man.

Phillips will be out of town and won't get to read the letter until the following week. But when he does read it, he will order the Dow Jones personnel director to respond; a job will be found for the man as a counselor in a New York halfway house for the emotionally disturbed, thus stopping his pathetic sit-in at the end of the second week. Meanwhile, a by now agitated rump group of *Journal* editors and reporters will take up a petition asking that all four of the remaining clipping clerks also be placed in Dow Jones jobs.

Steiger will invite anyone with gripes to show up at the big ninth-floor conference room one day late in April and—"even though he wasn't involved in the decision, he sat there and took a verbal beating for more than two hours," *Journal* Deputy National News editor Cathy Panagoulias will recall. Jobs will be found at Dow Jones for the other four clipping clerks.

Compassion is one of Steiger's traits that has served him best in times past. There had been a classic example of it a few years before he rejoined the *Journal*. Bob Dallos, an *L.A. Times* senior business writer in New York who was recovering from a heart attack, opened his eyes one day to find Steiger in his hospital room, fresh from Los Angeles. Paul spent about an hour with him and then left, Dallos recalls. About two hours later, when Dallos's wife came into the room, "I told her Paul had come to see me and she said: 'I know. He's been waiting with me in the lounge ever since.'" While Dallos would lavishly praise Steiger's intellect, truthfulness, and fairness, it was Paul's compassion that earned his dedication and loyalty.

Yet Steiger now finds he is forced to order or carry out some onerous aspects of the cost-cutting plan. Staffers will see his customary cheeriness fade in the coming months—amid a wave of warning letters, grave career-counseling sessions, and abrupt transfers that smack of demotions that sets off a quiet but steady exodus of reporters. By mid-1988, the *Journal* staff will be reduced by two dozen full-time employees from 500 at the end of October 1987.

So even his giant step closer to *The Wall Street Journal*'s top news job won't make the tasks in the months ahead any less irksome for Paul Steiger the genius; Paul Steiger the totally truthful, fairest man that Bob Dallos ever met.

APRIL 7, 1988, ■ Merrill Lynch offices, One Financial Place, Boston, 11:05 A.M.: Not all the victims of Black Monday are investors. Lonnie Gilchrist, now sitting in his boss's office, is a broker. And, except for the extraordinary event now beginning to unfold, his story would have remained untold under the awesome mountain of layoff statistics.

Without naming them, the SEC reported on the October 14–30 operating results of Wall Street's fifteen biggest investment banking and brokerage concerns. It wasn't pretty. Thirteen of the fifteen had losses ranging from a minimum of just under $5 million to more than $133 million, to a total of $796.6 million.

Merrill Lynch, First Boston, Goldman Sachs, and many others set layoffs, although not all firms announced them. By late January, the known Wall Street layoffs totaled 12,000, mostly among clerks and lower-ranking traders.

Salomon Brothers had already set 800 layoffs in a restructuring move that eliminated its municipal bond business shortly before the crash, and it didn't disclose any plans for additional layoffs afterward. But Solly lost $74 million, after taxes, in the fourth quarter, and by early in 1988, the King of Wall Street was eating generous portions of humble pie.

As Salomon Chairman John Gutfreund put it to a *Barron's* writer in January: "I think that a lot of our traders were probably arrogant, and I think that there are some who have had that knocked out of them. I think that of all the Wall Street people."

Huge trading losses in the October crash and customer defaults put E. F. Hutton on the selling block by late November 1987, when it was gobbled up by American Express's Shearson Lehman, itself a loser of $72 million in October. Hutton will set an unspecific layoff goal of up to 5,000 employees, and the layoffs will begin just before Christmas. L. F. Rothschild & Company, a large second-tier Wall Street firm with some 90,000 customer accounts, would post a fourth-quarter loss of $128.8 million and announce the layoff of 700 of its approximately 2,000 employees. By late February, Rothschild would have laid off another 100, and the firm would agree to be acquired by a closely held savings-and-loan institution in Ottawa, Kansas.

The SEC reports that some fifty-eight other, smaller firms—somewhat less than 1% of those registered to sell securities in the U.S.—went under during the crash. Three of the NYSE's fifty-five specialist firms were merged out of existence due to capital problems brought on by the crash, including Asiel & Company, the firm where Donny Stone's father had made his career.

In January Merrill Lynch announced that its fourth-quarter profits fell to just $3 million from more than $182 million a year earlier. And it laid off more than 2,500 employees. Lonnie Lee Gilchrist, Jr., BA, MBA, and a broker at Merrill Lynch for almost two years, survived that cut. But not this one, and he sits glaring at branch manager George W. Cook in their second anguished meeting this morning.

In his mid-fifties now, Cook has been with Merrill for thirty-one years, and this is the third Merrill branch office that he has run, each larger than the last. Like the 484 other branch managers in Merrill's vast retail financial services network, George's principal duty is to supervise and motivate brokers—eighty of them here at the big One Financial Place office. Supportive, yet firm and fair, he does that job as well as any Merrill manager in the country. Indeed, this branch ranks among Merrill's top ten in commission revenue per broker.

Nearly six months after the October stock market crash, with trading volume limping along at depressed levels, Merrill must continue to lean heavily on its highly professional broker force for extraordinary performance. And this at a time when some of its best brokers are being lured away by hard-pressed competitors stretching to increase revenue by upgrading their brokerage forces.

Despite Cook's repeated efforts to help him catch on, and just when outstanding performance is needed most, Gilchrist hasn't yet managed to turn in even an average performance. He produced only $17,051 of commission revenue in all 1987 and $4,590 in the first quarter of 1988. That's only a third of the firm's minimum acceptable level, a Merrill official will tell the press.

It's not that Gilchrist lacks the education or appearance to be an effective salesman. He is a distinguished-looking black man of forty-one, over six feet tall, solidly built, and, today, dressed in a dark, three-piece suit and a red tie. Colleagues see him as sensitive and intelligent. In 1975 he graduated with an MBA from the University of Pennsylvania's highly regarded Wharton School.

But a successful stockbroker needs to be unusually thick-skinned and emotionally resilient. Gilchrist seemed to be neither. He appeared always to suspect that the rejection he encounters is, at bottom, racially motivated. And some of his colleagues feel he resents their success, too. Nor is Cook alone in failing to get Lonnie to realize his potential. This is Lonnie's ninth job since leaving Wharton, and apparently he has little to show for nearly thirteen years of work. He still lives with his mother in a public housing-project apartment in the city's poor South End.

In recent months George had repeatedly warned Lonnie ("like an uncle," in the words of one colleague) that his performance would have to improve. Finally Cook had given up on Gilchrist and, yesterday, told Lonnie that he was fired.

Both yesterday and in the meeting Lonnie sought today, George has tried to be sensitive and professional about the ugly chore. It wasn't easy firing anyone, especially someone who wanted to succeed as desperately as Lonnie did. George makes it clear that Lonnie can continue to use his desk and phone at Merrill for several weeks while he looks for a new job and that he, Cook, will help him find one.

Perhaps it is all to the good. Since Gilchrist clearly isn't making it as a stockbroker, perhaps the dismissal is just what he needs to force him into a more promising new career. However, Lonnie doesn't see it that way, and he's asked for help in getting a broker's job with Merrill

Lynch competitors Prudential-Bache or PaineWebber. "You don't understand," George tells him. "You're just not suited to this kind of work," the *Boston Globe* will learn he said.

Later, Edna Pezzolesi, Lonnie's career counselor when he was an undergraduate at the University of Massachusetts Boston campus, will suggest to a *Boston Herald* reporter that the intensely proud and sensitive Lonnie Gilchrist may have taken George's solicitude as a patronizing final affront—a last straw, which caused him to use the gun he has brought with him into Cook's office.

According to charges against him, which he denies, and to witnesses' reports obtained by Boston newspapers, Gilchrist fires eight shots in all and clubs Cook over the head with a .22-caliber pistol. The murderous assault begins in George's office, and continues as Lonnie pursues Cook along a row of file cabinets outside. Finally, his face contorted with rage, Gilchrist kicks Cook as he lies crumbled on the floor, screaming at him: "No billionaire's going to run my life."

A glassy-eyed but still conscious George Cook tells co-workers that he can't breathe. He has bullet wounds in his arm, armpit, chest, and abdomen. In an hour and a half, at 12:35 P.M., he will be pronounced dead on the operating table at Massachusetts General Hospital. His wife, Marcia, and two of his three sons reportedly will rush to the hospital, but arrive shortly after his death. A third son is still in college in Colorado.

Later today, Merrill's chief of security, Patrick Murphy, who flew to Boston as soon as he heard of the shooting, will tell the *Boston Herald* that it doesn't appear that the murder is an aftereffect of the market crash.

Yet a Merrill official in New York will know to the dollar ($6,491) the amount of commission revenue Gilchrist has produced "since last October."

OCTOBER 20, 1987. ■ New York Stock Exchange trading floor, 3:59:50 P.M.: "Ding . . . ding . . . ding . . . ding . . ." John Phelan and Donny Stone, standing together in the ceremonial balcony, pull the lever that rings the electronic bell signaling the close of today's trading.

The Stock Market Crash of 1987 is over, although it is far from clear yet to anyone here. Today the Dow is up 102.27 points at the close, a record that will be eclipsed by a 186.84-point explosion tomorrow. Volume surged 4 million shares beyond yesterday's record, to 608.2 million shares.

Yet the stock market reversal is narrowly based. While the blue-chip Dow and the S&P 500 are up 5.9% and 5.3%, respectively, the broad NYSE composite is up a far smaller 3.6% and the American Stock Exchange composite and the NASDAQ composite of OTC stocks have plunged 8.6% and 9%, respectively. Astonishingly, today's record rise has come despite the fact that Big Board issues declining in price outnumbered those advancing by 1,445 to 509—circumstances more consistent rationally with a large decline in the Dow.

Donny and Phelan are waving and smiling now, but there will be little to wave or smile about in the months ahead. Trading will remain explosively volatile and frightening until November, and thereafter the market will walk a razor's edge above the abyss on several occasions.

Phelan and Stone will also find themselves walking a tightrope between the exchange's divided staff and members on the issue of program trading. The big securities houses, whose business is predominantly based on brokerage commissions, will reflect their large institutional and retail customers' opposition to program trading, which they blame for the crash itself and for the nervous and volatile market conditions that will later prevail. However, the big trading firms will win full approval to return to program trading through the DOT system by November 9. An NYSE staff that is itself divided on the practice will seek to reassure opponents of program trading. It will move to adopt a "circuit breaker" rule, denying the program traders access to the DOT system on days when the Dow moves beyond a specified threshold. In mid-January 1988, the exchange will begin a pilot test using a 75-point threshold, but will reduce it to 50 points in an operating rule that will be adopted later.

On the staff, exchange President Bob Birnbaum is an opponent. In a March 26, 1988, speech to an American Bar Association group, he will blame index arbitrage for intensifying price volatility in the stock market, note that it is used by "only a small number of brokerage firms and institutions," and he will flatly state: "I believe that index arbitrage should be eliminated." While he recognizes that such a move would cut both futures and stock trading volume, "In the long run, futures and equities institutions will be stronger and our markets better," he contends.

Birnbaum will also note an important but little discussed finding of the Brady Commission: "that a small number of institutions were largely responsible" for the Black Monday catastrophe. Perhaps it is time, Birnbaum will suggest, to consider some limitations on the size of portfolios or discounting the value of large positions. Liquidity is a valuable as well as limited commodity, and no institution should have unlimited access to what is available.

But adopting Birnbaum's radical recommendations would put the exchange on a collision course with the big trading houses and with at least some of its specialists. The recommendations won't be implemented, and Birnbaum will leave the NYSE on June 1, 1988, at the expiration of his three-year employment contract. Dick Grasso will succeed him. Torrenzano will stress that hiring Birnbaum away from the presidency of the American Stock Exchange had been an interim measure from the start, primarily to allow qualified young NYSE insiders like Grasso some time to gain added seasoning. The sixty-year-old Birnbaum will say he is leaving because "I've had about enough of stock exchange work. I want to leave while there's still enough time to do something else."

The exchange will eagerly embrace a principal recommendation of the SEC report—that the Big Board beef up its trading capacity even further. The exchange will gravely pledge to expand its trading capacity from less than 500 million shares at the time of the crash to 600 million by the end of the first quarter of 1988, to a stunning 1 billion shares a day by the end of 1989.

The more shares that trade on the NYSE, the more money its members make. And that's especially true for the specialists. According to secret exchange records to be obtained by *The New York Times* late in the spring of 1988, the specialists as a group rode the crest of the huge wave of program and other institutional trading in 1987. Despite their losses in the crash, the *Times* will report, the specialists' aggregate profit reached a record $369 million, or nearly half again more than in 1986.

As for the events that have brought John Phelan and Donny Stone to the closing bell today, neither the Brady Commission report nor the presumably exhaustive, 874-page SEC study of the crash will offer much enlightenment. Neither will confirm or rule out the charges of manipulation in the MMI futures pit after Black Monday. Neither will voice even a breath of suspicion about midday trading here today.

The question is, whether, after repeated failures, Phelan and the specialists finally succeeded in pulling the Dow out of its nosedive with the advance knowledge and tacit approval of the Federal Reserve, the Securities and Exchange Commission, and the White House. To this observer of the day's incredible events—and the explanations to be offered for them—the answer to this central question inescapably is yes. Yet, far from answering that question, the major studies of the stock market crash will not even raise it. It will seem a decision has been made at the highest levels that, even in America, some questions are best not asked.

Speaking only of the odd MMI futures trading, Bart Naylor, an investigator for the Senate Banking Committee, will state the dilemma that applies to all of today's strange happenings: "This is tricky," he will say. "You don't want to put people in jail for saving the market."

"Ding . . . ding . . . ding . . . ding . . ." There are no thoughts of a return to 2700 in John Phelan's or Donny Stone's mind as they close the day's trading. For now, it is good enough that the Dow has not gone to 1200, or 800, that the exchange has survived, and that, together, they have helped assure that outcome. "Donny and I grew up in the business together," Phelan will reminisce. And on the floor "they have confidence in him as a leader. He has had to make a lot of tough decisions and they have worked out."

"Ding . . . ding . . . ding . . . ding." Strip all the rest away and a man is left finally with just his life and his integrity. Long ago, John Phelan and Donny Stone had put their lives on the line for their country at war, and had walked away intact. And they are walking away from Black Monday intact, too.

"There were cheers and some people threw things up in the air," Rich Torrenzano will recall. "Nobody was thinking about tomorrow."

BIBLIOGRAPHY

BOOKS

Greider, William. *Secrets of the Temple: How the Federal Reserve Runs the Country.* New York: Simon and Schuster, 1987, p. 39.

LeFebre, Edwin. *Reminiscences of a Stock Operator.* Burlington, Vt.: Fraser Management Associates, 1980 (reprinted).

New York Stock Exchange. *Marketplace: A Brief History of the New York Stock Exchange.* New York, 1982.

Securities Industry Association. *Securities Industry Yearbook, 1987–88.* New York, 1987.

INTERVIEWS

E. Gerald Corrigan: February 26, 1988.

John J. Phelan, Jr.: March 3, December 31, 1987; March 25, May 25, 1988.

Scott R. Serfling: December 29, December 30, 1987; March 14, March 15, 1988.

Paul E. Steiger: November 24, December 4, December 11, 1987; February 19, April 4, 1988.

Donald Stone: January 12, February 1, February 25, 1988.

SELECTED NEWSPAPER/MAGAZINE STORIES

Anders, George. "Portfolio Insurance Helps Investors, But Hurts Market." *The Wall Street Journal,* October 19, 1987.

Anders, George, Cynthia Crossen and Scott McMurray. "Big Board Curb on Electronic Trading Results in Halt at Stock-Index Markets." *The Wall Street Journal,* October 21, 1987.

Andrews, Suzanna. "Moving out from Under Paul Volcker's Shadow." *Institutional Investor,* September, 1987.

Bennett, Amanda. "Top Dollar: Corporate Chiefs' Pay Far Outpaces Inflation and the Gains of Staffs." *The Wall Street Journal,* March 28, 1988.

Cole, Robert J. "Wall Street Point Man: John J. Phelan Jr." *The New York Times,* October 21, 1987.

Coll, Steve. "Crisis Chronology: The Day Wall Street Went Wild." *The Washington Post,* October 25, 1987.

Davis, L. J. "William Simon's Pacific Overtures." *The New York Times Magazine,* December 27, 1987.

Davis, L. J. "$60 Billion in the Balance: For CREF a 4% Move in the Stock Market Can Mean a $1 Billion Gain or Loss." *The New York Times Magazine,* March 27, 1988.

Feinberg, Andrew. "Blown Away by Black Monday." *The New York Times Magazine,* December 20, 1987.

Grant, Peter. "John Phelan vs. Program Trading." *Investment Dealers' Digest,* March 2, 1987.

Jones, Alex S. "Caution in the Press: Was It Really a 'Crash'?" *The New York Times,* October 21, 1987.

Kleinfield, N. R. "When Will the O-T-C Wake Up?" *The New York Times* (Sunday Business Section), February 14, 1988.

Lowenstein, Louis. "Wall Street, Take a Valium." *The Wall Street Journal,* November 9, 1987.

Mayer, Martin. "Don't Shoot the Computer: There's a Better Way to Curb Program Trading." *Barron's,* November 9, 1987.

Meislin, Richard J. "Yuppies' Last Rites Readied." *The New York Times,* October 21, 1987.

Meyers, Mike. "Corrigan Kept a Cool Grip on Black Monday Events." *Minneapolis Star Tribune,* January 25, 1988.

Oram, Roderick. "How Luck and Nerve Saved Financial Markets Round the World." *Financial Times,* October 26, 1987.

Smith, Randall, Steve Swartz, and George Anders. "Black Monday" (Crash of '87, Part II). *The Wall Street Journal,* December 16, 1987.

Stewart, James B., and Daniel Hertzberg. "Terrible Tuesday," *The Wall Street Journal,* November 20, 1987.

Taylor, John. "Hard to be Rich: The Rise and Wobble of the Gutfreunds." *New York* magazine, January 11, 1988.

Uchitelle, Louis. "Reliance on Temporary Jobs Hints at Economic Fragility." *The New York Times,* March 16, 1988.

SPEECH

Corrigan, E. Gerald. "Remarks before the Venezuelan Chapter of the Interamerican Council on Business and Productivity." October 16, 1987.

STUDIES

Bowsher, Charles A., Comptroller General of the United States, General Accounting Office. *Financial Markets: Preliminary Observations on the October 1987 Crash.* January, 1988.

Brady, Nicholas F., James C. Cotting, Robert G. Kirby, John R. Opel, and Howard M. Stein. *Report of the Presidential Task Force on Market Mechanisms.* New York: January, 1988.*

Katzenbach, Nicholas deB. *An Overview of Program Trading and Its Impact on Current Market Practices,* A Study Commissioned by the *New York Stock Exchange.* December, 1987.

Miller, Merton H., John D. Hawke, Jr., Burton Malkiel, and Myron Scholes. *Preliminary Report of the Committee of Inquiry Appointed by the Chicago Mercantile Exchange to Examine the Events Surrounding October 19, 1987.* December, 1987.

U.S. Securities and Exchange Commission Staff. *Internationalization of the Securities Market.* July, 1987.

U.S. Securities and Exchange Commission (Division of Market Regulation). *The October 1987 Market Break.* February, 1988.*

TESTIMONY (Before the United States Senate Committee on Banking, Housing and Urban Affairs)

February 2, 1988:
Greenspan, Alan, Chairman, Board of Governors of the Federal Reserve System
February 3:
Nicholas F. Brady, Chairman, Presidential Task Force on Market Mechanisms
Kalo A. Hineman, Acting Commissioner, Commodity Futures Trading Commission
David S. Ruder, Chairman, Securities and Exchange Commission
February 4:
Joseph R. Hardiman, President, National Association of Securities Dealers, Inc.
Kenneth R. Liebler, President, American Stock Exchange, Inc.
Leo Melamed, Chairman of the Executive Committee and Special Counsel to the Board, Chicago Mercantile Exchange.
February 5:
Richard L. Fogel, Assistant Comptroller General, General (sic) Government Programs, United States General Accounting Office
John J. Phelan, Jr., Chairman and Chief Executive Officer, New York Stock Exchange.

*Distributed by U.S. Government Printing Office, Washington, D.C.

INDEX